The Polygraph Test

The Polygraph Test

Lies, Truth and Science

edited by Anthony Gale

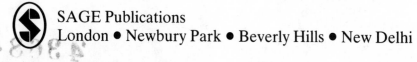

SAGE Publications
London ● Newbury Park ● Beverly Hills ● New Delhi

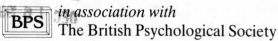

in association with
The British Psychological Society

First published 1988

The views expressed in this book are those of the individual authors
and not necessarily those of The British Psychological Society.

SAGE Publications Ltd
28 Banner Street
London EC1Y 8QE

SAGE Publications Inc
2111 West Hillcrest Street
Newbury Park, California 91320

SAGE Publications India Pvt Ltd
C-236 Defence Colony
New Delhi 110 024

SAGE Publications Inc
275 South Beverly Drive
Beverly Hills, California 90212

British Library Cataloguing in Publication Data

The Polygraph test: lies, truth and
science.
1. Lie detectors and detection
I. Gale, Anthony
363.2′54   HV8078

ISBN 0-8039-8122-8

Library of Congress catalog card number 87-062787

Printed in Great Britain by J.W. Arrowsmith Ltd, Bristol

Contents

Contributors

Gordon H. Barland, Director of Research, Research Division, Defense Polygraph Institute, Fort McClellan, Alabama, USA

Steve Blinkhorn, Managing Director, Psychometric Research and Development Ltd, St Albans, Hertfordshire, England

Raymond H. Bull, Professor of Psychology, Glasgow College of Technology, Scotland

Douglas Carroll, Lecturer in Psychology, Department of Psychology, University of Birmingham, England

Cyril Cunningham, formerly Senior Psychologist to the POW Intelligence Directorate and former adviser to the Ministry of Defence on International Interrogation Techniques and Systems; School of Management Studies, Portsmouth Polytechnic, England

Anthony Gale, Professor of Psychology, Department of Psychology, University of Southampton, England

Robert Grime, Professor of Law, Faculty of Law, University of Southampton, England

Gisli H. Gudjonsson, Senior Lecturer in Psychology, Department of Psychology, Institute of Psychiatry, University of London, England

Sarah E. Hampson, Research Scientist, Oregon Research Institute, Eugene, Oregon, USA

Edgar A. Jones Jr, Professor of Law, School of Law, University of California, Los Angeles, USA and Arbitrator

Ken Jones, Head of Research, Research Department, Society of Civil and Public Servants, England

David T. Lykken, Professor of Psychiatry and Psychology, Department of Psychiatry, Medical School, University of Minnesota, Minneapolis, Minnesota, USA

Tara Ney, Research Fellow, Department of Psychology, University of Southampton, England

David C. Raskin, Professor of Psychology, Department of Psychology, University of Utah, Salt Lake City, Utah, USA

Peter Thornton, Barrister at Law, and Past Chairman, The National Council for Civil Liberties, Temple, London, England

Introduction
The polygraph test, more than scientific investigation

Anthony Gale

The polygraph lie-detection test is used in three contexts: criminal investigation, security vetting, and personnel selection. Its use is extensive in the USA and evidence derived from the polygraph test is acceptable in certain legal systems and courts in the USA and elsewhere. Following the Geoffrey Prime spy case in the UK the British Government announced its intention to undertake pilot studies of the use of the polygraph test for security vetting purposes at its intelligence information centre, the GCHQ, at Cheltenham. In a statement to the Employment Committee of the House of Commons, the Government announced that the study would include the Security Services also. The Employment Committee, concerned at the Government's apparent faith in the polygraph test procedures and its implications for personnel screening and employment screening, set up an inquiry to examine the evidence for the efficacy of the test and its consequences for industrial relations. The report of the inquiry was published in 1985.

Many individuals and organizations submitted evidence both orally and in writing to the inquiry. The British Psychological Society, the main scientific and professional body for British psychology, and representing some 12,000 scientists and applied psychologists, submitted evidence prepared by Victor Dulewicz (Dulewicz, 1984). Dulewicz argued that the evidence in favour of the introduction of the polygraph test was very slender, and that its reliability and validity were in question, there being a need for systematic and scientific research into its accuracy. The Scientific Affairs Board of the Society decided to take the matter further and set up a working group under the chairmanship of the present author.

The present book is a result of the deliberations of the working group, which published its own report in 1986. That report, available from the Leicester offices of the Society, is the Society's official statement on the use of the polygraph. The report concluded that the published descriptions of polygraph testing procedures indicated that they were contrary to the spirit of the Society's Code of Conduct (British Psychological Society, 1985). The procedure seemed to involve: the use of non-standardized procedures; misleading the subject as to the efficacy of the test; participation which appears not to be voluntary; the induction of anxiety to induce compliance; possible intrusions into privacy; and potential difficulties in maintaining regulation of practice through the establishment of a registration body.

The report concluded: 'In such circumstances, it is difficult to see how Members of the Society could engage in work as polygraphic interrogators and claim that their conduct is consistent with the Society's current Code of Conduct' (British Psychological Society, 1986: 93).

The reader will note that this conclusion is not as firm as it might have been. Expressions like 'it is difficult to see how . . .', or 'current Code of Conduct' reveal a desire *not* to be wholly dismissive of polygraph testing procedures, nor to exclude the possibility that one day the Code of Conduct might alter.

Why did the Society stand back from more definite conclusions? The answer to that question is to be found in this book. The truth is that we do not know the full truth about polygraphic lie-detection.

Polygraph testing procedures and their accuracy

The procedures used by polygraphic examiners are described in the following chapter by Ray Bull; he also considers evidence by Ekman (1985) and others concerning other psychological methods of detecting deception. Distinguished scientists in the USA have engaged in prolonged controversy over the reliability and validity of the polygraph test procedures. The views of these antagonists are sampled in Chapters 7, 8 and 9, by Gordon Barland, David Raskin and David Lykken respectively. Gordon Barland is a distinguished and leading practitioner in the field of polygraph testing, with many years of experience in a variety of contexts, who has also conducted research on accuracy. As an advocate of the procedure, he sets out the most systematic and subtle arguments for its use. In the interests of balance he has been allocated a longer chapter than other contributors. David Raskin, while favouring the use of the polygraph in certain contexts, is a scientist with laboratory and field experience of its use. David Lykken is a vigorous and vocal opponent of the polygraph test, and his book *A Tremor in the Blood: Uses and Abuses of the Lie Detector* (1981) was one of the first attempts by a psychophysiological scientist to put lie detection under a critical microscope. The reader should note, however, that Lykken, in spite of several objections to current polygraph testing practices, nevertheless supports the use of the *guilty knowledge method*, a technique in which few polygraph examiners are trained, and which is rarely applicable in many of the contexts in which lie-detection tests are used. All three authorities agree that much of the research conducted into the accuracy of the polygraph test is inadequate.

Douglas Carroll, who gave oral evidence to the Employment Committee inquiry (House of Commons, 1984), presents a disinterested evaluation of research into the accuracy of the polygraph; he is particularly concerned to discover which component of the testing procedure accounts for its success in identifying the guilty and whether the polygraph chart itself contributes a great deal to the examiner's decision. The data which Carroll samples are also referred to by Lykken and Raskin, who offer further commentary and interpretation.

Psychological issues of relevance in assessing lie detection

Psychometrics

Psychology has developed an enormous battery of psychological tests for the evaluation of intelligence, personality and aptitude. Such tests are used widely in educational selection, assessment of individual abilities and interests, and employment selection and counselling. The question arises whether these procedures also may be subject to criticism, and whether psychologists should not be wary of criticizing others who seek to develop useful tests. Steve Blinkhorn (Chapter 3) explains the principles upon which psychometric tests are constructed and developed. Particularly important within test theory are the concepts of reliability, validity and freedom from bias. Blinkhorn demonstrates that polygraph test procedures fall short of the requirements of adequate psychometric testing. He challenges the view that polygraphic interrogation techniques are truly standardized or that they can be used to make decisions as to truth, honesty or deceptiveness.

There are two further issues of psychological importance which have a bearing on polygraph lie testing.

Truth and honesty

In employment screening the polygraph test is used to check whether applicants have been honest in completing job applications, but it also seeks to aid the employer in making judgements as to the general probity of the applicant. Sarah Hampson explains in Chapter 5 what psychology has to say about general personal characteristics or traits such as honesty and truthfulness. Both theoretical considerations and the results of many experiments indicate that it is difficult to offer such general characterizations, and that the individual's behaviour and conduct are often governed by the context in which they find themselves. She concludes that an individual's performance on lie detector tests currently in use is unlikely to give a reliable indication of how they might behave in different circumstances. She also points out that definitions of honesty and integrity also vary with social circumstance: telling the truth may be a sign of insensitivity and tactlessness in one situation, yet a sign of discretion and kindness in another. Nor is personal integrity necessarily a guarantee of loyalty to one's employer; the cases of Ponting and Tisdall, both of whom were disenchanted by their employers' actions, are referred to in Chapter 12.

The measurement of emotion
The problem of measuring emotion is one which has worried psychology for almost a century. Few polygraphic experts claim that their procedures measure a specific *lie response*. Rather, they claim that during testing, sensitive material about a specific event or the act of lying when one is guilty of a misdemeanour provoke an uncontrollable *emotional* reaction on the part of the subject. Tara Ney (Chapter 6) gives a brief account of current theories of emotion and emotional expression. She discounts the view that physiological recordings are a royal road to the unconscious. There is little consistency in the ways in which we give physiological responses, and different measures of bodily activity, such as respiration and blood pressure, do not yield very high correlations. Such evidence serves to undermine the view that there is some inner state (emotional reaction) which can be tapped into by measurement of a peripheral physiological change. Moreover, different theories of emotion make different predictions about emotional expression. Some claim that responses such as facial expression, cardiovascular response, bodily movements and subtle alterations in speech *parallel* each other. But different authorities claim that such aspects of emotional expression are *reciprocal* – skilled poker players can keep their emotions to themselves. Thus, for the latter school of thought, the very inner feeling of guilt could serve to *reduce* physiological responding. The findings which Ney reports also explain one of the major problems with lie detection procedures: while being accurate in detecting the guilty, they make many errors in falsely accusing the innocent. Physiological responsiveness is not easy to control, and many of us give responses at the suggestion of guilt, even when we are innocent.

The place of polygraph testing in national security vetting

The context of the House of Commons inquiry was the revelation of treachery in Government employees. The use of polygraph testing, it was argued, can help to protect national security from infiltration by alien agents, and to prevent disloyalty in individuals already employed in public service. Cyril Cunningham (Chapter 4) gives a detailed account of current vetting practices and the procedures employed in the special investigation of persons under suspicion of disloyalty. He points out that the requirement for security vetting is enormous, since the Government employs many hundreds of thousands of individuals, a high proportion of whom may be handling sensitive material or who may be suborned by enemy agents. For example, a humble cleaner in a Government establishment could reveal valuable information on the layout of a building, the hours of work of certain individuals or the location of offices dealing with highly sensitive material. Such a person, in casual conversation in a public house, could reveal such information quite inadvertently. The stereotype of security and espionage work neglects its opportunistic nature and the fact that much of the work depends on careful and systematic examination of databases which are not necessarily closed to public scrutiny. Cunningham concludes that within the context of existing security vetting procedures, and the capacity of the Security Services to engage in covert operations, the use of overt polygraph testing is a costly irrelevance.

One concern expressed by Dulewicz (1984) and others is that the use of polygraph testing in security contexts might be self-defeating. An alien espionage service, aware that its enemies employ polygraphic lie detection, might train its agents in methods of defeating the test. This could lead to a paradoxical outcome, for a government using polygraphic screening procedures could not only alienate its own employees by falsely accusing them of dishonesty, or exclude from employment individuals of a physiologically responsive disposition, but let through the screen individuals whose performance on the test, by virtue of their special training, is excellent. One of Lykken's favourite tales is that of Buzz Fay, who was imprisoned for murdering his friend, after failing two lie detection tests and in spite of protesting his innocence. While in gaol he claimed to have successfully trained several of his fellow inmates to defeat the test when it was used in the prison to detect misdemeanours. Do such counter-measures really work and can people be trained to defeat the test? Gisli Gudjonsson, a clinical psychologist and a former policeman with considerable experience of criminal investigation and the use of the polygraph for scientific and forensic purposes, explores the research literature on the use of counter-measures (Chapter 10). These include mental techniques (such as self-distraction, imagination), physical techniques (for example, placing a drawing pin in one's shoe and ensuring a vigorous physiological response to all questions asked), or methods involving use of chemicals and drugs (for example, those which attenuate physiological responding). As yet there is relatively little reliable evidence on the power of counter-measures.

Legal and civil rights issues

The issues considered so far focus on scientific and theoretical issues, as well as giving an account of current practice in polygraphic lie detection and security vetting procedures.

However, it is clear that scientific investigation alone cannot provide a comprehensive answer. The use of the polygraph has implications for legal procedure and the rules of evidence, public policy, personal privacy and personal rights, and management and industrial relations. Nor are the issues free of political consideration. Following the Geoffrey Prime spy case the Government withdrew trade union rights from its employees at the GCHQ while also introducing the pilot polygraph testing scheme; this provoked a vigorous response from several trade unions.

In the view of the report of The British Psychological Society's working party, such issues make it very difficult indeed to be wholly objective about polygraphic lie detection. It recognized that members of the Society might themselves have varying political beliefs, which might make them favour or criticize actions taken by governments to ensure national security. Moreover, one's view of individual rights might well vary, given the context within which the test is to be used: an individual might find polygraph testing acceptable in national security matters, but quite objectionable in day-to-day employment contexts. It has been claimed by advocates of lie detection procedures in pre-employment screening that questionnaire studies and opinion polls within the USA reveal that the general public is not opposed to testing. We cannot anticipate what the public response would be in the UK. Elliott (1982), a distinguished academic lawyer, warns that many American institutions have ultimately become accepted in Britain and continental Europe.

Thus, to make our review of polygraph testing complete, we have asked lawyers and a trade unionist to express their views. Peter Thornton, a barrister at law and a former member of the Executive

Committee of the National Council for Civil Liberties, presents the case for a Bill of Rights guaranteeing certain individual freedoms (Chapter 12). He illustrates his arguments by reference to recent notorious cases of breaches of the Official Secrets Acts. Thornton is wholly opposed to polygraph testing. Ken Jones, in Chapter 14, presents the viewpoint of the trade unions and their objections to government actions in relation to the GCHQ. While The British Psychological Society is in no sense a political organization and does not necessarily share views expressed in this book, it believes that any account of polygraph testing must be balanced. From a psychological point of view, it is essential to appreciate how different parties to a procedure might view its impact on their lives. Jones explains why, for trade unionists, polygraph testing is unacceptable.

One of the conclusions of the working party report was that polygraphic testing procedures contained elements which seemed incompatible with current legal practice. For example, in civil cases it is the judge who determines whether what is said is true; in criminal cases this is typically the job of the jury. Is the polygraph test like the breathalyser, a scientific instrument which provides a formal reading, indicating how much alcohol the accused person has absorbed? Tape recordings and video films are likely to be introduced in British courts as evidence – how different is the polygraph trace? Is the polygraphic interrogator like an expert witness? Such issues are considered by Robert Grime in Chapter 11. He warns us that definitions of evidence change with time; before the introduction of the breathalyser a variety of behavioural tests was used, of varying reliability. Moreover, our courts already have accepted practices which are not scientifically justifiable; for example, it is assumed that an individual will be telling the truth if he or she takes an oath. Grime explores those aspects of current procedure which would work against the introduction of polygraph evidence in current law.

Finally, from the home of polygraphic testing, the USA, where an estimated two million tests are carried out every year both by federal agencies and by private employers, Edgar A. Jones Jr examines the place of polygraph testing in the context of civil rights and in a country which, unlike Britain, has a written constitution. By exploring an extensive case law, some of it quite recent, he demonstrates implications for several aspects of tort, showing that the polygraph raises issues of battery, misrepresentation, wrongful discharge, invasion of privacy, intentional infliction of mental distress, defamation, and product liability. Edgar A. Jones Jr concludes that there is a burgeoning ground for litigation against polygraph usage in the civil courts. His analysis is particularly novel.

Conclusion

Advances in science and technology are unlikely to leave our lives untouched, and the polygraph is no exception. The polygraph is a scientific instrument used for research into bodily responses and their relationships with psychological processes. As an instrument, it is reliable in producing a record of bodily events. However, this does not imply that the *uses* to which the polygraph might be put are also reliable. Some members of The British Psychological Society have expressed concern that the use of the polygraph for lie detection might reflect badly on its use in basic research. Criticism has also been made of the term 'the polygraph test', a misnomer which is said to give lie detection procedures some respectability by their association with a scientific instrument.

The general lesson here is that the results of scientific and technological advances can be deployed for a variety of purposes. In preparing this book we were aware that much of the controversy in the psychological literature has focused on the accuracy of the polygraph as demonstrated by its reliability and validity. Claims of advocates of polygraphic lie detection have been challenged. For example, there are claims that polygraph testing is more than 95 percent accurate. Generally, accuracy in this context is defined in terms of its capacity to identify the guilty person. But critics have demonstrated that if one in twenty persons is guilty, then detection of that person can yield an accuracy score, so defined, of 100 percent. The difficulty is that the cost of so doing is to find ten of the twenty falsely accused of lying. There are five possible outcomes of the procedure: the guilty are caught, the guilty are let free, the innocent are seen as innocent, the innocent are falsely accused, and the outcome is inconclusive. It is misleading to take one of these outcomes and base accuracy estimates upon it.

But the issue of false positives, the false accusation of the innocent, raises non-scientific problems. These include the relative cost of the procedure in terms of negative reactions of staff, the recording of misleading information on personal files, and the interpretation that anxiety and fear are so much a part of the success of the procedure that they lead to the individual giving physiological responses indicative of guilt. This raises problems of the invasion of privacy and voluntary consent. At a time of high unemployment also, the introduction of pre-employment screening could be seen to be imposed upon volunteers who are truly under duress.

In compiling this collection of essays it was essential to seek to tell the whole story, and not to limit the account to purely scientific matters. It was also essential to ensure that all sides of the argument surrounding the polygraph were addressed; that is why advocates of polygraph testing were invited to contribute, although in the nature of things they are in a minority and often less vocal than their antagonists.

A result of this broad-based approach is that the book should be accessible and readable by several audiences. It will appeal to psychologists and psychology students. But it will also offer useful information to members of the police forces, personnel officers, managers and trade unionists. Lawyers and civil rights workers will also find that within one set of covers virtually all the key issues surrounding polygraph testing are addressed.

The sources referred to by authors are collected together in the reference section at the end of the book. There is also a brief glossary of some of the technical terms and a guide for students, together with an annotated bibliography to aid further investigation by the interested reader.

PART ONE

The Basic Facts

1

What is the lie-detection test?

Ray H. Bull

Throughout history it has been assumed that lying is accompanied by physiological activity within the liar's body. For example, it has been reported (Kleinmuntz and Szucko, 1984b) that the Chinese forced suspected liars to chew rice powder and then to spit it out. If the resultant powder was dry then the person was judged to have been lying. Beliefs such as this were based on the premise that lying caused the individual to experience emotion, and that this would be accompanied by a change in the body's physiological activity (for example, a diminution of saliva, the result of a change in the activity of the autonomic nervous system). Modern notions concerning polygraphic lie detection also make such assumptions.

Modern polygraphers, however, rarely make the mistake of believing that lying is accompanied by a *special* pattern of physiological activity. Instead they assume that *changes* in physiological activity in response to incriminating questions are indicative of lying. Many of them also seem to assume that lying is accompanied by changes in bodily behaviour such as foot-wagging, eye-blinking and the like (Reid and Inbau, 1977). However, although most of them do endeavour accurately to measure and to record a suspected liar's physiological activity, they neither quantify nor record such bodily behaviour even though it may well influence their judgement. Indeed, some polygraphers are trained to focus on bodily behaviour as well as on physiological activity (British Psychological Society, 1986), notwithstanding the considerable amount of research which has found that the observation of bodily behaviour is not very useful in the detection of deception (Bull, 1983).

Detecting deception via bodily behaviour

Ekman and Friesen (1969, 1974) have suggested that, when lying, people have more control over the movement of their face than of the rest of their body. If this were so, and if lying does in fact cause bodily movement (which is often described as 'non-verbal behaviour'), then the body might be a better source of cues to deception than would be the face. Research has, by and large, found this to be the case (see, for example, Zuckerman, De Paulo and Rosenthal, 1981). However, such research has often been naively taken to imply that bodily behaviour is a reliable clue to deception. This is not so. Although observation of a person's body may be of greater use numerically than observation of the face, it does not necessarily follow that bodily observation will occasion a *high* level of accuracy in detecting deception. De Paulo and Pfeifer summarized research on this topic by stating that

> The detection of deception from verbal and non-verbal cues is a very difficult task. Although most groups of subjects whose skills have been assessed have performed at a level that exceeds chance, very few groups have ever achieved an accuracy level greater than 60 percent (in tasks for which 50 percent accuracy would represent a chance level), and some have even performed worse than chance. (1986: 249)

They suggested that 'The skill profile of the human lie detector, then, is not a very impressive one.'

Proponents of the use of the observation of non-verbal behaviour in the detection of deception could argue that in most research studies the detectors have been mere students rather than people whose jobs may have provided them with far greater experience of attempting to detect deception in this way. There is, however, no evidence that people who have had years of such experience (for example, police officers) are any better than are novices (De Paulo and Pfeifer, 1986; Kohnken, 1987). Thus, given that the observation of bodily behaviour seems not to be a very useful index of lying, the notion that lying may be revealed by the physiological activity which a polygraph can record then assumes greater importance.

What the polygraph measures

The polygraph is a neutral, accurate scientific measurement device which can display, via ink writing pens onto charts or via a computer's visual display unit, a direct and valid representation of various sorts of bodily activity such as heart rate, blood pressure, respiration and palmar sweating. This electrical device, which nowadays can be compact and portable, quantifies blood pressure and heart rate in a way similar to that used by one's own doctor. Respiration rate is measured by placing a strain gauge or pneumatic tube around the chest. The activity of the palmar sweat glands is usually quantified by passing a minute amount of electrical current from one small piece of metal (an electrode) to another placed some distance away on the palm so that the changing resistance of the palm to the passage of this electricity can be measured.

The polygraph (from the Greek 'poly' = many, and 'grapho' = to write) is widely used by properly trained staff in many aspects of scientific, medical and psychological research because it is known to represent reliably such physiological activity. However, the status of the polygraph as a research instrument should not be confused with the validity of lie-detection procedures which employ it.

The procedures used by polygraphers

When an individual undertakes a polygraphic lie-detection test the first phase of this usually involves an interview with the polygrapher during which some biographical questions will be asked. Then the polygrapher will tell the suspected liar or job applicant the actual nature of the questions which will be asked during the lie-detection test. The polygrapher will ask whether the individual understands every question. Many polygraphers also use this first phase to obtain an initial impression of the testee and to judge whether the individual seems to be more of an honest, upright citizen than a deceiver. At this time the polygraph will not have been switched on, but now the polygrapher will explain its basic principles. He or she will connect the individual to the machine and show the testee how it works.

The second phase begins when the suspect is asked a series of questions to which the reply of either 'No' or 'Yes' must be given. The polygraph is switched on and now is out of sight of the testee, usually behind him or her. During this phase the various physiological activity which may accompany the testee's answers to the questions (some of these questions being incriminating) is displayed and recorded on pen charts by the polygraph.

Early polygraphic lie detection was based on the assumption that there might be a special physiological response that occurred only when a person was lying. Almost everyone who is today concerned with polygraphy, either as a practitioner or as a critic, agrees that no such response exists. However, as pointed out by Kleinmuntz and Szucko (1984b: 767), 'The public, with the encouragement of contemporary polygraphy, tends to believe that lying produces a unique set of measurable physiological responses that characterize lying and only lying.'

Notwithstanding this probable misunderstanding of polygraphy by members of the public, the basic principle underlying modern polygraphy is that of making a comparison between how a person responds to non-incriminating questions and how he or she responds to incriminating questions. This comparison does not look for any complex pattern of responding (for example, high heart rate and low respiration rate when lying, and the reverse when telling the truth), but at the magnitude and frequency of physiological activity to various sorts of questions.

Early polygraphic comparisons often employed what has become known as the 'Relevant/Irrelevant' question comparison procedure. For example, relevant questions might be those to do with a crime of which a person was suspected, and irrelevant questions might ask 'Are you in Manchester now?' Lykken points out that

> If the subject shows a strong polygraphic reaction to some or all of the relevant questions [when stating that he was not involved in the crime], but not to the irrelevant questions, then his answers to the relevant questions are classified as deceptive. Most psychologists will find it hard to credit that so simple-minded a procedure has been in constant use since the 1920s. (1981: 105)

To their credit the vast majority of polygraphers would not nowadays countenance the use of this 'Relevant/Irrelevant' technique since they realize that even an innocent person is much more likely to display more physiological activity when (truthfully) responding to the relevant questions than to the irrelevant ones.

In the criminal setting the two most widely employed types of questioning now in use by polygraphers are usually called (a) the control question technique (CQT) and (b) the guilty knowledge test (GKT). Each procedure examines a person's physiological reactions to certain questions.

The control question technique

In the CQT the person is asked a series of questions, some of which are relevant to the crime in question (for example, 'Did you kill Mrs Smith?'), some of which are believed to cause concern in the person but which are irrelevant (for example, 'Have you ever engaged in unnatural sexual behaviour?', 'Have you ever stolen anything?'), and some of which are termed 'neutral' questions (for example, those asking for the person's age or name).

The irrelevant (or 'control') questions are supposed to be chosen with special care by the polygrapher so that a person innocent of the crime in question will nevertheless lie when responding 'No' to them. If a testee replies 'Yes' to a control question it is revised until he gives a (presumed deceptive) 'No' to it. It is assumed that for the innocent person their (supposed) lying in response to the control questions will cause more of a physiological response than will responses to the relevant questions. A well-trained polygrapher may spend over an hour talking to the person in order to choose control questions likely to cause considerable physiological reactions. Some polygraphers choose for control questions topics which occasioned a behavioural response (for example, breaking eye contact) in the first phase of the interrogation.

The rationale behind the CQT is that an innocent person will respond similarly or more to the control questions than to the relevant questions, but a guilty person (who, of course, will be lying to the relevant questions – hence the need for using a lie detector) will respond more to the relevant questions. Just how different the magnitudes of the reactions to these two types of questions need to be to avoid an 'inconclusive' decision is still under debate.

This technique has several worthwhile aspects; for example, since it compares some of a person's responses with other of his or her responses it is not affected by the vast differences that exist between people in their physiological reactivity. However, its main fault is that it is extremely difficult to devise control questions that would ensure the eliciting of stronger reactions in an innocent person than would the relevant questions relating to the crime of which they had been accused.

Professional polygraphers try to play down this problem, but in many cases it may be insuperable. It is likely to be a particular problem when the person being tested is innocent and believes polygraphy to be error-prone and therefore likely to misjudge him. This problem may be one reason why the CQT may be much more efficient when suggesting that a person is telling the truth than in suggesting that someone is lying. That is, the CQT does seem to lead to a substantial proportion of truthful, innocent people being judged as liars (see Chapter 2 below, by Carroll).

The CQT has also been used in the United States as an attempt to determine whether women who claim to have been raped did not, in fact, consent to the proven intercourse. Relevant questions such as 'Did you willingly consent to have sexual intercourse with John Shapiro?' are asked on the assumption that a raped woman (who would therefore be telling the truth) would respond less to this than a control question! Again the problem is finding control questions that would be more arousing for a truth-teller than would the relevant questions. The devising of control questions depends totally on the skill of the polygrapher.

The guilty knowledge test

A few polygraphers still use questioning techniques, other than the CQT and the GKT, that almost all research on this topic has found to be useless (for a review of these see Lykken, 1981). Apart from the CQT, another type of questioning that is sometimes used in criminal polygraphic lie detection is the guilty knowledge test (GKT). This suffers from some of the shortcomings of the CQT, but because it is concerned with information that only the offender (plus the authorities and the polygrapher) would know about, an innocent person is less likely to be falsely deemed guilty. Unfortunately, most polygraphers' training does not include use of the GKT.

In the GKT, each of several different questions is followed by several alternatives. For example, one question could be concerned with the type of implement used to kill someone. The polygrapher would examine a suspect's reactions to a question such as 'Was Mrs Smith killed with a hammer (pause), or a screwdriver (pause), or a knife (pause)?' Several such questions covering different facts would be asked. If the suspect's largest physiological reaction for each question was often occasioned by the alternative the police knew to be correct, the suspect would be deemed to be guilty.

The GKT seems far less likely to suggest falsely that a person is guilty than does the CQT, but it suffers from the limitation that it must focus on facts known to the authorities and to the offender that could not be known (or guessed) by an innocent person. Like the CQT, it has been criticized on the grounds that an offender wishing to deceive may be able to enhance his reactions to certain alternatives or to the irrelevant questions so that he appears to react as an innocent person might, in that his responses to the relevant information will now be smaller than his artificially enhanced reactions to the irrelevant information. It is certainly very easy for a person to enhance his physiological reactions, but professional polygraphers say they watch for this. Research suggests that it is not easy for an offender to reduce his reactions to the relevant information (see Chapter 10 below, by Gudjonsson).

The relevant control test

The CQT and sometimes the GKT are used in connection with criminal investigations. However, neither is really suitable for the most frequent application of polygraphy, namely the screening of job applicants or of employees. In these situations the person taking the test is not usually suspected of committing a specified criminal act and therefore the CQT and GKT are not applicable. Instead what is often referred to as the relevant control test (RCT) is employed. This test involves a fairly large number of 'relevant' questions such as 'Have you ever stolen anything from your employer?', 'Did you answer truthfully all the questions on the employment application form?', 'Have you ever been found guilty of a criminal offence?', and a few 'irrelevant' questions such as 'Is it Tuesday today?' Each is phrased so that the answer should be 'No'. The rationale behind this test concerns the possibility that the testee's reactions when responding to some of the relevant questions may be larger than to other relevant questions. If this were so the polygrapher would assume that these answers may be deceptive. As with the CQT and GKT the polygrapher will go through the questions to be asked before turning on the polygraph and may conduct the polygraph test two or three times, with the questions being asked in a different order each time, so that checks can be made to determine whether the testee's physiological reactivity was similar each time he responded to certain questions.

An obvious problem with this test is that it assumes that for the honest person the relevant questions are equally arousing. This may well not be so. Another problem is concerned with professional ethics. It has been reported (Lykken, 1981) that some polygraphers in employee/applicant screening ask very personal questions concerning a person's sexual, political and other behaviours. Unless there is strong evidence supporting the validity of the RCT, such questions may well be not only improper but also unlawful. Even if the RCT were found to be a valid procedure in the hands of a professional, the ethical aspects of its use warrant debate.

During the polygraph phase, or at the beginning of it, what has become known as a 'stimulation procedure' or 'stim test' will sometimes take place. This is a procedure designed to convince the suspect of the polygraph's validity as a lie detector. The polygrapher may, for example, ask the person to choose a playing card from a pack, to note it (for example, 'Ten of Clubs') and to replace it in the pack. The polygrapher then instructs the person to respond 'No' to each of several cards he calls out while appearing to examine the person's responses on the polygraph. The polygrapher then informs the person that the machine has revealed that the card was the 'Ten of Clubs'. (Little does the person know that every card in the pack was a 'Ten of Clubs'.) Other procedures employed by polygraphers to persuade the testee of the standing of their procedures include having a well-appointed office with various framed diplomas and other certificates present on the walls.

Scoring the polygraph charts

In scientific research the polygraph's output is represented via sweeping pens onto paper charts or it is fed directly into a computer. In either case precise, numerical quantification and measurement of the physiological activity monitored by the polygraph is undertaken. Thus when testing for differences between experimental treatments, statistical tests can be carried out upon numerical data. However, in lie detection it is by no means the case that numerical scoring of the polygraphic charts is performed. Until fairly recently many polygraphers decided which questions had occasioned the largest responses by merely looking at the charts without bothering to measure each response. Since most polygraphers also interact with the testee, such impressionistic global scoring procedures were open to being biased by the polygrapher's expectations, among other factors. Nowadays, however, a growing number of polygraphers do measure and quantify each response in order to compare it with others. A few go so far as to pass their polygraph charts (plus a list of the questions used) to colleague polygraphers who then attempt to decide whether the testee was being deceitful or truthful or whether the charts are inconclusive. While this is a laudable though sadly rare procedure, it still leaves open the question of precisely how much larger certain responses have to be in comparison with others before a 'conclusive' truthful or deceitful decision is arrived at.

Conclusion

Chapter 10 below, by Gudjonsson, is concerned with purposive attempts (counter-measures) not to be judged a liar by a polygrapher. However, we should also ask whether all those individuals who might not respond truthfully to incriminating questions will display the reactivity expected by polygraphers. Not only is there debate concerning whether individuals with psychopathic or sociopathic personalities will demonstrate reactivity when being deceitful, there is also the possibility that some people actually are not aware that they are lying. Furthermore, the reactivity shown by people when lying to incriminating questions is likely to depend on how accurate they believe polygraphy to be at detecting deception. If a liar believes that the polygraph test is not accurate then he may not demonstrate differential responding to the various types of questions asked.

The major questioning techniques used by polygraphers have been outlined. However, it has been pointed out that many of them do not solely base their decision concerning whether the testee is being deceitful or not upon the record of the testee's physiological reactivity. Until it is made absolutely clear on which forms of the testee's behaviours and responses decisions about possible deception are based, there can be no proper scientific study of the validity of polygraphers' procedures.

Unfortunately, only a small number of people who use polygraphy in certain circumstances are themselves trained scientists with degrees in such relevant disciplines as physiology and psychology. Many polygraphers are former police officers who, while they may have gained some experience concerning the questioning of suspects, have at best only a rudimentary understanding of all the physiological and psychological factors involved. Even that small proportion of polygraphers who have attended a short course at a polygraphy school will not, at the end of the course, have sufficient knowledge to make a scientific appraisal of polygraphy. This may be one of the reasons why the vast majority of polygraphers, who may themselves be honest, decent citizens, seem not to question in any effective way the validity of what they are doing. It is hoped that they, as well as other groups in society, will benefit from reading this book.

2

How accurate is polygraph lie detection?

Douglas Carroll

The apparently straightforward question, 'How accurate is poly-graph lie detection?', has been subject to at least two different interpretations. Proponents of lie detection have generally under-stood the question to mean, 'How accurate are judgements of truth or deception based on polygraphic records plus all other available information?' Since, in practice, the polygraph examiner's assess-ment is derived from a variety of evidence (behaviour during the examination, case file information), we should, it is argued, give particular weighting to such global estimates of accuracy. However, in the absence of data on the independent contribution of these other sources of evidence, global accuracy measures of this sort are clearly insufficient. We simply cannot determine from them the particular role played by the polygraph. Critics of polygraph lie detection have generally understood the question to mean something different: 'How accurate are judgements of truth or deception based solely on the information available from polygraph charts?' This is an impor-tant question to ask. It brings us a lot nearer what should be the proper interpretation of our question: what is the polygraph's par-ticular contribution to accurate judgements of truth or deception? If the polygraph is indeed the main source of accurate judgements in practice, then we would expect estimates of accuracy derived from polygraph charts to closely approximate the accuracy rates found with global assessments, where polygraph charts are just part of the matrix of evidence available. It goes without saying that we would not simply expect correspondence per se, but correspondingly *high* accuracy rates.

Two sorts of data are available on accuracy: data from laboratory studies mainly involving mock crimes and data from field studies of actual criminal suspects. Both have mainly involved one particular questioning technique: the control question test (CQT), where suspects are posed three sorts of questions (*irrelevant*, neutral ques-tions usually relating to some innocuous biographical detail; *relevant*, accusatory questions relating to the crime at issue; and *control*, emotive questions but unrelated to the crime at issue).

Reliability

Before considering accuracy it is worth saying something about reliability. It is a concept which has been much misunderstood. As used by psychologists, reliability refers not to the accuracy of evaluations but to their consistency across time or among examiners. Validity is the term reserved for accuracy. The relationship between reliability and validity is important to grasp. Reliability is a necessary condition for validity, but not a sufficient one. Validity, then, will be low where there is little reliability. However, judgements may be highly consistent but essentially inaccurate.

Reliability, whether across time or among examiners, has been expressed either in terms of percentage agreement or by means of a correlation coefficient. Percentage agreement is simply the percentage of overall judgements on which, for example, two examiners concur. For instance, if two examiners are asked to make ten assessments and agree on eight of them, then percentage agreement is 80 percent. Correlation coefficients are indices of relationship that vary numerically from -1.00 to $+1.00$. A coefficient of $+1.00$ signifies a perfect positive relationship; -1.00 signifies a perfect negative relationship, and 0.00 signifies no relationship at all.

In the context of polygraph lie detection, two sorts of reliability have been investigated. One may be labelled intra-examiner reliability and refers to the consistency of an individual examiner's judgements across time. Hunter and Ash (1973) had seven examiners analyse twenty sets of polygraph charts on two occasions, separated by at least a three-month interval. The charts related to actual criminal cases and six of the examiners were highly experienced. Intra-examiner reliability, that is, occasion-to-occasion agreement, ranged from 75 percent to 90 percent for the seven examiners (the average was 85 percent).

More usually, though, studies have investigated inter-examiner reliability, for example, the extent of agreement between two or more examiners. In a laboratory study, using a mock crime procedure, Barland and Raskin (1975) considered the consistency of the judgements made by the original examiner and five additional, highly experienced polygraph examiners given access to the charts. All six examiners concurred on only 33 percent of the cases. However, at least a majority of the examiners agreed on 86 percent of the cases. Correlation coefficients were computed to explore the concurrences between pairs of examiners. Coefficients ranged from 0.78 to 0.95; the average coefficient was 0.86. In a study investigating, among other things, the impact of counter-measures on the incidence of detection, Honts (1982) found a similar level of concurrence when comparing the original examiner's judgements with those made by one additional expert examiner given access to the polygraph charts. In this case the coefficient of correlation was 0.89. Using a more sophisticated statistical approach, Horvath (1977), in a field study, found that the intra-class correlation coefficient, calculated to compare simultaneously the judgements of ten examiners, was 0.89. However, not all studies have found such impressively high reliability. Hammond (1980) in a mock crime investigation reported correlations between the judgements of the original and subsequent examiner of only 0.64 where subjects were innocent and 0.61 where they were guilty.

Thus while acceptably high reliability has characterized the judgements of truth or deception in several studies, it is by no means a universal feature. In a recent field study Kleinmuntz and Szucko (1984a) examined the consistency of the judgements made by six professional polygraph examiners given between them 120 sets of charts for evaluation. Inter-examiner reliability was uniformly low. The fifteen correlation coefficients used to test the concurrence between pairs of examiners ranged from 0.24 to 0.54 (the average coefficient was 0.43).

Laboratory studies of accuracy

Turning now to validity and, first of all, laboratory studies, the Office of Technology Assessment of the United States Congress (1983) recently identified fourteen laboratory studies of the CQT procedure. It was found that on average 88.6 percent of the guilty were correctly classified while 82.6 percent of the innocent were correctly classified. These have to be placed against chance detection rates of 50 percent. However, this survey encompassed studies whose methodology bore only marginal resemblance to field lie detection. A slightly different picture emerges if we focus specifically on those laboratory studies that closely mirror CQT practices in the field. The following inclusion criteria were adopted: studies should have monitored the full range of field physiological measurements; they should have involved reasonable sample sizes; they should not have involved subjects who had been administered a drug or instructed in the use of counter-measures. The results of studies meeting these criteria are summarized in Table 2.1. The first three studies listed had guilty subjects engage in a mock crime. In the Waid, Orne and Orne (1981) study guilty subjects had to conceal certain code words from the examiner, and in the Barland (1981) study guilty subjects had to lie about a biographical detail. While accuracy rates vary markedly among studies, the average success at detecting guilt is 85.4 percent,

Table 2.1   *Laboratory studies of accuracy*

Study	Status of subjects	Number of subjects	Percent accuracy	Percent guilty classified innocent (false negative)	Percent innocent classified guilty (false positive)
Barland and Raskin (1975)	Guilty	26	88.5	11.5	28.6
	Innocent	21	71.4		
Raskin and Hare (1978)	Guilty	21	100.0	0	8.7
	Innocent	23	91.3		
Hammond (1980)	Guilty	24	95.8	4.2	33.3
	Innocent	18	66.7		
Waid, Orne and Orne (1981)	Guilty	40	72.5	27.5	23.5
	Innocent	34	76.5		
Barland (1981)	Guilty	26	80.8	19.2	23.8
	Innocent	21	76.2		
Average accuracy[a]			85.4 76.9	14.6	23.1

[a] These averages were computed taking into account the different sample sizes.

almost the same as that found in the American study. However, the average rate for correctly identifying the innocent is noticeably lower, 76.9 percent.

However, this is the accuracy of detection when the examiner can exploit data other than those provided by the polygraph. Unfortunately, only a small number of laboratory studies have sought recourse to 'blind' evaluation, where judgements are made solely on polygraph charts. Barland and Raskin (1975) reported only that all six examiners in their study (the original plus five 'blind' examiners) managed accuracy rates of 79–86 percent; the average was 81.7 percent. Thus there would appear to have been little, if any, drop in accuracy when the polygraph charts were scored 'blind'. The data from another study (Hammond, 1980) are presented in Table 2.2.

Table 2.2   *Hammond's summary of results for global and blind examination*

| Classification | Original examiners | | Blind examiner | |
	Actually guilty	Actually innocent	Actually guilty	Actually innocent
Guilty	23	6	21	2
Innocent	1	12	0	4
Inconclusive	8	12	11	24

Source: Hammond (1980)

Ignoring the inconclusive cases for a moment, there would again seem to be no overall drop in accuracy from global to blind evaluation. However, it is also readily apparent that the 'blind' evaluator offered significantly fewer definite judgements, particularly in the case of the innocent. While the original examiners correctly identified twelve of the innocent subjects, the 'blind' evaluator was able to provide an unequivocal pronouncement of innocence for only four of them. This would seem to imply that there was sensitive information available during the original examination that was simply unobtainable from the polygraph charts alone.

Conclusion on laboratory studies
Laboratory studies of field CQT practices, then, suggest global accuracy rates of around 80 percent. There are more false positive errors than negative errors. False positive errors occur when innocent individuals are wrongly classified as guilty; false negative errors are where guilty persons are classified as innocent. Further, the evidence, such as it is, indicates that reliance on information solely from the polygraph would not appear to affect accuracy unduly; it also suggests, though, that in reaching a decision the original examiner makes considerable use of non-polygraphic sources of information, particularly in the case of innocent subjects.

Attention has so far focused on the CQT, since it has proved the most popular vehicle for laboratory researchers. However, in practice, particularly in employment screening applications where no specific crime has been identified, the examiner is usually reduced to asking only two sorts of questions: relevant and irrelevant. With decisions framed from the comparison of physiological reactions to just these two quite different sorts of questions (i.e. in the absence of control questions), one would suspect even greater scope for error, particularly false positive error, in such circumstances. Accordingly, it is unfortunate that this approach has been subject to so little formal analysis. I know of only two recent investigations, both laboratory studies, that deal with accuracy in this context. Correa and Adams (1981) had twenty subjects lie on a pre-employment questionnaire and twenty tell the truth. They reported correctly identifying all of the subjects, i.e. 100 percent accuracy. However, the liars in this study had to lie about virtually everything: six items in all on the questionnaire. It is perhaps not surprising, then, that identification was so easy. When we turn to the success at identifying individual lies rather than lying individuals, a different picture emerges. Only 75 percent of the lies were, in fact, correctly identified. In the other study Barland (1981) had thirty subjects lie about only one biographical detail, undoubtedly a closer approximation of reality.

Twenty-six subjects told the truth. Of the deceptive, 86 percent were correctly identified; of the innocent, however, only 76 percent were correctly classified. These data are remarkably similar to the averages reported earlier for the CQT, and it should perhaps be pointed out that the relevant and irrelevant questions were, in fact, embedded in a CQT protocol. As yet, we are without any sort of 'blind' chart assessment of the relevant–irrelevant question technique.

Finally, there are good grounds for suspecting the utility of laboratory studies for the purposes of evaluating accuracy in the field. The most compelling concerns the emotional significance of accusatory questions for innocent people in the two contexts. In the laboratory such questions are of little psychological significance; only the subject's acquisition of some minor incentive is at stake. Given that our biology is sensitive to significance, one would expect innocent criminal suspects to show relatively more responsiveness to accusatory questions than innocent laboratory subjects. In short, an analysis of polygraph data from the laboratory will yield unrealistically high estimates of accuracy regarding the innocent.

Field studies of accuracy

Designing field studies that conform to the highest principles of experimental design is no easy matter. The main problem is finding a satisfactory criterion for assigning guilt or innocence. Many studies have managed this in only a small proportion of cases, and accordingly accuracy rates so derived may be unrepresentative of accuracy over the full range of cases. There is one very parsimonious explanation for why someone who has failed a polygraph test does not subsequently confess their guilt – they are, in fact, innocent! The crucial attribute of any criterion is that it must be independent of the polygraph examiner's judgement. Thus retrospective comparisons of examiners' judgements against court dispositions, where the examiner's decisions are part of the evidence contributing to the disposition (for example, Peters, 1982), are unacceptable. By the same token, we should not place overly much reliance on the undoubtedly sincere, but nonetheless unsubstantiated pronouncements of polygraph examiners as to their success rates. Aside from criterion problems, we undoubtedly have to bear in mind that most general of human propensities: while we can generally recount our successes with ease, we frequently experience difficulty with our failures. Only a rather small number of field studies are sufficiently free of such problems to warrant serious consideration.

In a study that is frequently cited by proponents of lie detection, Bersh (1969) had four experienced attorneys judge the guilt or innocence of suspects on the basis of their evidential files, minus of course any reference to polygraph examinations. The four attorneys were unanimous in 157 instances and managed a majority decision in a further fifty-nine instances. The correspondence between their judgements and the original polygraph examiners' assessments are presented in Table 2.3. Accuracy rates were impressive where there

Table 2.3   *Bersh's summary of results of global evaluation*

Study	Status of suspects	Number of suspects	Percent accuracy	Percent false negative	Percent false positive
With unanimous panel assessment	Guilty	70	93.0	7.0	8.0
	Innocent	87	92.0		
With majority panel assessment	Guilty	34	70.5	29.5	20.0
	Innocent	25	80.0		

Source: Bersh (1969)

was a unanimous panel decision, although they were noticeably lower in instances of a majority decision. However, rather than clinch the matter in favour of polygraph lie detection, the Bersh study merely reveals the limitations of relying on global accuracy rates. High accuracy rates cannot be attributed in any significant measure to the polygraph where there exists other salient clues to guilt or innocence. As with the laboratory research already considered, Bersh's examiners could make use of a range of verbal and non-verbal behaviour exhibited during polygraph examination. Further in contrast to laboratory practice, but in line with general field practice, Bersh's examiners also had access to the evidential files upon which the attorneys based their judgements. The accuracy rates reported by Bersh are, in fact, precisely what would be expected had a fifth assessor judged guilt or innocence on the same information as the original panel of four. Considered together with Lykken's (1981) revelation that, in a subsequent study, Bersh's polygraph charts actually generated fairly inconsistent decisions regarding guilt or innocence, the suspicion must remain that the original polygraph examiners relied decidedly more on the case files than on the polygraph charts. There is certainly nothing in the study to allay such suspicions. A compelling case for the inclusion of the polygraph could be made in this instance only if it could be demonstrated that an interrogator with no polygraph but with access to the case files reached decisions that were significantly less in accord with the panel's judgements than were the polygraph examiners' decisions.

Table 2.4   *Summary of results of field studies that involved blind assessment of the polygraph records*

Study	Status of suspects	Number of suspects	Percent accuracy	Percent false negative	Percent false positive
Barland and	Guilty	40	97	3	55
Raskin	Innocent	11	45		
(1976)					
Horvath	Guilty	28	79	23	49
(1977)	Innocent	28	50		
Kleinmuntz	Guilty	50	76	24	37
and Szucko	Innocent	50	64		
(1984a)					
Average			83	17	43
accuracy[a]			57		

[a] These averages were computed taking into account the different sample sizes.

A requirement such as this is given particular force when one considers the results of field studies using 'blind' chart evaluation. The outcome of these studies is presented in Table 2.4. The Barland and Raskin (1976) study employed a panel of five experienced attorneys to ascertain guilt or innocence on the basis of evidential files. While Barland conducted the polygraph examination, Raskin, 'blind' to the case files, analysed the charts. Of the ninety-two original cases, sufficient panel agreement was reached on sixty-four of them. Of these, thirteen were classified as inconclusive by Raskin; accordingly, the data presented deal only with the remaining fifty-one cases. Horvath (1977) approached the matter of assigning guilt or innocence in a different manner. Guilt was presumed where there was a confession of guilt, and innocence where there was a confession of guilt by another. Horvath located twenty-eight examples of each from the police files and distributed the polygraph charts to ten trained polygraph examiners for 'blind' evaluation. Five of the examiners had more than three years' experience; five had less. Thus the data presented are, in fact, derived from 560 judgements. Aside from the data presented in Table 2.4, one other result is worth mentioning: examiner experience did not significantly affect accuracy. The recent Kleinmuntz and Szucko (1984a) study adopted a similar approach, selecting for evaluation the polygraph charts of fifty confessed thieves and fifty innocents who, although initially suspected of the same crimes, were subsequently cleared through the confessions of the actual thieves. The charts were distributed among six professional polygraph examiners for 'blind' evaluation of guilt or innocence. Aside from the data presented in Table 2.4, one other result is again worth mentioning. Overall aggregate accuracy of 69.6

percent (obtained by averaging 63 percent and 76 percent) conceals a range of individual examiner accuracy that never exceeded 80 percent.

These data largely speak for themselves; overall accuracy is generally low, and the rate of false positive judgements staggeringly high. Thus polygraph data per se would seem to be remarkably insensitive, particularly to a suspect's innocence. Expressed another way, the 'blind' evaluation studies strongly imply that the polygraph contributes nothing of worth to traditional means of establishing innocence. In fact, the data it provides probably mislead.

Given the discrepancy between these data and those reported by Bersh, it would seem clear that accurate assessments, particularly of innocence, in the course of a usual polygraph evaluation have little if anything to do with the pattern of a suspect's physiological reactions. On what, then, might the examiner be relying? The two most likely sources of information have already been mentioned: the data in the evidential files and the suspect's general demeanour during interrogation. Having said a little about the former, let us briefly consider the latter. In order to assess the utility of this possible non-polygraphic source of information it is necessary to add to the usual procedure, as a control, either an interrogator or an observer with no access to the polygraph. Such a control was included by Ginton et al. (1982) in a CQT investigation of Israeli policemen known to have cheated or not on a mathematics test. Unfortunately, only two dishonest subjects were available for testing, and so attention will focus on the thirteen innocent subjects. The data are presented in Table 2.5. There were three different assessors: the interrogator (access to polygraph data and subject's general demeanour); the observer (access only to demeanour); the 'blind' evaluator (access only to polygraph data). While the observer's accuracy matched that of the original interrogator, the 'blind' chart evaluator performed no better than chance. These data strongly suggest that the subject's general demeanour offers more accurate grounds for attributing innocence than the polygraph chart, and that the polygraph, in fact, brings nothing of merit to interrogation as far as innocent suspects are concerned.

Table 2.5 *Ginton's summary of results for innocent subjects*

Classification	Original examiner	Observer	Blind evaluator
Guilty	2	2	3
Innocent	11	11	7
Inconclusive	0	0	3

Source: Ginton et al. (1982)

Conclusion on field studies

The field studies, then, far from establishing a case for the polygraph, lead us to conclude that there is little or no case. The Bersh study offers no evidence that the impressive accuracy rates owed anything to the polygraph. Subsequent studies using 'blind' chart evaluation strongly suggest that Bersh and other field examiners rely heavily on non-polygraphic sources of information, since 'blind' evaluation yields aggregate accuracy rates that are no greater than 70 percent. Of particular concern, in this context, is the high level of false positives; 'blind' evaluation identifies the innocent at round about chance level. In addition, although few data exist, it would appear that an observer, regarding the suspect's general behaviour from another room, does just as well as an experienced polygraph examiner, and better than someone blindly evaluating the polygraph charts.

Overall conclusion

If proponents wish to convince the scientific community of the merits of polygraph lie detection, I submit that they will have to develop a more convincing case than the one currently on offer. Their case must be founded on studies which include the necessary controls for non-polygraphic sources of information, that is, studies which compare the accuracy of assessments derived from case-file material and the subject's demeanour during questioning with that based on these sources plus the polygraph record. I strongly suspect that such studies would confirm what the available data suggest: that polygraph lie detection adds nothing positive to conventional approaches to interrogation and assessment.

3

Lie detection as a psychometric procedure

Steve Blinkhorn

Mind and body are intimately interconnected, intertwined and inter-dependent – of this there is no longer room for doubt. If, once upon a time, it was possible to believe that physical and mental events belong to essentially different spheres, in contact only in the sense of a spiritual mind inhabiting the wondrous mechanism of the body, that is no longer so. And whilst we may know less in detail than we would like, we do know a great deal about the physiology of emotion and of stress. We can alter mental states by the administration of any of a long list of drugs; with training we can learn to alter some of our bodily functions at will. The lie detector is a procedure that takes advantage of this intimate interconnection of mind and body to discover facts about the mind from observation of physical responses to questions.

And that, at its simplest, is what the fuss is all about. In theory a polygraph examiner watches instruments detecting physiological changes associated with stress and emotion. Using one of several different questioning techniques, the examiner looks for responses which indicate *extra* emotional response or stress to pinpoint deceit-ful answers. There is little doubt about the relationship in general terms between the measures used – skin resistance, heart and respiration rate and so forth – and stress. The instruments used are fairly straightforward and well understood. The process can be taught in a few weeks.

In principle, then, we have a technique which is the stuff of the dreams of early scientific psychologists and of the popular novelist. There is ample evidence that most guilty people fail the lie-detector test – accuracy rates above 90 percent are quoted. Why should the test not be adopted far more widely?

But there is a dimension to the discussion of the polygraph test which has never been properly explored. In some important respects the polygraph test is very similar to other psychological tests used in screening for employment, in the diagnosis of mental disorder or in vocational guidance. And in pursuing this line of analysis we shall come to understand just how badly flawed the lie detector can be, noting in passing that many of its supposed successes could well be accidental.

What is a psychometric test?

In most people's minds psychometric tests are pencil-and-paper, questionnaire-type techniques for getting quick measures of intelligence or personality. But that is only part of the story. The theory of psychometric tests applies to *any* method which infers a person's mental state, behavioural tendencies or capacities from a standard sample of behaviour. And that theory is very highly developed – it is one of the outstanding durable achievements of scientific psychology.

So let us examine the lie-detector test from the point of view of psychometric theory: how does it measure up to the standards demanded of less glamorously scientific, more mundane psychological measurement techniques? For the only real difference is that the lie-detector test concerns itself with what are hoped to be involuntary responses, rather than with responses which – regardless of how they will be interpreted – are directly under the examinees' control.

Psychometric tests require standardization, guarantees of reliability, tests of validity and freedom from bias if they are to be used with confidence in the assessment of members of the general public. Information about these are to be found in the manual published with a test, along with a comprehensive account of the rationale for the test, statistical analyses of large sets of data relating to the test, and detailed discussion of a variety of technical issues surrounding the proper use of the test – for instance how it performs with regard to sex, race, educational level and so forth.

In this context *standardization* is a matter of independence of the procedure from the idiosyncrasies of the examiner; *reliability* relates principally to the extent to which independent examiners draw the same conclusions from the same charts; *validity* is to do with the extent to which the procedure yields accurate classifications on the basis of a genuine connection between the polygraph evidence and the states or procedures hypothesized; and *bias* could arise inter alia in the disproportionate misclassification of individuals belonging to social or ethnic subgroups, or having temperamental dispositions associated with chronically high or low physiological arousal.

Standardization

Psychological tests are usually standardized in two important ways. First, the test is the same for everyone who takes it. Everyone has the opportunity to answer the same questions or solve the same problems (though it may be that different questions, carefully researched and calibrated so as to be equivalent, are asked in some special types of test). Second, an examinee's score is compared with *norms* – the range of scores in a large sample of people who have taken the same test. The norms provide a standard of comparison for scores on a standard test – this is what makes the results of the test interpretable.

The purpose of all this is to turn the examiner into a nonentity as far as the examinee is concerned. Conditions of testing should be identical for all, to the extent that the establishment of rapport with the examinee is considered to be of the first importance.

Now obviously the lie-detector test does not always involve the same questions, nor is it possible to do the kind of calibration which is sometimes done with other tests. On the contrary, much of the skill of the polygraph examiner is held to lie in the choice and sequencing of questions. In the control question technique, for instance, it is important to choose questions which are stressful or emotionally arousing to the individual examinee as a baseline for comparison. In this respect, an attempt is made to standardize the measures *within* each examinee's record, and then identify responses which may be categorized as deceitful. So the decision as to whether an individual examinee is lying is taken on the basis of comparison of responses of that examinee only (and the experience of the examiner), *not* by comparison with other examinees' responses directly.

In other words the measure we are dealing with is normally the polygraph examiner's judgement regarding the examinee's responses, not the intensity of these responses in some absolute or hard scientific sense. But how well do different examiners agree in their judgements when considering charts from the same interrogation? Indeed, how consistent in general is the evidence of lie-detector tests? In psychometric terminology, this aspect of the matter is called reliability.

Reliability

There is a voluminous literature on the reliability of psychological tests. The more reliable a test is, the more immune it is to random effects causing error in scores. And there are many ways of estimating the reliability of a test. All textbooks on psychological testing give an account of reliability theory, and many general psychology texts include some treatment of the topic. Anastasi (1976) gives a clear conventional account; Cronbach (1981) is more sophisticated and treats the topic in a way favoured by more theoretically inclined measurement specialists.

The estimation of reliability involves deciding what counts as a source of error. For instance, if you have a cold on the day you take a test, it could well be that you perform less well than you would normally. Most tests are sensitive to some extent to factors like that. What is much more serious is if your score on a test depends heavily on who is conducting or scoring the test, or if it fluctuates markedly from day to day. So different methods for looking at reliability focus on different sources of error. Most of them result in a figure which represents the proportion of 'true-score variance' in scores. Without going into technical detail, a figure of 1.0 (never achieved in practice) represents a rock-solid measure. A figure of 0.0 represents random, unreliable results.

There are two particularly useful ways of looking at the reliability of the polygraph test: do the different *measures* (heart rate, skin resistance, respiration) tell the same story; does the same *examiner* interpret the same *charts* the same way twice running? Barland and Raskin (1976) present evidence which is very much to the point. First, as regards the different measures, the correlations amongst the different measures can politely be described as modest (Table 3.1).

Table 3.1 *Correlations amongst component measures*

	Respiration	SRR	Cardio	Total
Respiration	1.000	0.185	0.089	0.552
SRR	0.185	1.000	0.395	0.863
Cardio	0.089	0.395	1.000	0.632
Total	0.552	0.863	0.632	1.000

Source: Barland and Raskin (1976)

The cardiographic and respiration measures are virtually unrelated; skin resistance has some slight relationship with the other two measures. The only sizeable relationships – between each measure and the total – are the result of a statistical artefact known as part–whole overlap. To put some scale on these figures, consider that different tests of mental ability commonly correlate well above 0.70, and even different supervisors' judgements of workers' performance, which are notoriously unreliable, are often correlated about 0.60. So, rather than the three component measures providing mutual support, they appear to tell substantially different stories. Any coherence between them is mostly in the imagination of the examiner, rather than on the charts.

In psychometric terms, these results count as no evidence at all of the reliability of the lie detector. On the contrary, they suggest it is a most unpromising technique. As to the agreement between scorings of the same charts by the same examiner, Barland and Raskin's Table

1 gives values between 0.80 and 0.92 after a six-month interval. These would be very acceptable for a complete retest (a new examination, followed by comparison of charts across a six-month time interval), but for a rescoring of the same charts they are disturbingly low – especially since the examiner remembered his overall judgement in each case. One would expect little short of perfect agreement if the examiners' judgements were really based on the evidence of the charts. Certainly, any normal test which showed such great variation on rescoring by independent scorers, let alone the same scorers, would get and deserve a pasting in the technical journals.

When independent examiners rescore charts, the almost invariable tendency is for them to produce fewer definite conclusions, and more inconclusive results, than the examiner who conducted the original questioning. The natural interpretation of this is that examiners tend to base their conclusions in part on evidence which is not represented in the polygraph charts. In other words, they exercise observational skills and combine their observations of the examinee with what is represented in the charts to produce a scoring of the charts. In confusing their subjective judgements with the apparently scientific evidence of the polygraph they attribute qualities to the instruments which they do not have (see Chapter 2 above, by Carroll).

Thus, such evidence as there is of the reliability of the polygraph test is very unsatisfactory. The different measures used do not cohere at all well; when the original examiner rescores the same charts he does not replicate his original results; and independent scorers see less certainty in a set of charts than the original examiner. These results alone are enough to raise serious doubts about the credibility of evidence based on polygraph examination.

Validity

When all is said and done, however, what matters most is whether the lie detector accurately detects lies. This is where most of the research effort has been concentrated.

Investigation of the validity of the ordinary run of psychological tests focuses on correlations among tests, and between tests and independent criterion measures – such as job performance, school achievement or the results of therapy.

In the case of the lie detector, the independent decision of a jury, the judgement of an expert panel or independent evidence from a contrived experimental situation provides the criterion measure. But the most remarkable thing about the published evidence concerning the validity of the lie detector is how ineptly and inappropriately it is presented on both sides. Most usually the percentage of 'correct' decisions, the percentage of guilty subjects detected and the percentage of innocent subjects exonerated are the statistics given. But from the point of view of a psychometrician these figures are neither here nor there. In fact they are often positively misleading.

If most of your subjects are guilty, and most are found deceptive by the polygraph, then most of the decisions based on polygraph evidence will be correct. Similarly if most are innocent, and most pass the lie detector, then most decisions will be correct. A large number of published studies are unbalanced in this way. But lie detection works the other way round; it is not a matter of how many guilty people fail, or how many innocent people pass. The real issue is, how many who fail are guilty? Or, to put it another way, if you are on a jury and the evidence says the prisoner failed a lie-detector test, what are the chances that he is guilty?

In fact the only relevant questions concern those who fail the test. Consider the (hypothetical) figures in Table 3.2.

Table 3.2   *Sample figures*

	Innocent	Guilty
Pass	72	1
Fail	18	9

A hundred people are tested: 81 percent are correctly classified; 90 percent of the guilty fail; 80 percent of the innocent pass. And yet of these who fail, only one in three is guilty. This contrived example demonstrates how misleading talk of 'percent correct decisions' can be – especially when most of those tested are innocent.

Now for some real data. Horvath (1977) presents results from ten examiners' judgements of charts derived from 112 criminal suspects, balanced to ensure equal numbers of guilty and innocent subjects, verified and unverified cases, person crime and property crime (see Table 3.3). The statistics for verified cases of person crime are

Table 3.3   *Polygraph examiners' judgements of charts compared with verified results for person crime*

Polygraph examiners' judgement	Verified	
	Deceptive	Truthful
Deceptive	78.6	50.0
Truthful	21.4	50.0

Figures are column percentages.
Source: Horvath (1977)

representative. Notice that there is a tendency for more truthful answers to be classified as deceptive than vice versa. What is more, given the known equal numbers in each column, it is plain that the polygraph results offer only a modest improvement over guessing – only about 61 percent of those judged guilty by the lie-detector examiners were in fact deceptive.

Now these results are representative of how badly the blind evaluation of polygraph charts can reflect what is called in the jargon 'ground truth' – yet they could without deliberate dissimulation be held to show 78.6 percent accuracy in detecting the guilty. More properly they could be said to show a small improvement over chance. The trouble is, you have to work the sums over again for every set of data, and for any future use of the polygraph test we of course do not know what proportion of these tested will in fact be trying to deceive.

There is no straightforward way of summarizing all the information in tables like these, and certainly not in a single figure. Investigators who report 'highly significant correlations' or 'significant chi-squared statistics' show little appreciation of the nature of the statistics they are using or of their relevance to the point at issue.

In fact, the general finding is that innocent subjects are more likely to be classified as deceptive (except where the guilty knowledge technique is used) than guilty subjects are to be classified innocent. Horvath's data are just a particularly stark case of this effect. There is even some evidence that the *victims* of crime are more likely to be classified as deceptive than subjects with no involvement.

Wider issues

So far, the lie detector looks rather unhappy judged on psychometric criteria. But there are two issues that are worth pursuing further and wider.

The first of these concerns the use to which the lie detector is put. It is used to yield a *decision* not a *measure*. Now decisions often depend on measures: governments watch economic indicators and adjust policies in the light of what they suggest; medical treatment is prescribed on the basis of measures of physiological indicators; half a hundred everyday decisions are based on informal measures of what will fit our pocket, our pretensions or our prejudices: too expensive, too demeaning, too left-wing.

When psychometric tests are used for making employment or educational decisions, the measures are clearly distinguished from the decision criteria. The measures are independent of the criteria they are meant to predict. You can shift your criteria without changing the measures. Someone who does badly on an employment screening test *might* have proved successful in the job, but the employer will probably have found equally successful candidates from amongst those who did well. High scorers are more likely to do better: the decision is based on probability. The unsuccessful can try again elsewhere another time. When there is only one opportunity, or only one test, then quite rightly there is great public concern about the validity, the fairness and the reliability of the test used.

The lie detector purports to ascertain fact on a yes/no basis – facts which have severe consequences for the future of individuals. If you are convicted of a crime on the basis of polygraph evidence, you cannot try again in another court later. This would matter little if there were never false positive results, if the innocent were never wrongly implicated, if all the errors were failures to detect. But that, as we have seen, is not so.

Secondly, the fact that there tend to be more false positive than false negative results suggests that there is more than just *random* error at work in lie-detector studies. The sort of asymmetries that Horvath found, replicated in less extreme form elsewhere, are actually rather unusual in psychological assessment. They suggest that two different processes are at work, whose combined effects are represented in the outcomes.

For instance, suppose that the lie detector gave a positive result if the subject was *either* lying *or* had a more reactive autonomic nervous system than average. In this case exactly the sort of pattern that is observed in the published data would be expected to result. Add in a dose of random error for good measure – and there is no test yet devised free from random error – and you end up with some guilty subjects being correctly detected, not because the polygraph picks up symptoms of deceit, but because it picks up evidence of nervous reactivity in general.

This is a line of research that has been more or less neglected: what do false positive subjects have in common? Researchers are far more concerned with counter-measures the guilty can take, and whether psychopaths can successfully evade detection. But there is a mass of evidence supporting the view that just the kinds of indicators used in the lie detector relate as well to stable measurable temperamental and constitutional differences amongst individuals, although there is much disagreement as to how to explain these findings in detail.

What if the over-reactive individual is over-represented in the false positives? In real uses of the lie detector, would the evidence be discounted if a personality test showed the suspect to be of a nervous disposition? And what if he tried to fake the personality test?

It could even be that very perceptive individuals detect small shifts in the voice, posture or manner of the examiner when the critical questions are asked, shifts which neither examiner nor subject are consciously aware of, yet to the significance of which the subject's biology is sensitive. Such suspects might well become false positives.

Changes in voice patterns have provided a basis for the detection of stress, using electronic detection techniques. Many cases of animal 'genius' (horses and dogs doing arithmetic, for instance) have proved to depend on the animal's sensitivity to slight and unconscious signals from their trainers. Indeed, almost all cases of 'psychic' phenomena which are not either straightforward fraud, conjuring or exploitation of human credulity turn out to involve the perception of very slight and subtle responses which normally go unnoticed.

Polygraph examiners always know which are the significant questions – the examination techniques require that they know in most cases. Unwittingly, they may be signalling to the examinee which questions have significance for the investigation, and provoking a response amongst the sensitive. *Any* examination technique which involves live interaction between two people is potentially undermined by unwitting communication. The whole research enterprise which has popularized the notion of 'body language' stands as witness to this fact. Yet the lie detector is treated as if it were simply a matter of the attachment of laboratory instruments, and the polygraph examiner himself is seen as a detector of signals rather than as engaged in a complex and highly loaded social relationship with the examinee.

Honesty tests

We have concentrated on the lie detector in the context of detecting specific lies, where there is a specific issue of criminal guilt or innocence. An alternative use of the polygraph is to establish a subject's honesty in general, by asking questions which implicate him in relatively minor dishonesties, immoral or illegal acts, or the falsification of a job application form.

Whatever the accuracy or otherwise of the judgement of the polygraph examiner as to whether the subject is lying, the inference to judgement of his overall honesty is unjustified. The same is true of paper-and-pencil 'honesty' tests which purport to put a figure on the extent of an individual's honesty. Indeed honesty is notoriously not assessable in a way which holds across a wide variety of situations.

Fifty and more years ago a classic study of honesty as a personality trait demonstrated just how problematic the notion is. Honesty, for most people, is tied to situations. Consider the politician, scrupulously honest with his close colleagues, a practised liar for good professional reasons when appearing in public, and carrying on an affair with his secretary whilst concealing the fact from his wife, yet beyond reproach in handling the office petty cash. Honest or dishonest? Honesty tests are an exercise in printing, publishing and marketing, not in psychological measurement.

Why does the lie detector seem to work?

It is too cynical to claim that the polygraph lie-detection process has achieved a measure of acceptance merely on the basis of the gullibility of the public. A reading of the research data suggests that original examiners do better when they take account of their observations of the behaviour and demeanour of the subjects than when they score charts blindly. And of course this makes a good deal of sense. Polygraph practitioners sometimes specifically make the claim that it is the whole process of examination that has validity, not the simple scoring of polygraph charts. They have the opportunity of watching the subject over an extended interview in which they explore various sensitive areas in his life.

This in itself is a fairly good way of forming a judgement as to whether a suspect is lying about a particular topic – it often happens in the course of criminal trials. And we may suppose that people who do this for a living may become more expert at judging their fellow citizens in this context than most of us need to or choose to.

But this is not an argument for the use of polygraph instruments in lie detection. It is an argument for giving special credence to evidence given by practised interrogators who happen, by way of a side-show, to strap various wires and cuffs onto their victims, meanwhile assuring them of the infallibility of their gizmos.

The choice of question, the timing of questions, the scoring of charts, the interpretation of scores in combination with the observation of behaviour and demeanour – all these depend heavily on the skill of the examiner. Indeed the dependability of their conclusions derives solely from that skill. It is difficult anywhere in the process to detect a standardized element which would allow the attribution of quality in results to the characteristics of the test rather than the characteristics of the tester. Yet the reputation of lie detection rests on its being a measure of behavioural biology, not on its being conducted by an accredited admitted member of some latter-day Guild of Inquisitors.

What polygraphers propose is lie detection as Craft, not lie detection as Science. Any jurisdiction which chooses to give credence to polygraph-based evidence is creating a special class of witness, deemed to have privileged access to knowledge of the truthfulness of other witnesses. It is not recognizing the special scientific status of the polygraph, for that status is a matter of science fiction not of demonstrated fact.

Conclusions

The polygraph used as a lie detector falls very far short of acceptable standards for psychological tests. It is essentially unstandardized; it is internally inconsistent; rescoring of charts is unreliable; no retest reliability information is available for examinees; it produces a disproportionate number of false positive results; it has not been investigated for adverse impact on social and ethnic subgroups; it involves measures sensitive to aspects of temperament.

There are no good reasons for placing credence in the results it produces.

4

Vetting, investigation and interrogation

Cyril Cunningham

The number of people who become eligible for vetting or re-vetting in the United Kingdom is probably well in excess of 100,000 per annum. This includes applicants for and incumbents in jobs in the armed forces, the Civil Service, police, Customs and Excise, the Post Office and British Telecom, the public utilities and a large number of people involved in the design and manufacture of equipment. The annual turnover is enormous and the vetting task is very large and clearly precludes extensive and indiscriminate investigation in every case. Nor is it necessary.

All jobs are not equally sensitive, or indeed sensitive for the same reasons. Some jobs are classified because of the access they afford to politically embarrassing material; others because of their financial or economic implications, as in the Treasury. Others require vetting because of the opportunities they provide for sabotaging vital communication networks, or installations or services vital to the nation. The proportion of jobs directly related to high-grade military or intelligence secrets runs into a few thousands, though the figure is considerably higher for jobs related to technical secrets.

No security intelligence or counter-espionage organization would be very effective if it relied entirely upon gratuitous or fortuitous information. To do so would render it entirely reactive and dependent upon chance to an unacceptable degree. A positive approach is essential for the initiation of information in anticipation of events.

However, not even the most oppressive surveillance measures operating in the worst kind of police state can be all-seeing, all-knowing all the time, and they have never managed to eradicate or to predict sudden disaffection and defection in every case. To attempt to do so is utterly absurd and simply is not feasible. Security in a police state is based upon a philosophy of distrust and gives rise to immense and stifling bureaucracies and widespread controls as existed to a lesser extent in the United Kingdom only during the Second World War. The financial cost of widespread, intensive and continuous surveillance and its social and political conseqences are unacceptable in a democracy in peacetime and in any case must always be set against the probability and cost of damaging leaks.

The United Kingdom system is based upon trust and upon an assumption of the inherent trustworthiness of citizens and their willingness to co-operate voluntarily with official enquiries. It is accepted that trustworthiness and willingness are not evenly spread among the population, that there are regional, social, political, economic and age variations.

A system of vetting and security intelligence such as exists in the United Kingdom has obvious weaknesses. The net may be cast widely but the meshes may be coarse and full of holes. Any kind of sampling technique is bound to omit specific instances. Even the most stringent of systems will fail where suspicions have not been aroused early (because of a lack of awareness), and subsequently may escape notice despite a trail of evidence of nefarious or suspicious activity.

One of the problems for the security services is how far and wide it is politically and socially permissible to cast the net in order to pick up a trace without intruding upon freedom of speech and conscience, and democratic rights. This issue becomes very tricky in the light of evidence of concerted, persistent and pernicious attempts by unfriendly or allegedly friendly nations to use well-meaning citizens and organizations to damage or destroy the state. The response to threats to the state must depend upon the nature and degree of the threat and it is the very invidious task of the security services to balance the response according to the degree of threat from particular organizations, individuals and situations. This is not just for economy of effort; it is a matter of politics.

The polygraph, by its very nature, is a particularly intrusive device which also requires considerable co-operation from the individual. It is far more intrusive than most forms of investigation and more so than all but one of the various forms of interrogation. Like every other mechanism of prediction, investigation and surveillance, its intrusiveness, its financial, social and political costs and consequences must be balanced against the degree of threat from individuals and from the whole population under scrutiny. In other words the criteria that apply to other devices must also be applied to the polygraph and they will include the yield of legally, socially and politically acceptable evidence of individuals' movements, actions and affiliations.

Vetting

The system of vetting that has evolved in the United Kingdom has two aspects. The first concerns the opportunities, type and level of access to classified material or services afforded by an enormous variety of manual, clerical, technical, professional and administrative occupations. The second concerns assessing the risk of employing particular individuals. These two vetting tasks are usually carried out by separate divisions of security organizations.

The classification of jobs, and also information, has two dimensions, namely level and scope. Level means the degree of secrecy or confidentiality considered necessary for protection. The lowest level is Restricted; the highest includes special categories well in excess of Secret. At the lowest level, classification is a sectional or departmental responsibility. At the very highest levels it is the responsibility of special departments and a variety of specialized committees.

Scope concerns the range of classified areas to which a job gives access or to which access may become necessary for carrying out the job. In assessing this, the so-called 'need to know' system of compartmentalization is applied to the higher grades of classification. The more sensitive the material the more restricted the access.

Every job is classified by level and scope. Unfortunately jobs involving genuine secrecy spawn other jobs for their protection, similar in nature to the stone dropped into still water. Unfortunately, too, the jobs at the periphery afford access, eventually, to the centre, unless an ingenious cut-out can be provided. They also become more numerous as the circles expand, providing more opportunities for penetration for those bent on mischief or espionage. The penetration agent in the grand tradition, as exemplified before and during the First World War by the British secret agent Sidney Reilly, the so-called Ace of Spies, is now a very rare phenomenon. Today we hear of 'sleepers' and 'moles' – disaffected citizens in positions of trust who have usually been got at from the periphery. The trend of our enemies these days is peripheral saturation.

In other words, the status of a job gives little guide to its security implications or to the level and scope of access that it provides, a fact which is extensively exploited for espionage and counter-espionage purposes. The filing clerk or registrar may have access to a broader scope and higher levels of secrets than the initiators of the documents they file. Even the most secret of secret installations require all kinds of services including cleaning. From an enemy viewpoint the cleaner is a potential source of a great deal of valuable information, such as the geography and security of a building, the routes of its communication and electrical wiring, the names, fingerprints and possibly the appearances of occupants, their work routines and timekeeping habits, possibly their office and home phone numbers, their eating haunts and habits, car types and registration numbers and so on. They are also in a position to retrieve the contents of wastepaper baskets and dustbins and also to plant listening or other surveillance devices, and bombs!

Opportunity is the keyword. Espionage and terrorist organizations will go to considerable lengths and expend much effort upon identifying the holder of a job with access to target information, regardless of the affinities and affiliations of the unfortunate job-holder. That issue comes later.

The existence of circles of access must be borne in mind in considering who shall be screened by the polygraph, or any other screening device or procedure. The protection of people with genuine secrets starts at the periphery in social terms as well as in the physical terms of wire fencing, security guards, passes and pass keys.

It is the job itself that determines the level and scope to which an individual needs to be cleared, and every change of job, every promotion or transfer may involve re-vetting and re-clearance if a higher level or broader or different scope is involved. The clearance procedure can slow down or delay movements from job to job or it may have to be conducted retrospectively which may involve unnecessary additional risks.

Fortunately, for the majority, clearance is required at relatively low levels and broad scope. A minority require clearance to high levels (that is, above 'Secret') and the higher the level the narrower the scope is likely to be.

In assessing the risk of employing particular individuals, the consequences of infringement for the individual have to be taken into account. These include the economic consequences of the loss of a job, pay, benefits and pension rights. Sometimes it involves naturalization rights. There are also social consequences and consequences in professional and ethical terms. The higher the status, professionally and socially, the more the individual has to lose. The consequences for a married person with a large mortgage are likely to be more damaging than for a single person living in a rented room. Such risk assessments are not peculiar to security clearance; the cues used will be very familiar to bank managers and credit agencies.

The consequences of infringement are not evenly distributed through the vetted population. There are economic, social, political, religious, education and age variations in the degree of risk, and perhaps actuarial tables exist that can be used routinely before embarking upon specifically security procedures.

The extent of specifically security vetting clearly varies according to the needs of the job, and a system of negative and positive vetting has evolved. It must be stressed that within each of these two categories there are degrees of vetting effort so that, for example, negative vetting can vary from the superficial to a pretty extensive search of public, police and security records.

Negative vetting. This consists of checking an individual's identity against public records and against an index of people who have come to the notice of the police or security services. There has long been much public concern about the possibility of individuals being on record by witting or unwitting association with genuine police or security suspects. From a security point of view the existence of 'circles of access' must always be a consideration as also is the often strong possibility that the individual may be unaware of the nefarious activities of associates and some affiliations used as cover or recruiting grounds by intelligence agencies from all over the world, operating in the United Kingdom. The total number of foreigners working on intelligence assignments in the United Kingdom is mind-boggling, and the chances of brushing shoulders with one, especially in London, are far greater than the public imagines.

It is very important to stress that the individual being vetted has no part to play in the negative vetting procedure and therefore the majority of people requiring clearance will be unaware of being negatively vetted.

If a trace is found by the negative vetting procedure, clearance or refusal of clearance for a specific job will depend upon the reason for which the individual 'came to notice' and the degree of involvement in suspect activity. If there is reasonable suspicion, the suspect will not be offered the job. Refusal of clearance will simply debar the individual from jobs for which higher levels of confidentiality or secrecy are involved.

Positive vetting. This means that in addition to negative vetting, positive measures are taken to collect additional evidence to assist in the assessment of the risk of employing a specific individual in a specific job. The individual will be aware of being screened and will be asked to participate in some of the procedures. The individual may be interviewed at length by a security officer who will ask questions about one's career, family, associates, travel and work experiences. Referees will usually be required to vouch for the individual's identity, movements, affiliation, associates and 'character'. The referees will be visited and questioned in detail, and relatives, previous employers and workmates may also be questioned. The size of the circle of acquaintances involved will depend upon the sensitivity of the job to be done.

If a high level of clearance is required, the applicant or incumbent may be placed under routine domestic and job surveillance. This is not quite as sinister as it sounds since it would probably involve routine management and supervisory scrutiny in the first instance. The individual might also be placed under communications surveillance and be watched and followed on a sampling basis, if the required degree of clearance justified the expense and effort.

Special investigations. These can be initiated at any time for potential, new or existing employees in sensitive jobs if suspicions are aroused. Many of the cases that have made headline news in the post-war years have been partly due to departmental and managerial failures to initiate special enquiries despite ample evidence of behaviour indicating accelerating risk. Drunkenness especially seems to evoke sympathy from colleagues anxious to cover up for the alcoholic; this applies as much to the intelligence community as it does to most other occupations.

Depending upon what is at stake, a surveillance operation can be initiated using a variety of techniques including human and audiovisual surveillance on a round-the-clock basis, in addition to telephone tapping and mail interception, all of which has to be properly authorized. If necessary the individual may be literally surrounded by observers recruited for the situation by the security services. In suitable cases the suspect may be fed with traceable information, sometimes of a very high grade, to see what happens to it subsequently. The suspect may also be subjected to a range of decoy and deception techniques.

In suitable cases, the forensic sciences, radio and coding experts and many other technical specialists may be employed to obtain evidence of nefarious activities.

In determining whether behaviour is nefarious, investigators are always on the alert for what David Cornwall, alias John le Carré, has described in his novels as 'trade craft'. The trained agent will always leave the signature of training in his or her *modus operandi* and in the equipment employed. This signature has been the downfall of many a secret agent. The signature may be especially evident in agents' avoidance techniques, that is, the avoidance of each of the forms of surveillance.

The amount and type of effort brought into operation by the security agencies will usually depend upon the nature and level of secrets involved. If they are disproportionate they are likely to give rise to political scandals, should this leak out to the media.

The realities of interrogation

The first and very important point that must be made (as far as the United Kingdom is concerned), is that vetting is principally investigative, not interrogative. The proportion of cases that reach the stage where interrogation becomes necessary is infinitesimal, if by interrogation one means the popular idea of it. The popular notion is confrontational and overt close verbal examination, by an identifiable interrogator with powers to punish or imprison the suspect for failure to respond.

The reality, in the security context, is that very few cases get beyond the investigation stage, and for those that do, detailed examination can, and usually does, take less obvious and perhaps covert forms. There is no divine edict which compels an interrogator to reveal his identity as such, nor any compulsion to question suspects in a blatantly obvious manner or in circumstances indicative of interrogation, except where criminal proceedings are likely to ensue. Even then it is a matter of fine judgement as to the point in the proceedings at which the detailed examination will become overt.

The fact is that the confrontational form of interrogation so beloved by dramatists and fiction writers and so commonly in use universally, is amateurish and extremely crude compared with other available methods.

I have often said that the popular idea of interrogation is also a state of mind in the interrogated person. Carried out in an officious manner in formal surroundings, close questioning will be perceived as an interrogation. Effected in a pleasant manner in either formal or informal circumstances, it will be described as an interview. Conducted by an acquaintance in a restaurant or bar, it may be perceived as an interesting discussion. Yet the selfsame set of questions about identical issues can be asked in all three settings, which very roughly correspond to the three traditional interrogation techniques called the direct, the indirect and the clandestine methods.

Why hurl oneself at a barricaded front door if there is an option of sneaking round the back? More subtly, tap interestingly at the front door while simultaneously effecting an entry at the back!

It is a matter of history that where physical force is debarred by legal constraints or political or moral scruples there has been a development of and a greater reliance upon an ingenious variety of 'back door' methods of investigation and examination, of which the forensic sciences are perhaps the most obvious and best known. Such developments often bring howls of protest at their introduction from the physically unharmed, morally outraged, and intellectually outwitted victims of detailed examination or 'questioning' without knowledge or consent. The reader is invited to ponder upon the social, political and physical demerits of physically violent interrogation, and intrusive confrontational interrogation (including the use of the polygraph), as compared with simple or scientifically aided stealth!

The popular idea of an interrogation has very ancient origins in both religion and the law and both rest upon the untenable supposition that a sacred oath or trial by ordeal will evince the 'truth'; also that the 'truth', when told, will be readily recognizable as such by inquisitors and jurors alike. If this was really true there would be no need for the polygraph and a variety of other so-called 'aids' to interrogation (by which I do *not mean* electrocution and other tortures). The popular notion ignores the development and commonplace use of the forensic sciences and several potent traditional methods that are capable of 'questioning' without the suspect's knowledge or assistance. In the past half century there have been very rapid developments in audio, visual and other monitoring devices. However, as these are 'dumb', that is, not reactive and cannot ask questions from the information received, arguably they will never replace the ancient device of the spy or the witting or unwitting informant or 'stool-pigeon'. The recruitment, placement and control of the human agent is, and always has been, an essential element in every interrogation system, and is considered by many professionals to be the nub of the interrogator's skill. This is quite contrary to the popular idea, which regards framing questions closely as the essence of interrogation; indeed it is defined in the dictionary as such.

The effect of the little-known aspects of interrogation is that suspects may be closely questioned and investigated without their knowledge or witting participation. There is nothing unique to security in this. In principle it is no different to well-known criminal investigation techniques and procedures. From the security viewpoint, the more there is at stake, the more likely that a truly clandestine approach will be adopted because of the risk of alerting suspects and their contacts. In suitable cases the resources and resourcefulness of state security services may be almost limitless, and may involve elaborate decoy and deception techniques of breathtaking daring and complexity. Such cases do not always result in prosecution, as was evident in the case of Anthony Blunt, a member of the Philby, Burgess and Maclean complex, who, in exchange for information, was not prosecuted. There is always the issue as to whether a detected agent or traitor should be prosecuted, amnestied or turned into a double agent in what has become known as the 'double cross system'. But for the amateur being sucked into some nefarious peripheral spying activity there is usually the option of scaring them off in preference to prosecution. Prosecution tends to be too revealing of methods, and when trials are held in camera they attract too much adverse publicity.

Interrogation systems

To regard interrogation as merely a matter of close questioning, or more precisely as overt verbal examination, is inaccurate and mis-leading and removes it from its proper context. It compares with attempting to play a violin without music or the ability to read a note, and in ignorance as to where to place the fingers on the strings. Banging it against a wall will produce a sound of sorts, as will scraping it with a bow. But it will never produce music without score to play or expertise in fingering and bowing.

And so it is with interrogation. It should be obvious, but seldom is, that one cannot ask pertinent questions unless one knows what issues are pertinent and whom to question. Questioning, especially close questioning, presumes previous knowledge of people, situations and events. In this respect interrogation is no different from any other form of interviewing. Successful interviewing depends upon doing one's homework thoroughly on all available evidence, a lesson which psychologists have been preaching with seemingly little success for the past hundred years!

It is when one asks how interrogators obtain this previous knowledge that one opens up a wide area of essential intelligence activity, of which overt or clandestine investigation and examination are integral parts, not isolated activities. Interrogation agencies almost always consist of five main areas of intelligence activity which are:

1   creating and maintaining an intelligence environment for scanning and monitoring people, situations and events;

2   identification of suspect people, situations and events;

3   investigation of them;

4   information research and collation; and

5   examination and verification (i.e. 'interrogation').

It is when one or several of the essential support activities are omitted from a system, or are denied for economic or political reasons, or out of ignorance, that interrogation becomes either ineffectual or brutal. Every one of these five areas is politically controversial in democratic societies and their essential inter-relationship has never really been understood by politicians, authorities or the public. In fiction, drama and in the public imagination, interrogators are apt to be vested with supernatural insight and intellects, in order to be able to frame questions closely and have inspired guesses; everything takes place in the interrogation chamber! The reality is much more mundane. The insight is more likely to have come from patient investigations by others, and from the use of concealed monitoring devices, including agents; and the intellects are likely to be those of the hidden army of researchers and collators. The idea that interrogation is a duel of wits is utterly absurd. The victims are probably pitting their wits against all the complex and extensive resources of a state or an international intelligence system.

Creating an intelligence environment. This means organizing willing or unwilling, or unwitting, helpers. As was stated earlier, no security intelligence system can afford to rely entirely upon fortuitous or gratuitous information alone, but both are nevertheless fairly essential to intelligence systems. In the context of ordinary police work it has public relations connotations. Without a large measure of public co-operation a network would be severely handicapped, starved of basic information and active assistance. The organization and operation of fortuitous and gratuitous information networks is an important and innocuous aspect of security intelligence work that is easily overlooked. It extends to employers, employees, clubs and groups of great variety and it provides routine cover across a broad spectrum of activities.

In the security context people do give a lot of help when asked. There are also the traditional 'old boy' networks that riddle our society in all directions. These can be harnessed in two ways. The first is for surveillance; the second is to provide an enormous reservoir of voluntary experts for the evaluation of an equally enormous variety of topics and data. A professional interrogator cannot possibly be expert in every topic and issue that he may be asked to investigate, from the geography of a city to highly technical matters. Nor would it be feasible for an interrogation agency to keep all the necessary experts on its payroll, awaiting suitable opportunities to exercise their knowledge.

The alternative to voluntary assistance is the recruitment and organization of what I will call pernicious informer and helper networks, and trained agents to penetrate suspect groups and activities. This normal police technique is widely used by a variety of agencies such as Customs and Excise, and in the security context is an integral activity to bridge the gaps with voluntary informants.

Identification of suspects. The identification of suspect situations and events and the people associated with them results in 'coming to notice' and then a 'trace'. In some intelligence systems whole departments exist for the sole purpose of raising and maintaining trace cards and dossiers. The problem of searching these data for links was highlighted by the Yorkshire Ripper and other murder enquiries, where the volume of manual records and the lack of adequate collation facilities prevented the much earlier identification of the murderers. Computers have revolutionized this kind of activity and greatly enhanced the collating facilities and speed of operation. Identification is not confined to suspects but also includes the identification of people in a position to help.

The whole area is politically controversial. Controversy centres upon the issues of definition of potential threats and the diameter of the circle of affiliation and association that is placed upon record.

Investigation. This consists of 'police work', employing where necessary some highly technical aids such as fingerprint analysis (by computer), still, movie, and video photography, the forensic sciences, audiovisual monitoring and recording, human surveillance, document analysis and many specialized skills. Each can be brought to bear once suspicion has been aroused, but usually not otherwise. The case officer's skill lies in knowing which 'aid' to use and the sequence in which the aids should be introduced. This is especially so in the introduction of human agents and the use, if necessary, of penetration agents or voluntary 'links'.

Information research and collation. This is sometimes described as the intelligence section of an interrogation agency. Its task is the gathering, collation and evaluation of relevant specific and background knowledge and information, from a wide variety of public and intelligence sources. It is easy to overlook the fact that any particular agency is a part of a much wider intelligence system involving many agencies which share relevant information through co-ordinating bodies. A particular agency can easily recruit the assistance of other agencies where needs arise.

Intelligence research shares the same problems of information processing, methodologies and inference as any form of scientific research.

There is a world-wide tendency for police and security agencies to underrate the importance of the role of intelligence collation and research; it is almost always subordinate to the active departments (i.e. investigation and examination).

Examination/interrogation. This means, in effect, the use of the suspect as a source of information about his or her activities. In the context of a security investigation, suspects are clearly not the only sources of information about themselves and only an amateur would rely upon the individual as a principal source. In the case of United Kingdom nationals a surprisingly large volume of information is available from such sources as the Inland Revenue, the Department of Health and Social Security, local authorities, the public utilities and of course from employment and employee records, and it requires very little effort to bring this information together. Very routine police enquiries (apart from surveillance) can provide much information without recourse to specialized technical assistance. Most people seem unaware of the ease with which any citizen can gather detailed information on any fellow citizen using quite public sources. An authorized agency can raise a formidable dossier without much effort before calling for the services of the police or the Special Branch, or the Post Office, telephone or other specialized investigation agencies. In addition, security agencies have their own investigators and surveillance teams which, although without police powers, are very effective in gathering information.

No individual suspect would reach the stage of examination without previous extensive investigation. Once it has been decided to undertake an examination, its nature will be carefully considered in the light of what is at stake and whether the suspect is to be exploited, amnestied or prosecuted. The risks of alerting the suspect and associates and the degree of resistance likely to be met with will also have to be considered. The professional spy (identifiable by his or her trade-craft signature in their *modus operandi*, among many other things) will almost certainly be subjected, initially, to clandestine approaches in order to obtain sufficient legal evidence to justify a warrant for arrest and prosecution and provide a substantial 'hold' over the suspect. Clandestine examination might involve disguising the interrogator and the interrogatory situation and also might involve elaborate decoy and deception situations. The ingenuity is boundless and does not necessarily lead to arrest and prosecution. The trap may never be sprung as far as the individual or his or her associates may be aware. There is always the option of frightening them off by making it obvious that their activities have been well and truly noticed.

Obviously, a suspect cannot be interrogated in the popular sense, that is, overtly questioned, without alerting the suspect and associates that their activities have become suspect. If this stage is reached, sufficient evidence of nefarious activity will have been collected to justify an application for prosecution. Arrest is a powerful motivator for all but the professional spies of a few, select nations with bargaining powers.

Conclusions

I hope I have made it obvious that compared with many traditional methods commonly employed on people requiring positive vetting, the polygraph is, to say the least, a trivial and uncertain device which bears poor comparison. It cannot be a substitute for surveillance of an individual's activities or the verification of identities or the mass of objective clues provided by the forensic sciences and other scientific aids. Above all it cannot be used covertly. It is positively intrusive and is based upon uncertain prediction of actual behaviour from very uncertain verbal indications, in other words admissions. The normal devices employed by investigators are not predictive; they monitor actual behaviour, and associations, covertly. The polygraph is an irrelevance.

PART TWO

Psychological Issues

5
What are truthfulness and honesty?

Sarah E. Hampson

An infallible technique to discriminate between people of 'good' versus 'bad' character has an undeniable appeal. All employers would be eager to be able to avoid recruits who are likely to engage in various dishonest behaviours at work (such as lying, pilfering, and swindling) and some would welcome a reliable means of screening out applicants who are potential risks to security (for example, by leaking information or by betraying their country). With current levels of unemployment, the business of shortlisting appropriate candidates from the mountain of applications has become a serious problem and a topic for study in its own right (Herriot, 1984; Herriot and Wingrove, 1984). A pass or fail test of good character would be invaluable in this process. Although to many the idea of such a device appears naive, there are those who claim that this instrument exists and has been used successfully for years. The instrument, of course, is the polygraph.

The polygraph test appeared as early as the 1920s and, from the 1960s onwards, it has been used extensively in the United States both in criminal investigations and for pre-employment screening in the private sector (Lykken, 1983). It has been estimated that approximately 25 percent of major firms in the United States routinely use the polygraph in employment selection (Sackett and Decker, 1979). However, virtually all the field and laboratory research into the reliability and validity of the polygraph as a detector of deception has been conducted in the context of its use in criminal investigations (Saxe, Dougherty and Cross, 1985). At present, polygraph procedures are rarely used in psychological assessment in Britain. However, the signs are that this state of affairs is on the point of change (House of Commons, 1985), and therefore now is the time to consider the many scientific and ethical issues raised by the polygraph test.

The purpose of this chapter is to examine some of the *psychological* issues raised by the use of the polygraph test. In particular, I shall evaluate the use of the polygraph test as an assessment device in the light of contemporary personality psychology. The discussion will be limited to the use of the polygraph as a means of detecting someone of 'good character'. The issues concerning its use in criminal investigations are discussed in other chapters.

This chapter is organized in the following way. First, the differences between using the polygraph as a lie detector and as a way of assessing personality traits such as truthfulness and honesty will be described. Then the measurement of truthfulness and honesty will be examined more generally. The polygraph test has its own limitations, but any means of measuring underlying personality traits from observed behaviour is subject to practical and theoretical problems.

One of the enduring problems in the psychology of personality is the consistency of behaviour. Do people tend generally to behave consistently across time and situations? The usefulness of personality assessment depends upon a fair degree of stability of behaviour in order that predictions about subsequent behaviour, made on the basis of a trait measure, will be reasonably accurate. Some representative research on behavioural consistency will be described and the implications for polygraphic assessment of good character examined. The polygraph does not emerge unscathed from this analysis. It is concluded that there are enormous difficulties to be overcome in any attempt to assess such abstract and ambiguous qualities as moral character traits and that the polygraph test offers no new solutions to these old problems.

Personality assessment and the polygraph

The polygraph monitors psychophysiological responses (for example, respiration, blood pressure, galvanic skin response). Therefore it does not yield a single measure, but several records which together indicate a pattern of psychophysiological responding. The principle of polygraphic interrogation is to compare the polygraph charts for three kinds of questions: relevant questions, concerning the matter under investigation; control questions, which are designed to be as similar as possible to the relevant questions without referring to the matter; and irrelevant questions, such as asking the person's name (Lykken, 1983). If the polygraphist regards the physiological responses to the relevant questions as being consistently different from the responses to the other kinds of questions, then the record is deemed deceptive. Two questioning techniques have been developed: the control question technique and the guilty knowledge technique, but only the former is typically used in employment contexts.

In criminal investigations, or in investigations of thefts or misdemeanours in the workplace, polygraphic interrogation is used to determine whether a person is lying about his or her involvement in that *specific* incident. In pre-employment screening and irregular post-employment screening, the polygraph is used as a more general personality assessment device for the purpose of identifying people who *may* steal from work or who *may* be potential security risks. The principle of comparing responses to relevant, control and irrelevant questions is the same for both purposes although the nature of the relevant questions is different. For pre-employment screening the domain of relevant questions could include the person's entire background, but typically sensitive areas may be singled out, such as past dishonest behaviour or involvement in unwelcome political activities. In addition, relevant questions may probe the veracity of the person's responses on the job application form. Indeed, the polygraph test can be used in this way to deter people from making false claims when applying for jobs. However, there are three important differences between using the polygraph in criminal investigations and using it as a personality assessment technique in employment screening.

The first concerns accuracy. In the employment context the high rate of false positives typical of the polygraph test is a matter of particular concern: blameless individuals misclassified as potentially undesirable solely on the basis of their polygraph test will be denied a job and may then be handicapped by the slur of failing the polygraph in their subsequent search for employment. In criminal investigations the results of the polygraph test would only be part of the evidence. A second difference is that in employment contexts polygraphic interrogation may be used to make multiple judgements (for example, Does the applicant have a history of theft, and/or drug abuse, and/or absenteeism?) which necessarily result in lower accuracy levels compared with the single judgements made in criminal contexts (for example, Did this person commit the crime?). The third and most important difference is the identification–prediction distinction. Whereas in criminal contexts the polygraph is used to identify a person guilty of a past misdemeanour, in employment contexts the polygraph is used to predict which persons will be guilty of *unspecified misdemeanours in the future*. This is a substantially different use of the polygraph and it is the central issue in the evaluation of the polygraph as a personality assessment device.

The measurement of truthfulness and honesty

In our culture we make a number of assumptions about personality. For example, wherever security is a priority employers will aim to recruit employees of 'good character', and it is commonly believed that traits such as truthfulness and honesty are to be found in these people. It is assumed that a general and abstract way of classifying a person (for example, good versus bad character) can be broken down into specific components such as truthfulness, honesty, and perhaps reliability, trustworthiness, conscientiousness, and so on. In order to determine whether a person is of good character, it is assumed that all or some of these components must be assessed and the more general classifications will proceed on the basis of the outcome of these specific assessments. The same principle is adopted in our everyday judgements about people. Of course, we do not give new acquaintances actual personality tests, but we do instigate our own informal and perhaps relatively unconscious assessment processes. What is her occupation? What newspapers does she read? Or even, what does she like to eat? The answers to these kinds of questions provide us with concrete data which we use to infer abstract psychological characteristics such as intelligence, social attitudes or personality traits. None of these psychological properties of the individual can be examined directly, because they do not exist in a tangible form. Instead, we construct them on the basis of what we can observe, which is behaviour (using that word in its widest sense).

An important consequence of the inferred nature of personality is that it is possible to make mistakes when taking the inferential leap from observed behaviours to the underlying personality traits. These mistakes may be traced either to the person making the personality inference (the observer) or to the person who is the target of the inference process (the actor). In the case of the observer, the error is the result of an inappropriate inference from the data (for example, assuming that working at a university is a sign of high intelligence or that vegetarianism is a sign of neuroticism). In the case of the actor, the error may be the result of a deliberate attempt to mislead observers. We are all able, in varying degrees, to control our publicly observable behaviours in order to create a desired impression. However, not all psychological characteristics are equally vulnerable to misrepresentation. It is difficult to get away with appearing more intelligent than one actually is. Some personality traits such as anxiety or shyness are virtually impossible to hide behind a veneer of the appropriately relaxed and socially adept behaviour. However, many personality traits are inferred from behaviours which are under the actor's conscious control, and the signs of good character such as truthfulness and honesty are prime examples.

The appeal of the polygraph test lies in the belief that its combination of psychophysiological measures will allow the examiner to cut through the consciously manipulated aspects of self-presentation (for example, the fine speeches, the carefully controlled facial expressions and patterns of eye contact) to expose the real person behind the façade. The actor's public display of honesty may appear highly convincing to the observer, but the polygraph chart is believed to provide the ultimate check. However, once it is appreciated that there are no hot lines to personality traits – since they may only be inferred from overt behaviour and never observed directly – then it follows that the personality data generated in polygraphic procedures are of the same status as any other personality data. They may be useful indicators, but only so long as the observer (in this case the polygraphist) is correct in assuming a connection between the observed behaviour and the underlying trait, and only so long as the actor (in this case the person under polygraphic examination) is not able to exert conscious control over the responses being recorded. We have already seen in earlier chapters how neither of these assumptions is justified: physiological signs of emotionality do not necessarily accompany expressions of untruths and dishonesty, and the polygraph test is prey to deliberate distortions.

The prediction of truthfulness and honesty

So far, two of the assumptions underlying the assessment of personality have been discussed in relation to the polygraph test: the inferred nature of personality traits and the two kinds of errors to which these inferences are prone (errors of inference made by the observer, and deliberate distortions introduced by the actor). Already, the polygraph is not looking particularly impressive as a measure of good character since there is only a tenuous link between the data it generates and the traits in question, and these data are not immune from attempts at distortion. However, there is a further problem. Even if the polygraph could reliably identify when a person is being dishonest, would it be correct to infer that this person has a dishonest personality and therefore can be expected to behave dishonestly in the future? The concept of personality entails the assumption that behaviour is both temporally and cross-situationally consistent and, as a result of behavioural consistency, personality provides the basis for prediction. Once a trait has been inferred from observed behaviour, the trait inference is used to make subsequent behavioural predictions. These predictions are of two kinds: temporal and cross-situational.

Temporal consistency refers to the stability of the same or similar behaviours in much the same situation across occasions. Cross-situational consistency refers to the stability of psychologically equivalent behaviours across situations. For example, to be truthful on the polygraph test today and the same time next week is to demonstrate temporal consistency; but to be truthful on the polygraph test today and to resist the temptation to steal from the workplace tomorrow is to be cross-situationally consistent. The use of the polygraph as a personality detector depends upon the temporal and cross-situational stability of behaviours associated with being of good character. Having determined that a person behaved honestly or dishonestly in one particular situation, namely the polygraph test, the following assumption is made: the behaviour observed in the polygraph test is predictive of psychologically equivalent behaviours in a wide variety of situations. To put it simply, the assumption is that if a person lies on the polygraph test then he or she is likely not only to lie in other situations, but to inform, leak, deceive and so on as well.

Is behaviour consistent?

To what extent is behaviour observed in one situation predictive of behaviour in the same or different situations on subsequent occasions? This question has long been of central importance in psychology. If behaviour proved to be neither temporally nor cross-situationally consistent, then the concept of personality would be meaningless and personality assessment would be a pointless exercise. It is not surprising that the behavioural consistency debate has been so prolonged and so heated. There have already been three eras of behavioural consistency research over the last sixty years and each has yielded somewhat different findings.

Early studies of behavioural consistency
The early work in the 1920s and 1930s is best illustrated here by the work of Hartshorne and May (1928) on moral character (but see also Dudycha, 1936; Newcomb, 1929). They adopted a hierarchical view of the relations between behaviours, traits and personality: coherent patterns of consistent behaviours were subsumed by traits, and coherent patterns of consistent traits formed the more general personality categories such as 'moral character'. If there was insufficient evidence of behavioural or trait consistency, then the validity of the personality category would be threatened.

Hartshorne and May were looking for evidence of behavioural consistency from which to infer traits such as honesty, helpfulness, co-operativeness, persistence and self-control, all of which they believed were components of 'high' versus 'low' character. Several hundred children were given a wide variety of behavioural tests of these traits. The findings may be summarized as supporting temporal consistency but failing to establish strong cross-situational consistency. For example, one measure of deceit was the incidence of cheating on a self-scored test. Performance on this test correlated 0.70 with performance on another occasion on a similar self-scored test (temporal consistency). In contrast, cheating on the self-scored test only correlated 0.30 with cheating by failing to stop answering questions after time had been called, and only 0.20 with another index of cheating outside the classroom (cross-situational consistency). The comment of a contemporary reviewer summed up these findings as follows:

> The conclusion from this is that a single test of deceit has little symptomatic value of deceit in general. The value of a single test as an honesty test depends on the degree to which the single situation has features which are common to all the situations in which honesty may be displayed. (Symonds, 1931, 317)

These and the other research findings of the 1920s and 1930s cast some doubt on the role of traits in the determination of behaviour. If moral character is made up of moral traits such as honesty, then a person should behave in consistently and predictably honest ways in different situations. However, situational factors appeared to be more important in determining behaviour than had been suspected, even for qualities apparently so stable and dispositional as moral character traits. One honest (or dishonest) act did not reliably predict another.

Mischel's critique of traits

The second era of scepticism about the role of personality was initiated by a number of disillusioned personality psychologists, of whom Mischel is probably the best known. Mischel's (1968) critique was based primarily on his comprehensive review of personality research and his conclusion that it had failed to provide convincing evidence for cross-situational behavioural consistency. He accepted that behaviours often demonstrated high levels of temporal consistency, so it was cross-situational consistency that was at issue. When a person's behaviour in a particular situation is predicted from his or her score on a personality test, the cross-situational consistency of behaviour is assumed (that is, the behaviour in one situation, the personality test, predicts a different behaviour in another situation because both behaviours are determined by the same underlying personality trait). Mischel concluded from his survey of the research that personality test scores had not proved to be good predictors of subsequent behaviours. Indeed, he coined the derisory term 'personality coefficient' for the correlation of around 0.30 which was typically found between a trait measure and a behavioural measure. Such a small correlation between the honesty test and honest behaviour means that the majority (around 90 percent) of the factors determining honest behaviour cannot be accounted for by the test. In other words, Mischel argued that knowing how a person scored on a paper-and-pencil test of honesty, for instance, would not permit an accurate prediction about how honestly that person would behave in a subsequent, different situation. Mischel's review was seen as a serious challenge to the belief in stable personality traits and their part in the determination of behaviour. It led to a period of stagnation for the personality concept during which psychologists emphasized the role of situational as opposed to personality variables in controlling how people behave.

The return of the trait

Although psychologists may have been impressed by the research findings, the news that personality traits do not predict behaviour did not filter through to the rest of the world – or, if it did, the common-sense view of the everyday lay psychologist prevailed. Trait terms did not suddenly disappear from conversation, nor did employers stop asking for character references. Even the most sceptical personality psychologist probably reverted to believing in personality when he or she left the laboratory. Indeed, this is the paradox that the third era of consistency research is currently addressing: despite the evidence to the contrary, people continue to operate in their daily lives as if behaviour is cross-situationally consistent, predictable and determined to a significant degree by underlying, stable personality traits. The faith in the polygraph's power to identify the dishonest and untrustworthy is an expression of this belief.

The evidence against behavioural consistency accumulated in the previous two eras of consistency research is currently being re-evaluated both methodologically and theoretically. Contemporary research is providing some empirical vindication for the lay conviction in the value of the personality concept. On the methodological front, estimates of behavioural consistency have, in some studies, been doubled or trebled in size by the sensible expedient of correlating trait measures with aggregated behavioural measures (e.g. Epstein, 1979; Green, 1978). Several observations of the criterion behaviour are taken and averaged, and this aggregated measure is used in assessing behavioural consistency. This technique ensures that the behavioural measure reflects the way the person typically behaves, and is not the reflection of some chance factor as can happen with a one-off observation. Another methodological refinement has been the recognition that there may be individual differences in behavioural consistency: some people may be more consistent than others (Bem and Allen, 1974). When a mixed group of people are studied there is the possibility that these individual differences will cancel each other out, leaving the 'finding' that the group as a whole exhibited no behavioural consistency. Although this approach makes intuitive sense, investigators have yet to pin down the individual difference dimensions that produce variation in consistency levels (Chaplin and Goldberg, 1984).

On the theoretical front, new ways of thinking about the concept of personality are changing the kinds of questions psychologists ask about behavioural consistency. Perhaps too short-term a view has been taken in the past. Investigations were concerned with consistent patterns of behaviour over days or weeks, whereas the kind of personality consistency with which the lay person is familiar takes a lifespan perspective (e.g. Block, 1971). We see patterns of continuities between the child and the adult or between decades of an adult's life, and we are not dismayed by the inconsistencies that characterize the smaller-scale comparisons. What looks like an inconsistency close up may make sense in the broader scheme of a lifetime.

Taking a lifespan view requires, among other things, taking a flexible view of the behavioural indicators of personality traits. For example, the behavioural expression of aggressiveness differs considerably between adults and children. Traits vary in the range of behaviour from which they may be inferred: a wide range of behaviour is relevant to more abstract, broad traits (for example, conscientious, active, talented) whereas only a narrow range is applicable for more specific, narrow traits (for example, tidy, athletic, musical). Higher levels of behavioural consistency are expected in studies of narrow traits (say, talkative) than of broad traits (say, extraverted) (Hampson, John and Goldberg, 1986). More care is needed than has been shown in the past in deciding which behaviours are relevant to which traits. No wonder people appeared inconsistent when researchers made mistakes like predicting that hard-working students would leave their beds tidy in the mornings (Bem and Allen, 1974).

The distinction between broad and narrow traits is important with regard to using the polygraph as a test of good character. What could be a more abstract and broad trait description than 'being of good character'? Almost any behaviour, given the right context, could reflect good character, so the polygraph test is being used to predict an enormous range of behaviour on the basis of a tiny sample of highly specific behaviour – lying under polygraphic examination.

After extensive research into behavioural consistency we are not able to provide a definitive answer to the question 'Is behaviour consistent?' However, we can say that the accumulated evidence suggests that consistent patterns of behaviour can be found under the appropriate circumstances. These include using all the methodological refinements available to increase the reliability of the measures, ensuring that the behaviours under study are carefully selected for their relevance to the trait in question, and conducting longitudinal studies where necessary. Behavioural consistency is now viewed as relative, not absolute. Mischel's derisory personality coefficient of 0.30 does not look so bad if it is obtained in a longitudinal study where a trait score obtained in childhood predicts an adult behaviour thirty years later.

What are the implications of these conclusions for personality assessment in general, and for the polygraph test in particular? The reliable prediction of complex behaviour patterns now appears to be a delicate procedure requiring painstaking care and ingenuity to arrive at the right personality measures. The most unreliable predictions are made when the outcome of a personality test is used to predict the likelihood of subsequent behaviours that are very dissimilar from the test itself. Unfortunately, the polygraph as a test of good character is an excellent example of the worst conditions for reliable prediction.

So far in this chapter the polygraph test has been discredited as a measure of the traits of good character on three counts. (1) There is no convincing link between the responses measured by the polygraph and the traits in question. (2) The polygraph is vulnerable to deliberate distortion. (3) Using the polygraph test to predict undesirable behaviour relies on higher levels of cross-situational consistency than have so far been demonstrated in behavioural consistency research. These counts alone are sufficient to outlaw the polygraph as a means of assessing personality. However, there is one final argument against the polygraph that must be presented, since it applies particularly to its use as a measure of truthfulness and honesty. This argument derives from the fact that truth and honesty are not inherent qualities of behaviour but depend on the meaning of behaviour in a particular context.

The social construction of truthfulness and honesty

One reason why good character is so hard to assess accurately and to predict reliably is that the traits associated with being of good character have a large socially constructed component (Hampson, 1982). Behaviour in the raw does not tell us anything about personality. It is only when it is understood in trait terms that it takes on significance for personality. The process of adding meaning to behaviour relies heavily on the context in which the behaviour is performed and the intentions of the actor revealed by the behaviour. For example, there is nothing inherently dishonest about the behavioural act of cheating on a self-scored quiz by copying from the key (one of the acts in the studies by Hartshorne and May). Nevertheless, when viewed in the light of our classroom norms the intentions we may infer from this behaviour lead us to label it as dishonest. However, it is possible to construct alternative scenarios (for example, from the child's perspective) in which the same behaviour would be labelled very differently (say, sensible, daring, clever).

The importance of the social construction of personality is even more acute where adult behaviour is concerned. Although we teach our children that lying is wrong, we know that life is really more complicated and that sometimes lies can and perhaps should be told for admirable reasons. The polygraph has been strongly advocated as a screening device for government employees in the hope that it will help identify the truly patriotic and cut down on the seepage of secret information which appears to be a growing problem these days. However, a spy need not necessarily be lacking in moral character traits. On the contrary, some spies have been motivated by lofty ideals and have been morally scrupulous in other aspects of their lives. Similarly, trustworthy government employees do not have to (and perhaps cannot) be paragons of virtue. There are occasions when a civil servant is called upon to engage in behaviour that from one perspective would be labelled as untruthful and dishonest, but from another would be labelled as loyal and discreet. Leaks of secret information to the press are not always perpetrated by delinquent mischief-makers, as advocates of polygraph testing seem to imply, but sometimes by people of exceptionally high moral character who, after a period of mental anguish, conclude that it is their duty to expose a grave wrong.

Telling a lie acquires its moral significance from the context in which it was told. The act of lying acquires meaning through the social constructions of observers. We are all capable of telling lies, so to catch someone out in the act of lying is not necessarily particularly informative. What may be more interesting is knowing to which question or under what circumstances the person lied. In employment screening the examiner is using the polygraph as a way of finding out if there is anything undesirable about the applicant in relation to the job in question. So on closer inspection it emerges that it is not so much the telling of the lie that is relevant, but rather it is the additional information about the applicant that has been exposed by the lie. For example, as a result of a deceptive response on the polygraph chart to the question 'Is there anything in your past which makes you vulnerable to blackmail?' the examiner has gained a potentially valuable piece of information about the applicant that perhaps no other source had revealed. However, in view of the sophistication of today's vetting techniques it is extremely unlikely that the polygraph examination will expose something new (see Chapter 4 above, by Cunningham). Indeed, the examiner has to have some idea of what may be a sensitive area for the examinee before he or she conducts the test. Therefore some prior investigation is essential, and the additional information revealed by the polygraph may be superfluous.

Conclusions

The use of the polygraph as a measure of good character in general, and of truthfulness and honesty in particular, rests on several dubious assumptions. It is assumed that good character can be specified in terms of measurable personality traits which are the major determinants of behaviour. It is assumed that if a person is dishonest on the polygraph test, then he or she will behave in other undesirable ways on other occasions. It is assumed that truthfulness and honesty are inherent qualities of behaviour. However, half a century's research into behavioural consistency has shown that it is not possible to make highly accurate cross-situational behavioural predictions. This research has led to a questioning of the trait concept and an appreciation of the socially constructed nature of many personality traits, particularly those pertaining to being of good character such as truthfulness and honesty. The polygraph may or may not be a lie detector, but it could never be a personality detector.

6

Expressing your emotions and controlling feelings

Tara Ney

Why is emotion relevant to a discussion on lie detection? The answer is almost obvious: an individual who is subjected to a series of often probing questions in an attempt to distinguish between his telling the truth and telling lies, knowing full well that his answers are being 'scientifically' scrutinized by a rather nervous machine that he is electrically connected to, is bound to be experiencing a number of emotions. Indeed, the act of lying is itself an emotional experience for the majority of people and may invoke any number of emotions.

But emotions are a funny thing – funny peculiar, that is. Sometimes you can deliberately invoke an emotion by thinking about a particular memory or inventing a scene. Other times an apparently insignificant event can elicit a completely unanticipated and unstoppable emotional response. In other words, emotions function within the dynamics of an internal–external and deliberate–spontaneous matrix, and all of this is compounded by time, personality and situations. In short, emotions are not things that can be confined to a simple cause–effect relation: pain is more painful when you're feeling sad; joy can be greater when shared with a friend; guilt can sneak up long after the event. The complexity of emotion is not to be forgotten when we discuss its significance with respect to the lie-detection test.

In lie-detection testing the machine used to detect a lie is called a polygraph. It responds to, and displays, the amount of physiological arousal the autonomic nervous system is generating. However, interpreting the polygraph's scribbles is problematical. Interpreters and users may assume that a physiological response (an increased scribble) indicates a lie. The premise is quite simple: telling lies is supposed to cause some stress or anxiety, and this stress or anxiety is somehow echoed physiologically and recorded on the polygraph.

The problem with the above reasoning is that emotional arousal or difficulty in thinking, as measured by physiological responses, may be caused by a number of different factors other than the act of lying.

For example, a situation which threatens to undermine an individual's honesty will be likely to stimulate emotional responses. Thus the physiological response may be reflective of anger, fear, shame, guilt or any combination of these and other emotions, as well as other thoughts. Such variability in responding may be dependent upon the personality of the suspect, the past relationship between the lie-catcher and suspect, the suspect's expectations, or even the suspect's knowledge of how a lie-detection machine operates.

Take the following example. A quiet individual, unaccustomed to speaking her mind, is told she must be tested by the lie tester about the theft of some money belonging to her boss. The ultimatum is made that if she does not undergo the test she could be dismissed from her job. The lie-catcher poses the following question: 'Did you steal $50.00 from your employer?' The suspect, already having reported denial of the charge, may now feel so resentful of being tested about her honesty that a feeling of anger is experienced in response to the critical (relevant) question: the anger is accordingly displayed in a physiological response on the polygraph. This is in spite of the fact that the victim is not lying. The innocent victim may then be wrongly assessed as a liar. In short, *the physiological response measured by the polygraph can only tell that some kind of reaction is taking place within the victim; it cannot, however, tell what that reaction is.*

The correlations between what people feel and how they physiologically express what they feel are not at all straightforward or simple. Nor indeed are the relationships between how people behaviourally or facially express themselves and how they physiologically respond. Of the literally hundreds of theories of emotions, each theory represents a different view of what emotion is, how it functions, how it can be studied and what its purpose is. Yet the assumption made by the lie-detection test supports only one of the hundreds of theories of emotion, and moreover one that has been hotly contested.

Lie detection: assumptions

Lie detection assumes: (1) that individuals cannot *control* their physiology and behaviour; (2) that specific emotions can be *predicted* by specific stimuli; (3) that there are *specific relationships* between parameters of behaviour (such as what people say, how they behave, and how they respond physiologically); and (4) that there are *no differences* between people such that most people will respond similarly. But these assumptions are false, and I want to explain in the remainder of this short paper why this is so.

Control

The first assumption which underlies the use of the lie-detection test is that individuals cannot control their behaviour. In other words, the guilty person is incapable of controlling the stress, anxiety or guilt which may accompany a lie. The assumption is, therefore, that the liar reflexively emits a physiological response when lying. Such an assumption may contain an element of truth in that individuals cannot monitor, disguise or control all modes of behaviour at one time. But most people are capable of concealing or falsifying what they believe others will likely attend to. For a liar undergoing a lie-detection test, and only modestly good at the task of lying, it would be most important to control what is said, and thereafter, in descending order, it is important to control physiology, the face, the body and the voice. It is sometimes held that only a very good liar can control what is said while also controlling non-verbal behaviour such as facial expression, body movement and voice intonations (Ekman, 1985).

But experience tells us everyone can learn to be a liar of sorts, and everyone can learn to evolve their own personal techniques of controlling their physiological responses. 'Getting over your nervousness', 'getting rid of the butterflies', 'take a deep breath', and even 'stay cool' – these are all common ways of expressing some attempt to control physiology in the face of emotional stress.

With respect to the issue of control one may refer to the literature on biofeedback. Biofeedback is the technique of acquiring voluntary control of internal bodily processes, such as heart rate, blood pressure or sweat gland activity. Under normal circumstances there is no reason to acquire voluntary control over such internal processes: indeed we could imagine it a great inconvenience were it necessary to supervise sweat gland activity during a game of tennis. However, such autonomic control is often accomplished by the Zen masters and yogi practitioners – usually for the purposes of achieving a calming effect. Jet-fighter pilots learn to control their emotions (and therefore their physiology) in order to operate with maximum efficiency under extreme physical and psychological stress. Internal control can also be achieved by the layman, including the liar. The theoretical workings of biofeedback are still not well understood, since it is not clear whether skeletal or somatic responses are mediating the biofeedback effects. But the point here is that directly, or more likely indirectly, *visceral or autonomic responses can be learned to be controlled*.

The implication of this observation in lie-detection testing is that an individual, only vaguely familiar with the procedures of lie-detection testing, may produce physiological responses on opportune occasions and thereby portray himself as an innocent victim.

Predictability

Can emotions be predicted by the presentation of specific stimuli? For example, when a spider is presented to different individuals it is unlikely that all individuals will have the same emotional response. Some may be horrified by the sight of the spider, while others will be unaffected, and still others may be pleasantly attracted to the spider's presence. Similarly, when the lie-catcher poses the relevant question (emotional stimulus), can one predict that the liar will respond with one kind of emotion, and the innocent victim with no or another emotion? The answer to this question is negative.

One theory of emotion which accounts for this phenomenon is Lazarus's cognitive appraisal theory of emotion (Lazarus, Coyne and Folkman, 1984). In this theory of emotion the causal role of cognition in emotion is emphasized. The theory suggests that cognitive processes (what people think) are primary in emotional responding; that elicitation of an emotion requires first and foremost a cognitive evaluation. In other words, what a person *thinks* will determine the emotional response. Furthermore, the quality and intensity of an emotional reaction are determined by the cognitive appraisal processes.

If this theory has correctly identified the role of cognition in emotion, then it follows that an individual may *reappraise* or misread the stressful stimulus. In other words, during a lie-detection test the victim has the opportunity to control thoughts, which then elicit the emotion: tell the truth and think of something painful and the truth may appear on the polygraph as a lie.

The critical aspect of cognitive reappraisal of an emotional stimulus is that there are no rules, at least no simple rules, about the determinants of appraisal. Appraisal is a highly individualized process. Therefore the flaw in the assumption that an emotional stimulus can predict emotion is precisely that an outside observer (the lie-catcher) cannot know how an individual has cognitively appraised a potentially emotional situation.

The implication of this assertion is that the guilty victim may not respond with anxiety if he does not cognitively interpret the act of lying, or being caught lying, as an anxious experience. Likewise, for any number of reasons, the innocent victim may cognitively interpret the relevant question as particularly stressful, and consequently be wrongly assessed as guilty.

Problems between parameters of behaviour

Sometimes, but not always, a polygraph examiner will make a judgement about whether a suspect is lying not only from the polygraph chart, but also from behavioural cues such as the subject's facial expressions, voice, gestures and manner of speaking. So what does the research on emotion tell us about the relationship between these parameters of emotion?

In emotion research it is generally agreed the operationalization of emotion must include at least three parameters of behaviour. For example, Hodgson and Rachman (1974) have examined the fear responses of neurotics and propose a 'tripartite response system' model of emotion. This system includes verbal–cognitive, motor, and physiological events which interact through interoceptive (neural and hormonal) and exteroceptive channels of communication. There are several permutations on the response parameters. In some cases the relationship between these events may be demonstrated by complete synchrony between events. Thus the fearful person may report feeling fearful, demonstrate avoidance behaviour and display physiological disturbance. Given such a response pattern, the lie-catcher should have little problem in correctly detecting the lie. Nor should the lie-catcher be troubled if there were a physiological response and avoidance behaviour, but no report of fear.

However, what happens when other combinations of the response systems do not necessarily work in a co-ordinated fashion? Under different circumstances, or with another individual, desynchrony may be demonstrated in numerous ways. For example, what happens when the individual feels afraid, but does not display physiological disturbance or avoidance behaviour? Or a person may feel frightened, engage in avoidance behaviour, but not exhibit any marked physiological change. There may also be problems for the lie-catcher who overemphasizes the importance of non-verbal cues in an individual who refrains from carrying out any avoidance behaviour, despite the presence of physiological disturbance and subjective fear. An individual may even display avoidance behaviour in the absence of feeling fearful or physiological disturbance. Of course there is always the possibility that there is no response in any of these response parameters. Thus we see the emergence of a matrix where response parameters may covary, vary inversely, or vary independently.

Facial feedback and discharge theory. The tripartite theory of Hodgson and Rachman, described above, was developed from observations taken from clinical populations. It was designed to explain and help overcome problems with individuals who experience or display abnormal emotional processing. But what might be the relationship between parameters during emotional processing in normal subjects?

The research which examines this question is divided into two camps: the facial feedback hypothesis and the discharge theory of emotion. The facial feedback hypothesis is a Darwinian notion in that it suggests that non-verbal displays, by way of wired-in circuitry from the facial muscles to sites in the brain, regulate the experience of emotion. The essence of the hypothesis is that the degree or quality of non-verbal behaviour is causally and positively related to the feeling of emotion. To support the hypothesis one would expect to find a positive relationship between non-verbal displays and self-reports or autonomic responses. Thus, for example, smiling should cause the smiler to feel good, and frowning should produce bad feelings.

The discharge theory is a Freudian-type notion, in that it incorporates notions of repression, 'leaking' of emotional expressivity, and intrapsychic conflict. This theory has been treated as diametrically opposed to the facial feedback hypothesis. Such a cathartic or hydraulic view suggests that verbal, facial and physiological responses are alternative channels for releasing emotion; if one channel is blocked, the response through the other should increase in intensity. Thus one expects an inverse relationship between non-verbal display and physiological responses: if one feels angry, and yells and bares her teeth, she should then have reduced physiological tension and feel better.

In sum, the former of these two theories suggests that to repress emotion is to 'soften' it, while the discharge or Freudian theory maintains that to repress the emotion is to intensify it. The research findings supporting these two schools of thought are as contradictory as are the theories themselves.

Although the research at present has not been able to give us any clear-cut answers, commonsense tells us that probably both a facial feedback and discharge theory may be operationalized by different people in different situations. An alternative view, supported by some preliminary research, suggests that for some people a specific pattern of physiological responding may characterize a specific emotion (Ekman, Levenson and Friesen, 1983). At this stage, however, it is not clear what precisely are the mechanisms involved in emotional responding. The various views of emotion examine the relationship of expressivity for emotion. But they demonstrate different ways of expressing: ways that need not be contradictory. How people feel and how they think about how they feel, and how they physiologically express how they think and feel, are not necessarily co-ordinated or correspondent. What emerges here is that there can be either synchrony or desynchrony between various parameters of emotion.

The implication of such a conclusion to lie-detection testing is that there are not set patterns of behaviour that reflect a liar. There are many ways to express a lie, just as there are many ways of feeling about expressing a lie.

Reliability. The inconsistencies in the above described area of research may also, in part, be accounted for by the unreliability of the skin conductance measure (SC) – the measurement used in lie-detection tests. In many studies SC has been difficult to interpret. For example, to help phobic patients overcome a fear they may be 'desensitized' from the fear object. This is done by training the individual to relax at a time when fear or anxiety is normally experienced. However, the success of desensitization (the term given to such a technique) has been found to be unrelated to a reduction in SC response (SCR). In other words, SC, in these studies, was unrelated to a reduction in anxiety. It was concluded from such studies that 'SCR is a multi-system response which is only loosely coupled to subjective anxiety' (Hodgson and Rachman, 1974: 324).

Perhaps an explanation of this conclusion is found in a recent study by Arena et al. (1983) where the aim was to assess the reliability of psychophysiological recording. In this study fifteen normal subjects were assessed on multiple response measures (forehead electromyographic activity – EMG – and forearm flexor EMG, heart rate, skin resistance level, hand surface temperature and cephalic vasomotor response), under multiple stimulus conditions (baseline, self-control, cognitive and physical stressors), on multiple occasions (days 1, 2, 8 and 28). Three forms of reliability coefficients were computed for each response measure: coefficients on absolute scores, coefficients on change scores from baseline to stressful conditions and coefficients on percent change from baseline. Of all these measures, SRL demonstrated the lowest reliability: in fact, it appeared completely unreliable. The correlations indicate a low internal reliability across time, across situations, and with other measures. *Skin conductance is worst, that is to say, the most unreliable, of all physiological responses*. These findings suggest that we can have little credibility in skin conductance as a physiological measure.

Individual differences
In emotion research, investigators are becoming more interested in the issue of individual differences. The premise of individual differences research is that people differ from one another in significant and consistent ways. In the context of lie-detection testing, acknowledgement of such differences is critical. For example, a lie-catcher may interpret a raised pitch in the voice as an indication of lying. For some individuals this may be the correct clue. However, failure to show a sign of emotion in the voice is not necessarily evidence of

truthfulness; some individuals are very skilful at controlling their behaviour, while others never show emotion, at least not in their voice. And even people who are emotional may not be so about a particular lie.

In our own research we have found that there are no simple relationships between variables which are the same for all people (Ney and Gale, 1987). While some individuals are responsive to situations with their face, others are responsive with their voice, and yet others are responsive physiologically. Even *within* a particular variable, say for example the physiological variable, individuals may simply be responsive or variable.

Thus the notion of individual differences has implications for users of the lie-detection test. Some individuals may be more predictable than others on physiological measures.

Conclusion

Lie-detection testing is a haphazard technique for four reasons: (1) the biofeedback literature demonstrates that individuals may control their physiology; (2) specific emotional stimuli cannot predict emotion because we can never be sure how an individual cognitively evaluates what appears to be an emotional stimulus; (3) research examining the relationship between different parameters of emotion is methodologically weak, and further, physiological measures which have been used have demonstrated unreliability across time, situation and with other physiological measures; there are no clear-cut answers in this area of research; (4) some preliminary research in our laboratory demonstrates how individuals may vary between themselves across a number of parameters of emotion.

For the lie-detection test to be effective, perception of emotion (stress, anxiety) is singularly important. But anyone who insists that all or even most individuals will respond to stress similarly, or that emotion will be expressed on a single index by all people in a single way, or that presentation of a particular question will elicit the same response in all people, may themselves be fooled by the results. The lie detector may tell lies about the truth.

PART THREE

The Polygraph in Practice

7

The polygraph test in the USA and elsewhere

Gordon H. Barland

To many people the polygraph is as American as apple pie or the Statue of Liberty. But just as Miss Liberty was fashioned in Paris, scientific lie detection had its origins in Europe before the turn of the century. The main interest in scientific lie detection was in Italy, Germany, Austria and Switzerland from 1895 until the First World War. Before looking at the history of instrumental lie detection, it is necessary to mention the unsuccessful search for psychological tests to identify criminals.

Psychological guilt detection

In 1904 Wertheimer and Klein published a sensational paper in which they originated the concept of *psychologische Tatbestandsdiagnostik*, that when a person commits a crime it creates a complex within the mind which can be detected under appropriate conditions. Dozens of psychologists in Germany, Austria and Switzerland – and, later on, also in America – worked on developing psychological tests of guilt for use in criminal investigations (for an excellent review, see Herbold-Wootten, 1982). The main test, known as the word association/reaction time test, consisted of twenty relevant words which the guilty person would recognize as pertaining to the crime he was suspected of having committed. These words were embedded within a list of an additional eighty innocuous words. The psychologist then slowly read each word to the suspect, who was instructed to reply as rapidly as possible with the first word that came to mind. The psychologist recorded both the associated word and the length of time it took for the suspect to reply. The test was based upon the principle that whenever the guilty person would recognize one of the relevant words, the first word which would come to mind would be likely to relate to the crime. The suspect then had to make a decision. He could either speak the associated word and risk revealing his guilt directly, or he could try to come up with a less incriminating association, in which case he would risk indirectly revealing his guilt by the additional time required to come up with the second association. Although this test showed some promise in criminal investigation, its use never caught on. There may have been several reasons for that: it required a team of three or four people to administer it, it took a day or more to evaluate the results, the results were often ambiguous, and because (in America, at least) it was eclipsed by instrumental lie detection, the polygraph.

Instrumental lie detection

Possibly as early as 1881, even before the interest in word association/ reaction time tests, the Italian criminologist, Cesare Lombroso, was the first to report using an instrument to detect lies (Lombroso, 1881, 1895). His device, a hydrosphygmograph, measured changes in the amount of blood in the arm of a criminal suspect undergoing an interrogation. The changes were permanently recorded on a chart or graph, which allowed Lombroso to make a detailed analysis of it following the questioning. Because only one measure was being recorded, the chart was not a *poly*graph, but simply a graph.

Mosso (1878), an Italian physiologist who worked closely with Lombroso, found that breathing patterns changed in response to various stimuli. Wertheimer and Klein (1904), German psychologists, proposed that respiratory changes might be of use in criminal investigation. A few years later in Austria, Vittorio Benussi, a professor at the University of Graz who was studying problems in psychophysics, decided to test Wertheimer and Klein's suggestion. He recorded respiratory patterns, and found that the inspiration–expiration (I/E) ratio changes when people lie. Shortly after his finding was published in 1914 the gale force winds of war extinguished the flame of interest in lie detection throughout all of Europe.

The Americans took the separate ideas from Europe and dropped some, modified others, and combined them to form today's polygraph technique. The catalyst for American interest in scientific lie detection seems to have been a flamboyant German-born professor, Hugo Münsterberg, then at Harvard University. Without citing the European researchers by name, he published a remarkable book in which he suggested that research be done with a variety of psychological and physiological measures including the pneumograph, the plethysmograph, heart activity, and electrodermal activity to detect guilty knowledge (Münsterberg, 1908: 123–33). One of Münsterberg's students, William Marston, discovered in 1915 that systolic blood pressure changes are associated with deception (Marston, 1938: 46). He developed the systolic blood pressure deception test in which the systolic pressure was intermittently measured while a person was being questioned. In 1917 or 1918 Marston used his technique to help the military solve espionage cases (Marston, 1938: 66–7).

If any single moment was the watershed in the development of the polygraph as we know it today, it occurred in late 1920 or early 1921, for it was then that August Vollmer, chief of the Berkeley Police Department in California, had John Larson develop a 'lie detection' apparatus to solve a case then under investigation. Larson's device was the first true polygraph used for lie-detection purposes. It measured respiration and, by means of a modified Erlanger capsule, a continuous recording of cardiovascular changes on a Jacquet polygraph which apparently also included an event marker (Larson, 1932: 276). Within a few years the polygraph was made portable and an electrodermal channel added. A number of sensational successes by Larson and one of his protégés, a college student named Leonarde Keeler, quickly popularized the technique, which was initially confined to criminal investigations. The first examiners were either self-taught or underwent tutorial training by the practitioners. By 1942 Keeler was teaching a two-week course for police and military examiners; he expanded it to a six-week course in 1948, by which time it was a formal school (Keeler, 1984: 162). Today the demand for polygraph examiners has resulted in the creation of over thirty polygraph schools accredited by the 3,000-member American Polygraph Association. The private schools have at least a seven-week curriculum, and the US and Canadian government schools last fourteen weeks.

Although there are no reliable figures indexing the growth of the polygraph field in America, it seems to be growing exponentially. The first thirty to forty years evidenced a slow but continual growth, with the polygraph being used primarily for criminal investigation. In 1931 the entrepreneurial Keeler was introducing the polygraph to businesses to solve internal thefts and possibly to screen applicants (Keeler, 1931). It is not known when the business use of the polygraph overtook the police use, but that probably occurred by 1970. Despite the fact that the polygraph is now routinely used in criminal investigation – nearly every police and sheriff's department in America has at least one officer assigned full-time as a polygraph examiner – perhaps 80 to 90 percent of all polygraph examinations administered in America today are employment-related.

The explosive growth in polygraph screening by business is now being echoed by the government. For more than thirty years, only the CIA and NSA conducted screening examinations. Due to a series of damaging spy cases recently, the number of federal employees subject to polygraph examinations has been increased, with the result that most of the military services have started major polygraph screening programmes. The number of examiners trained by the government is being nearly tripled. The increased government polygraph activity is not confined to security screening. Throughout most of the 1970s about eight government departments had a polygraph capability. Today, the list includes at least fourteen: the Army; Air Force; Navy; Marine Corps; the FBI; CIA; NSA; the US Postal Service; the Secret Service; the Drug Enforcement Administration; the Bureau of Alcohol, Tobacco and Fire Arms; the US Marshal's Service; the US Customs Office; and the Defense Investigative Service. All told, there are now over 300 active federal examiners. If the average salary is $25,000, the Government is spending more than $7.5 million annually for examiner salaries alone! When the cost of equipment, office space, travel, training and research is included, the total is in excess of $10 million.

The dramatic increase in polygraph usage in the US, particularly for screening, has been matched by a surge of legislative, judicial and scientific interest in the polygraph. Within the scientific community the two main empirical issues are the accuracy of blind chart analysis, especially at detecting the truthfulness of the innocent criminal suspect, and the validity of the polygraph screening tests where the base rate for deception is low. Most of the available research is limited to the polygraph's accuracy in criminal investigation. There is a growing belief that those studies contain significant deficiencies in design or execution which may severely limit the generalizability of their results. Virtually no research has been conducted on the polygraph in screening applications. As long as the polygraph remained low-keyed there was no pressure on the Government to allocate money for polygraph research. With little research money available, the scientific community had scant interest in conducting studies. The dearth of scientifically trained researchers who were also familiar with lie-detection procedures resulted in paradigms and methodologies that are increasingly being viewed as inadequate. Only now are superior paradigms being developed which combine the ground truth of the laboratory with the realism of field applications (see Iacono and Patrick, 1987). Such paradigms are essential for estimating the accuracy of the polygraph with innocent suspects.

International use of the polygraph

The rapid expansion of the polygraph in America is being paralleled internationally. Although isolated efforts at scientific lie detection had been made prior to the 1930s in Europe and Japan, they did not prove practical, despite the fact that a Japanese named Togawa used skin conductance for testing a spy (Fukumoto, 1982). The internationalization of American lie-detection technology started slowly in the early 1950s, largely as a result of its use within the US armed services stationed abroad, but has accelerated sharply within the past five years. Prior to 1980 there was only a handful of countries known to have any polygraph capability. Today, there are six countries with a major capability (see Table 7.1), and at least thirty others – perhaps as many as fifty – that have one or more examiners conducting tests on at least a part-time basis.

Table 7.1 *Countries with a major polygraph capability*

Rank	Country	Estimated number of examiners	Population/examiner ratio
1	USA	5,000–10,000	29,000
2	Canada	110– 120	213,000
3	Japan	90– 110	1,165,000
4	Turkey	60– 65	723,000
5	Korea, South	40– 50	881,000
6	Israel	40– 45	95,000

Numbers of examiners are estimates based upon personal communications with examiners from various countries. The population per examiner ratio was based upon the author's best estimate of the number of examiners and 1980 world population figures.

Japan appears to have been the first country outside America to use scientific lie detection officially as a routine method of criminal investigation, for a Japanese-made psychogalvanometer was adopted in 1947 by the Metropolitan Police. The Japanese police received polygraph training from the American army as early as 1951 (Fukumoto, 1982), and today rank third in the number of examiners. The National Institute of Police Science in Tokyo has perhaps conducted more research on lie detection than any other laboratory in the world. The police examiners are trained at their own school which emphasizes the peak of tension test. The control question test is used primarily to supplement the peak of tension test.

In Germany, despite the presence of the American army, the situation was different. Following a spirited debate within the legal community, the German supreme court ruled in 1954 that the polygraph could not be used because it compelled a person's body to reveal the truth despite a conscious decision to lie, thereby violating the freedom of the will (Kaganiec, 1956). A renewed debate within legal and scientific circles (e.g. Tent, 1967; Undeutsch, 1975, 1979) was quashed in 1982 by the supreme court's refusal to hear an appeal.

Korea is another major polygraph user. As with Japan, the initial examiners were trained by US Army examiners in the 1950s. Unlike the Japanese, some Korean examiners have been trained outside their country, primarily in America and Japan. Consequently, both the control question and peak of tension tests are used in criminal investigation.

Canada is second only to the US in its use of the polygraph. It was slow to start using it, no doubt because of the British influence on its investigative and judicial processes. However, the Canadian use of the polygraph is so heavily influenced by the American model that there are few differences in its application. All Canadian examiners were trained in American schools until the Canadian Police College opened its own polygraph training course in 1978; and that school is patterned after the US Department of Defense Polygraph Institute. In Canada the polygraph is used primarily for criminal investigation and seldom for screening, be it by government or industry. As in America, the control question test is the technique of preference in criminal investigation.

Perhaps because they felt the need to offset their small numbers with technological efficiency, the Israelis were also early to accept the polygraph. Some of their examiners have been trained in America, but most are trained in their own school. Unlike the Japanese, who have no private examiners, about a third of the Israeli examiners are retired police examiners who now have a private practice. They rely heavily upon the control question test in criminal investigation.

Turkey is an example of the speed with which a country can acquire a major polygraph capability. As recently as 1984 there was not a single examiner known to be in Turkey. Today it has sixty to sixty-five examiners, all trained in American schools and using the latest polygraph equipment and techniques. Despite the precipitousness of their polygraph build-up, they have taken care to establish quality control procedures modelled after that used by the American federal government. Although it is too early to assess the effectiveness of their programme, it is obvious that the Turks are making every effort to ensure high standards.

Other countries which have at least a modest polygraph capability include Great Britain, India, the Philippines, Poland and Yugoslavia. The polygraph seems not to be used by the Soviets, apparently because they consider it to be a capitalist tool for repressing the proletariat (Nikolaichik, 1964; Radio Moscow, 1980). It is something of a paradox that two of the more repressive regimes of the twentieth century with fearsome reputations for extracting information against the will of their victims – the reigns of Hitler and Stalin – never once used the polygraph.

A rationale for lie detection

Every event leaves traces behind for the scientist to discover. Some of the traces are of short duration, such as body warmth imparted to a chair by someone seated in it. Others, such as fingerprints, may last indefinitely if preserved under optimum conditions. Science is continually improving the technician's ability to discover those traces. Some four decades after attempts to develop a latent fingerprint from an incriminating document had failed, the FBI recently was able to identify a Nazi spy using laser technology to recover the print.

The polygraph is a means of detecting biological traces of an event which are stored as memories in the brain of a perpetrator or witness. The memory cannot be detected directly; but the body responds to them, and those perturbations are recorded by the polygraph, however slight they may be. However, the body reacts not only to memories, but also to original thoughts and to changes in its external environment. The central problem in lie detection is to arrange the testing conditions in such a way that extraneous reactions can be eliminated, controlled or explained. Then, if unexplained reactions to a question persist, the only reasonable alternative is that the person is lying or holding back information he considers important. Although it may at first seem to be an impossible task, it can often be successfully accomplished. To the extent that the required degree of control can be achieved, the test will be accurate.

Extraneous reactions caused by aural and visual stimuli can be eliminated by conducting the examination in a quiet room free from uncontrolled sights and sounds. Reactions caused by orienting responses (ORs) are controlled by inserting one or more irrelevant questions to absorb the ORs. The effects of habituation can be controlled by reordering the question sequence from one chart to the next in the relevant–irrelevant (RI) test, or by the judicious juxtaposition of control and relevant questions in the control question test (CQT). Reactions caused by random thoughts are easily controlled by repeating the question sequences. By definition, random reactions will be evenly distributed among the various questions and can thus be factored out. Non-random reactions caused by innocent associations to a specific question can be identified by incorporating the subject's explanation into the wording of the questions, and continuing the examination.

For example, let us assume that a person is suspected of killing his wife, Mary. He claims to have come home from work one evening to find her body in the bedroom. She had been stabbed repeatedly, and blood was splashed throughout much of the room. He was administered a control question test, and appeared deceptive; that is, he reacted more to the question 'Did you kill Mary?' than to the control question 'Before the age of 24, did you ever hurt anyone who loved you?' When asked why he was reacting to the question about killing his wife, he claims that there were two reasons. First, the name Mary evokes an emotional response because of his great love for her. Second, whenever the relevant question was asked, he involuntarily had a vivid recollection of the crime scene in his mind's eye, and re-experienced the shock of finding Mary's body.

These explanations can be directly tested by asking a series of additional questions on a follow-up relevant–irrelevant test. In order to assess how much of the reaction was caused by the name Mary, that name would be included in most or all of the questions, including innocuous questions. In order to factor out the emotionality caused by viewing the crime scene, some of the questions would include that, whereas others would not. The questions might include: 'Do you love Mary? Did you ever argue with Mary? Did you ever want to kill Mary, even for just a moment? Did you see Mary's body in the bedroom? Was Mary already dead when you first entered the bedroom? Did you stab Mary, yourself?' If the suspect is innocent and he is telling the truth about why he reacted, he should react more to the initial questions than to the later ones, and he should react the most to the question of seeing her body in the bedroom. On the other hand, if he killed Mary himself, the earlier questions should not bother him as much as the later ones, and he should show his largest reactions to the last two. Note that the fourth relevant question asks about 'seeing' the body, not 'finding' it, for the latter phrasing would not allow the examiner to differentiate between the innocent and guilty person; both would be expected to show large reactions to it, for the guilty person would be lying about having found the body.

Factors affecting the accuracy of the polygraph technique

How accurate is the polygraph? Not long ago this was the primary question that researchers were trying to answer, but that question is too broad to be answerable, too simple to be useful. We are at an exciting stage in the development of polygraph science, for we now are able to ask much more precise questions. Perhaps the single most important distinction that must be made is the polygraph's accuracy in detecting lies versus its accuracy in detecting truthfulness. Other major distinctions involve the test format (such as the RI, CQ, POT and GK tests), the type of examiner (government, police or private), the examiner's level of training and experience, the manner in which the charts are evaluated (numerically or non-numerically), and the accuracy of the clinical examiner's judgement versus the blind analysis of polygraph charts. Some of these factors are discussed in this section.

The detection of deception versus truth
Is the person being tested innocent or guilty, truthful or deceptive? There appears to be an interaction between this variable and the type of test being administered. With the RI and CQ tests, the polygraph seems to be more accurate at detecting the deception of the guilty person than detecting the truthfulness of the innocent person, though the opposite seems to be true with the POT and GK tests. Indeed, both the critics and the proponents of the polygraph are in general agreement that the RI and CQ tests are quite accurate at detecting deception. It is generally believed to be in the range of about 85 to 95 percent. The controversy centres on the accuracy of those tests in detecting the truthfulness of the innocent person. A growing number of scientists claim that the CQT cannot do so at all, that the accuracy is no better than chance (Kleinmuntz and Szucko, 1984b; Lykken, 1981). If they are correct, the polygraph's sole value is not scientific but utilitarian: information obtained through adroit questioning with the polygraph as a backdrop.

It has been argued (Iacono and Patrick, 1987) that this vital question cannot be resolved by research employing the conventional mock crime, for the psychodynamics of the mock-innocent subject is quite different from that of the innocent suspect in a real-life criminal investigation. They believe that studies using the conventional mock crime to estimate the accuracy of the polygraph at discriminating between guilty and innocent real-life suspects are seriously flawed, and that more rigorous methodology must be employed before the question can be answered. They urge the development of a more realistic paradigm in which the subjects are blind to the research nature of the examinations. One of the many paradoxes of lie detection is that not long ago it was believed that the mock crime was capable of providing a realistic estimate of the accuracy of the polygraph with real-life innocent people but that it underestimated the accuracy with real-life guilty ones. Now the situation is arguably the reverse. The accuracy rates for the detection of lies in mock crime and real life appear to be similar; it is the difference in the psychodynamics of the innocent suspect which seems to be the more important limit on the generalizability of mock-crime results.

Examiner qualifications

The quality and experience of the examiner have a significant effect on the accuracy of the polygraph. One reason why it is difficult to compare various studies is that this variable is often ignored. Elementary texts on experimental design stress the importance of sampling from the population to be generalized to. Recent research on lie detection has taken this into account when sampling subject populations by recruiting from the community or from prisons. Unfortunately, most studies have failed to sample from the examiner population. The examiners have too often been selected from the opposite extremes of examiner competence. Most studies have used whatever examiner was most convenient: students in polygraph schools (Kleinmuntz and Szucko, 1984a) or even untrained college students at the low end, or examiner-scientists at the other extreme (e.g. Raskin and Hare, 1978). This is not to say that atypical examiners ought not be studied, for they can shed valuable light on the upper and lower limits of examiner accuracy; but when trying to generalize to the typical field situation the researcher has an obligation to sample from the typical examiner population.

Defining the typical examiner is difficult, because there is a broad range of examiner training, test techniques, what type of non-polygraphic data (if any) are included in the examiner's decision, and the type of quality control system (if any) within which the examiner works. In America the federal examiners undergo fourteen weeks of polygraph training as compared to seven for most police and private examiners. All federal examiners work within a compulsory quality control programme, whereas fewer police examiners do and almost no private examiner does. Some unknown proportion of police examiners include varying amounts of non-polygraph information such as behavioural cues when making their decisions, as do virtually all private examiners conducting screening tests. Many examiners accustomed to testing criminal suspects may thus be at a disadvantage when examining experimental subjects, as the range and intensity of the subjects' behavioural cues may be markedly diminished in mock-innocent and mock-guilty subjects. The effect of non-polygraphic data upon examiner accuracy has not been systematically studied. In view of the diversity of examiner experience and decision-making strategies, it would seem necessary to exercise far more caution when generalizing from experimental results than has thus far been the case.

Even when a typical field examiner is selected, the use of only one examiner to conduct a series of tests creates the additional problem of lack of independence between the examinations. An examiner conducting tests on fifty subjects in a mock crime views the last subject differently than he did the first, even when kept blind about the accuracy of his decisions. The problem is particularly insidious when a series of studies are conducted employing the same paradigm, examiner and subject population, for here the examiner knows his success rate on the earlier studies. In an effort to maximize the effectiveness of the test, the procedures are debugged and modified from one study to the next. In the beginning the changes are usually major and are quite deliberate; later they may be more subtle and done quite unconsciously. To the extent that the increases in the experience and sophistication of the examiner(s) are not matched in the field, the later experimental results may overestimate the polygraph's field accuracy.

Suspects and victims

The polygraph may be more accurate with criminal suspects than with victims. Some thirteen theories have been proposed to explain why people react when they are deceptive, although none can yet account for all of the facts. One of these theories is the conditioned-to-crime theory. It states that the guilty person reacts when lying because the relevant questions tend to elicit the emotions or arousal that existed at the time the crime was being committed. It predicts that victims are at increased risk of false positive errors if the relevant questions impinge upon the emotionality present when the crime occurred. Let us suppose that a woman reports having been raped, and the investigation has raised the possibility that no force had been employed. If the question on the polygraph test were: 'Did that man hold a knife to your throat before you had intercourse with him?', the conditioned-to-crime theory would predict that the truthful victim should react precisely because she is telling the truth! Accordingly most examiners would not ask such an emotion-evoking question. Rather, they would subtly shift the psychological focus of the question away from the time of the alleged rape by asking, 'Did you lie to the police when you said that you were forced at knifepoint to have sex?' Incidentally, another theory, the conditioned-to-punishment theory, does not posit any increase in false positives with victims.

Type of issue

Another variable thought to affect the accuracy of the polygraph is the type of issue under investigation. The polygraph is believed to be most accurate when a person denies having physically committed a specific, usually illegal, act. It is probably less accurate when the suspect admits the act, but denies criminal *intent*. For example, a defendant may admit fatally shooting a friend, but claim it was an accident. Here the issue is not as distinct; it calls for an interpretation which may be subject to distortion or rationalization. The more vague or nebulous the issue, the greater the chance of error, particularly false negatives. These difficulties are magnified when the criminal act is more mental than physical, such as what was said in a possibly conspiratorial conversation that occurred months earlier. Nonetheless, in situations where no physical evidence bearing upon that type of issue can be obtained the polygraph may be the best means of assessing the suspect's claim. It is important that those receiving the examiner's report be aware of the increased likelihood of error, however.

Base rate for deception

The base rate for deception may also affect the accuracy of the polygraph, although no research has yet been conducted on this important issue. As the base rate for deception (BR(d)) decreases, the possibility of making a false negative error likewise decreases, and the proportion of false positive errors within the total population of errors must increase. When the BR(d) is zero, obviously only false positive errors can occur.

In addition to affecting the FN/FP ratio, high or low base rates for deception also affect the overall accuracy of blind chart analyses. If the polygraph were 90 percent accurate with deceptive subjects and only 50 percent accurate with truthful subjects, the mean accuracy of the polygraph would be 70 percent only when BR(d) = BR(t) = 1/2. As either base rate approaches zero, the mean polygraph accuracy becomes increasingly skewed. As shown in Table 7.2, when the BR(d) is only 1 percent, as it might be in some screening situations, only 0.2 percent of the examiner's truthful decisions would be in error because there are so few guilty subjects in the total population. However, fully 98 percent of all decisions of deception would be false positives if the polygraph is not able to detect truthfulness beyond chance levels. The overall accuracy in this illustration would be 496 correct detections out of 1,000 exams (49.6 percent), instead of the 70 percent that would occur if the BR(d) were 1/2.

Table 7.2 *Predicted accuracy of polygraph outcomes when accuracy with guilty subjects is 90 percent, accuracy with innocent subjects is 50 percent, and BR(d) is 1 percent*

Polygraph outcome	Ground truth			Error rate %
	Guilty	Innocent	Total	
Deceptive	9	495	504	98
Truthful	1	495	496	0.2
Total	10	990	1,000	
Error rate	10%	50%		49.6

Effect of base rates in screening tests

Because of the impact of base rates on polygraph accuracy, it has been argued that the polygraph ought not to be used for screening except in limited cases where the social structure requires it, such as with police applicants (Lykken, 1974) or for governmental security screening (Raskin, 1986b). However, the argument may not be as compelling as the statistics would suggest. Even in the bleak scenario presented in Table 7.2 in which the polygraph is only randomly accurate with truthful subjects, half of the 990 innocent subjects have been cleared at the cost of one (10 percent) false negative error. The successful elimination of 50 percent of the truthful subjects with 90 percent of the guilty subjects still under suspicion represents a considerable saving of investigative effort.

However, theoretical projections of false positive rates to be expected in screening situations very likely overestimate the error rate. They include an assumption that has never been explicitly stated, but which is almost certainly false in most screening situations. This implied assumption is that the examiner's awareness of the probable base rate for deception does not affect his decisions, and thus the false positive error rate. Another implied assumption is that the examiner is unable to discover potential false positive errors and take effective corrective action prior to the time that he renders his report; that is, whenever a subject reacts to a question on the polygraph, the test is halted and the person is reported as being deceptive.

Examiners who specialize in screening tests tend to view the polygraph differently than those who test criminal suspects. Examiners testing criminal suspects typically equate responses with deception. However, examiners experienced in screening view the polygraph as an 'emotion detector', and approach positive results more cautiously. Before discussing how the examiner's awareness of base rates works to reduce the number of false positives, it is necessary to discuss the definition of errors.

Psychophysiologists focus on the decision based upon blind analysis of the polygraph charts, whereas the examiners focus upon the decision reported by the examiner, even though that may contain extrapolygraphic data such as the examiner's observation of the subject's behaviour. I will refer to this distinction as 'chart decisions' and 'clinical decisions'. Thus, it is possible for a chart decision to be a hit (true positive or true negative) and the clinical decision to be a miss (false positive or false negative) if the examiner misreads the charts or disregards them in favour of misleading extrapolygraphic data. Obviously, the reverse could also occur. There are no hard data to indicate whether chart or clinical decisions are more likely to be correct in the event of a conflict. It may be that FPs occur more often than FNs with chart decisions, but that the reverse is true of clinical decisions. If that is the case, then both types of errors might be minimized at the expense of increasing the inconclusive rate by making a definite decision only when the chart and clinical decisions are in agreement.

With respect to ground truth, there are five possible polygraph outcomes: true positive, true negative, false positive, false negative, and no decision (inconclusive). These terms are self-evident in many criminal applications. If a suspect denies having committed a crime when in fact he did it, the polygraph outcome is a true positive if the examiner concludes that the suspect was deceptive, and a false negative if he concludes that the suspect was truthful. With an innocent suspect, the polygraph outcome is a true negative if the examiner concludes that the suspect was truthful, and a false positive if he concludes that the suspect was deceptive.

There are cases in which the distinction between hits and misses is less clear-cut. Let us consider, for example, a crime committed by two persons. One shot a person to death while the other drove the getaway car. Only one suspect – the one who actually did the shooting – has been apprehended and has agreed to take a polygraph examination. The police suspect that he drove the getaway car, but for some reason do not seriously suspect him of being the one who pulled the trigger. His defence attorney wishes to have his client examined by a private examiner. The relevant questions on the polygraph test are therefore limited to the issue of 'Did you drive the getaway car?' If the suspect appears deceptive on the test, should that be considered a hit or a miss? On the one hand, the suspect was literally truthful when he denied being the driver, and a positive outcome would thus be a false positive. On the other hand, most psychologists studying deception in contexts other than lie detection consider lies of omission to be just as deceptive as lies of commission, since the intent is to mislead the investigator (e.g. De Paulo, Stone and Lassiter, 1985; Ekman, 1985). If one accepts that definition of deception, then as long as the suspect intentionally minimizes or denies his actual involvement in the crime, a positive test outcome would be a true positive. Most criminal investigators, including polygraph examiners, would likely subscribe to that view. I must admit that I find it the more persuasive, in part because the body itself does not seem to distinguish between lies of commission and omission; both are readily detected through polygraphic means.

The inclusion or exclusion of lies of omission in the definition of deception is an important issue, for such omissions occur frequently in screening situations, where people are trying to present themselves in the best possible light. Whether deception is defined narrowly or broadly to include lies of omission has a profound effect not only on the definition of hits and misses but also on the base rate for deception. If the withholding of significant information constitutes deception, then the definition of hits and misses depends both upon the reason why the examinee withheld information and upon the threshold required for the withheld information to be considered significant.

Suppose a job applicant admits stealing $10 from a previous employer over a six-month period, but the applicant specifically remembers stealing $1,000 and believes that it could have been as much as $2,000. Most would agree that the withheld information is significant, and that a positive test result to the question 'Have you stolen more than $10 from a previous employer?' would be a true positive. However, if the applicant admits to stealing $1, but believes it could actually have been $2, *should* the polygraph outcome be positive or negative for it to be scored as a hit? Both alternatives could reasonably be argued. The required threshold probably depends more upon how certain the applicant is that he is withholding anything and why he is withholding it than upon the absolute magnitude of the discrepancy.

Now let us return to the question of how the examiner's knowledge of the base rate for deception may alter the false positive error rate. The approach taken depends upon whether the screening test is a short, one-hour exam being conducted for a businessman by a private examiner, or whether it is a more thorough security examination conducted by a federal examiner. Private examiners tend to take a more clinical approach than federal examiners. I will therefore discuss the two individually.

Screening by private examiners

With examinations conducted for the commercial employer, the economic realities of the free enterprise system place financial constraints on the employer, and hence on the examiner, that are not present in government screening examinations. The examinations are thus shorter and less detailed. When questionable reactions are observed, private examiners tend to rely upon observations of the applicant's behaviour during the test as an aid to assessing their significance. As Brett, Phillips and Beary (1986: 544) put it using a medical analogy, '. . . a positive exercise stress test in a 25-year-old symptomless woman does not imply the same probability of coronary artery disease as a similar result in a 60-year-old man with exertional chest pain'. Similarly, the clinical examiner looks for variables associated with deception to help assess the significance of marginal reactions on the chart. He looks first at the question, for different questions have different base rates for deception. He also looks at the age and lifestyle of the applicant. Marginal reactions to a question regarding the use of illegal drugs on past jobs are less likely to indicate deception with a 60-year-old housewife than a 25-year-old hippie merely because of the differing base rates of drug usage. The examiner also looks at the behavioural cues evident when the various topics were being discussed during the pretest interview. Finally, he notes the behaviour of the applicant when the questionable areas are brought up for discussion.

This is not to say that the examiner bases his decisions on extra-polygraphic data, for when the charts are clearly truthful or clearly deceptive there is little reason for the examiner to look elsewhere. Extrapolygraphic data are most influential in those cases in which the charts show reactions that may or may not be suspicious, depending upon those factors impinging upon the likelihood that the person is holding back information to that particular question. Not unexpectedly, private examiners have low inconclusive rates in screening examinations because of their incorporation of extrapolygraphic data. It is likely that private examiners underestimate their error rates because mistakes can seldom be discovered.

Screening by federal examiners
Most federally administered polygraph tests are checked by quality control officers who review the charts without having seen the behaviour of the subjects. Unless the charts support the examiner's decision, the examination is continued or the subject is scheduled for a re-examination. How, then, does knowledge of the base rates help prevent errors? There may be two mechanisms. First, both the examiner and the quality control reviewer may be predisposed to discount the significance of marginal reactions to questions in which the a priori probability of deception is remote, especially when numerical scoring cannot be employed, as with the RI test. Second, knowledge of the various base rates for deception on the individual questions help the examiner decide whether (and how extensively) to resolve reactions through interrogation or through additional testing. Every effort is made to avoid false positives by rewording the relevant questions in an effort to first discover, then resolve, any innocent associative complex through additional testing, a test within a test. Some potential false positive errors are readily detected and resolved prior to the completion of the examination. Others may be detected upon re-examining the subject after some days or weeks have elapsed. It is thus obvious that there are several practical methods of increasing the validity of deceptive polygraph outcomes: incorporate extrapolygraphic data which sheds light on the a priori

probability of guilt, incorporate behavioural observations of the subject, and retest subjects classified as deceptive (Garwood, 1985).

How effective are those procedures at reducing false positive outcomes? A recent report by the US Department of Defense (1986) discussed the results of polygraph examinations administered to 2,976 government employees with high security clearances being screened to determine if they had deliberately revealed secret information to unauthorized persons or if they were spies. The examinations were being conducted as a result of a new programme of heightened security measures, not because any of the employees was suspected of misconduct. Of the 2,976 employees screened under this programme, only eight produced inconclusive or 'no opinion' results. Of 2,969 decisions (there is a discrepancy of one case in the reported figures), an astonishing 2,958 (99.6 percent) were reported as truthful. This stands in sharp contrast to the many hundreds of false positive results expected on the basis of theoretical projections involving low base rates of guilt.

A careful reading of the report reveals several factors not taken into account by the theoretical projections. First, persons who admitted security violations during the pretest interview, but who appeared truthful on the polygraph when they denied any additional violations, were reported as truthful. Thus a true negative polygraph outcome is not synonymous with innocence. The report does not indicate how many cases of that type may have occurred, and hence does not disclose what the probable base rate of innocence was. Nor does the report indicate how many persons reacted to initial charts in the examination but were able to obtain a truthful outcome without revealing any information (a potential false positive error prevented by a test within the test through habituation or adaptation), idiosyncratic information of no security significance (either a potential true or false positive reversed by a test within the test through the resolution of an emotional complex), or significant security information (a potential true positive reversed by a test within the test through admissions).

Another factor involves re-examinations. The report does not explicitly state how many employees required a re-examination to clear up a positive outcome, but it implies that there were not more than nineteen cases (0.6 percent). It is possible that this figure may be much larger, however, depending upon how an examination was defined. Of the nineteen cases, five resulted in an outcome of 'no opinion'. One of these tests was discontinued before any decision could be made because the examinee was not medically fit; in the other four cases the examinees reacted to one or more of the questions on the test, and failed to appear to be re-examined. They apparently were classified as 'no opinion' because the Government normally conducts a re-examination before rendering an official decision of deception in screening situations, but most scientists would classify them as a positive outcome. It is not known if they were true or false positives.

Eleven individuals were officially reported as being deceptive. Seven of the eleven were true positives, as they were verified by admissions of security violations in which there was minimal damage to national security. At least three of the remaining four positive outcomes were verified by confessions to more significant security violations. Whether they would be classified as true or false positives would depend upon the definition of a true positive. Whether the final case was verified or whether it was a possible false positive was not reported. Although many details are lacking, it is clear that the large numbers of false positives that have been predicted in screening situations do not seem to be occurring. Even if the final, unverified case, the three questionable cases and the four 'no opinion' examinations are all categorized as false positives, then the maximum false positive error rate is less than 0.3 percent, far below the theoretical projections. The small number of positive outcomes raises the distinct possibility that the more frequent type of error in screening may be false negatives!

Utility and disutility

An important aspect of polygraphy is its utility in furthering an investigation. One type of utility is the effect of the chart interpretation or the examiner's decision in changing the direction or scope of the investigation. This is the type of utility that has historically been the focus of scientific attention.

A quite different type of utility is information obtained during the course of the examination. Even if the charts are inconclusive, the test has utility if the suspect provided additional information. This information may occur during the pretest interview (especially in screening situations), during a post-test interrogation, or even between the polygraph charts in the absence of any questioning. It often opens up fresh, productive avenues of investigation. In some cases the information could not be obtained through other investigative means. Perhaps the main reason why employers increasingly use the polygraph for pre-employment screening is the wealth of pertinent information obtained through polygraphic interviews. The information can be very accurate, since it comes directly from the individual concerned. As long as the questions being asked are appropriate, the pre-employment test is a fair means to learn the answers, as the applicant can decide for himself how much information to reveal and how best to present it. For example, if the applicant decides to reveal that he was fired from a previous job, he is able to present any mitigating or extenuating circumstances which might not have been revealed had the new employer obtained the information from a third party who did not have the applicant's best interests at heart. The value of this type of information in predicting the quality of the employee has not been scientifically investigated.

Another type of utility is the deterrent effect of the polygraph, particularly in screening situations. If a person knows he may be subject to a polygraph examination, that prospect may prevent him from engaging in proscribed behaviour such as theft, drug usage or espionage. For example, convicted criminals are sometimes offered early paroles if they agree to being tested periodically on the polygraph to determine if they are starting to commit crimes during a probationary period. Preliminary reports (Abrams and Ogard, 1986) suggest that the polygraph may have a deterrent effect, for the rate of recidivism was lower in such a programme as compared to a control group of parolees who were not polygraphed. Further evidence of deterrence is provided by the testimony of convicted spies such as Geoffrey Prime, Christopher Boyce, Ronald W. Pelton, John Walker and Bennett, who have either stated that they refused or would have refused to apply for certain intelligence positions requiring mandatory polygraph examinations out of fear that their espionage activities would be detected. That their fear may be realistic is demonstrated by the fact that Sergeant Jack Dunlap and Sharon M. Scranage were spies who first came under suspicion as a result of their being administered a pre-employment or aperiodic polygraph examination.

There has been no systematic attempt to define, quantify and study the utility of the polygraph. The other side of the coin, disutility, has likewise received little attention. Disutility does not mean the same as the cost of the examination, for costs in time and money are not normally considered a disutility. All disutilities are costs, but not all costs are disutilities. One type of disutility is when the polygraph outcome is in error, for the investigation may be misdirected if the error is a false positive or prematurely terminated if a false negative. Another type of disutility is any increase in negative attitudes towards the polygraph as a result of its use. For example, a study found that college students who read a job application scenario which included a polygraph test expressed more negative attitudes towards the employer than did students whose scenario did not include a polygraph test (White, Lopez and Haney, 1982). Although such a study must be replicated in real life before we can know how much confidence we can have in such a finding, it does raise an interesting possibility. It is conceivable that the polygraph could have an unintended counter-deterrence effect. That is, if employees feel that employers who use the polygraph do not trust them, they may steal more rather than less. They may do it because they feel the employer does not deserve their loyalty or perhaps because they want to beat the system. Parenthetically, in some cases use of the polygraph may engender positive attitudes in individuals or groups; that, of course, would be a utility.

Illustrations of polygraph usage

Criminal investigation

Most readers are undoubtedly familiar with the use of the polygraph with criminal suspects. Even though polygraph results are seldom admitted as evidence in court, they often play a major role in police investigations and in helping prosecutors decide whether to indict a suspect and what to charge him with. A number of books provide a wealth of case histories in which polygraphs helped clear the innocent and solve crimes (e.g. Block, 1977; Gugas, 1979; Keeler, 1984).

Every examiner has been involved in so many interesting cases that it is hard to select one or two which best illustrate the efficacy of the polygraph. Rather than select any of the spectacular or unusual cases which stand out from the mass, I prefer to illustrate the polygraph's role in criminal investigation with a very typical case. One which gave me considerable satisfaction was when I became involved in the investigation of the kidnapping of an 18-year-old Navajo girl, Sally. She had been abducted by a half-drunk 20-year-old male Indian of the Hopi tribe who was visiting Utah from his reservation in Arizona. Her abductor seized her in a parking lot in Salt Lake City, and drove her northwards towards Idaho. Fortunately, he took a wrong turn and was stopped by military police when he inadvertently tried to drive onto an air base. The moment the car was halted, Sally jumped out and sought the protection of the police.

Her abductor was arrested and put in jail pending his trial. The investigation proceeded rather slowly, however, as the Hopi could not speak English at all, and Sally's English limited her to a halting description of what had happened. After twelve weeks the investigators knew little more than they had the first day. I do not know what made the police question Sally's story – perhaps it was merely her inability to provide details that they were accustomed to hearing – but I was asked to administer a polygraph test on her. When she arrived in my office it was obvious that she was a very quiet, demure young lady who was somewhat daunted by the prospect of undergoing a mysterious, technological test at the hands of a stranger. The pretest interview was difficult because of her inability to express herself adequately in English and my total ignorance of Navajo. I struggled to phrase the questions just as simply as possible, and she indicated that she understood them.

I frankly was doubtful about obtaining a conclusive result under such trying conditions, but I decided to proceed nonetheless. As I was placing the electrodes on her in preparation for the test, she broke down and confessed. Sally lived with her uncle, who had strictly forbidden her to drink any beer. One day she went shopping in Salt Lake and had struck up a conversation with a handsome Hopi whom she met by chance in the parking lot of a supermarket. One thing led to another, and they decided to buy a couple of six-packs of beer and go for a drive in the country. Having polished off the beer quickly enough, they wanted to buy some more. They were looking for a liquor store when he drove onto the air base and was stopped. Believing that the police would report her drinking to her uncle, Sally did some quick thinking and came up with the kidnapping story. She let her new-found friend go to jail for several months so she could avoid being spanked by her uncle! Because the polygraph was brought into play, an innocent man was released from jail. There was an interesting postscript: once she had decided to confess, Sally's English turned out to be at least as good as mine!

Criminal screening

It is rare that the polygraph is used to screen a hundred or more suspects in a murder investigation in order to narrow the scope to one or two suspects, but such a case occurred in 1980. A US Army paratrooper fell to his death when his parachute failed to open during a practice jump at Fort Bragg, North Carolina. The investigation revealed that his static line had been cut. Any one of the 160 parachute riggers employed by the airborne division could have done it. Because it was possible that other parachutes had also been sabotaged, the whole division was grounded until the saboteur could be identified. The Army assembled a team of polygraph examiners who started testing the riggers. Five days after the murder the saboteur was identified as a result of the polygraph and confessed (Department of Defense, 1984: 8). Although the Defense Department did not report whether there were any false positive errors, some would be expected whenever the base rate for guilt is small and a large number of suspects is being tested. Had the murderer not confessed, the polygraph would nonetheless have been of value in reducing the number of suspects to a more manageable number. A retest of those who initially tested positive would be expected to clear a number of the errors.

Security screening
The polygraph has been instrumental in detecting a number of spies during routine security screening examinations, spies who had not been under any suspicion prior to the polygraph. Jack Dunlap was an Army sergeant working for the US National Security Agency, with access to some of the most sensitive secrets America had. He was passing much of that information to the Soviets. As he was about to be routinely transferred to a non-sensitive assignment overseas, he decided to apply for a civilian position at the Agency, so he could continue providing invaluable information. All civilian employees of the Agency were examined on the polygraph prior to being assigned to sensitive duties, but military personnel were exempted from that requirement. Now that Sgt Dunlap was applying for a civilian position, he was required to take a polygraph examination. During his test there were emotional reactions to the questions about espionage, but Sgt Dunlap claimed that a mistake had been made. A re-examination produced the same outcome. An investigation was started which provided confirmation that he had spied, but before he could be questioned Sgt Dunlap committed suicide. It is impossible to know how long his activities might have continued undetected had it not been for the polygraph, but if the recent Walker case is any indication, it could have been for a long time indeed.

Conclusions

Although it is not without problems, the polygraph is a valuable tool when properly utilized. There is no evidence to support the belief that mass screening produces a high rate of false positive errors. On the contrary, the little evidence presently available suggests that the number of false positives is several orders of magnitude below predicted levels, and that false negatives may be more of a problem than false positives. The current mathematical model for predicting errors when the base rate for deception is very low appears to be fundamentally flawed by its inability to account for the effect of the examiner's a priori knowledge of the base rate for deception, his ability to rectify potential false positive errors before the examination is concluded, and the effect of re-examinations.

The prevailing use of the term 'deception' in the context of polygraph screening ignores the concept of lies of omission, which are accepted by most psychologists studying deception in other contexts. As a result, the current definitions of true and false positives are inadequate to handle the complexities of screening situations and may seriously underestimate the base rate of deception. Thought must also be given to defining the concepts of utility and disutility, and to collecting objective data on them. Research in lie detection has suffered from the twin problems of poor design and flawed execution, problems which have not always been kept in mind when generalizing experimental results. A greater level of rigorousness in the design and execution of polygraph research is required to provide the hard data necessary for informed decisions regarding the proper role of the polygraph in society.

Note

The views expressed in this chapter are those of the author and are not necessarily those of the Department of Defense or the Defense Polygraph Institute.

8

Does science support polygraph testing?

David C. Raskin

In 1923 the US Circuit Court of Appeals in Washington, DC, ruled that the results of a 'systolic blood pressure deception test' conducted by Harvard psychologist William Marston were inadmissible as evidence on behalf of the defendant in a criminal trial (*Frye v. United States*, 1923). In response to that first effort to introduce the results of a lie-detector test in a court proceeding, the court ruled that:

> while the courts will go a long way in admitting expert testimony deduced from a well-recognized scientific principle or discovery, the thing from which the deduction is made must have gained general acceptance in the particular field in which it belongs. We think that the systolic blood pressure deception test has not yet gained such standing and scientific recognition among physiological and psychological authorities as would justify the courts in admitting expert testimony deduced from the discovery, development, and experiments thus far made. (*Frye v. United States*, 1923)

Attitudes of the scientific community

Since the time of the Frye decision there has been a great deal of research, development and experience with various techniques that employ physiological measures for assessing credibility with regard to specific acts, events or knowledge (Raskin 1982). Therefore it is useful to examine contemporary attitudes toward polygraph tests among the relevant scientific community. That was done in a recent civil case (*Kramer v. Drinkhall*, 1982) in which the defendants attempted to introduce the results of a control question polygraph test. In support of their motion they offered the findings of a scientific poll in which one fifth of the members of the Society for Psychophysiological Research were individually interviewed (Gallup Organization, 1982).

The findings of the poll indicated that 30 percent of the respondents had used polygraph tests for assessing credibility, either in research or teaching (19 percent) or professional applications (11 percent). The respondents were asked: 'Which of the following four

statements best describes your own opinion of polygraph test interpretation by those who have received systematic training in the
technique, when they are called upon to interpret whether a subject is
or is not telling the truth?' The findings for the 137 respondents who
held doctoral degrees are presented in Table 8.1. It can be seen that

Table 8.1 *Opinions about polygraph tests for interpreting truthfulness*

	Percent of responses
'It is a sufficiently reliable method to be the sole determinant'	1
'It is a useful diagnostic tool when considered with other available information'	62
'It is of questionable usefulness, entitled to little weight against other available information'	34
'It is of no usefulness'	1
'No opinion'	1
Other	1

the large majority of the relevant scientific community expressed a
relatively positive attitude concerning the usefulness of polygraph
tests for assessing credibility. In fact, among those who held doctoral
degrees and considered themselves to be very informed about polygraph tests, only one respondent considered them useless.

In spite of the generally positive attitude among knowledgeable
scientists, at my instigation the American Psychological Association
adopted a somewhat negative policy regarding polygraph tests, especially when used on victims of crimes or for employment purposes
(American Psychological Association, 1987). Some have urged that
polygraphs be totally abolished (Lykken, 1984a), while proponents
promote them with little reservation (Ansley, 1984; Barland, 1984).
The uses of polygraph tests raise complex issues that involve scientific, social and political judgements. This chapter attempts to eluci-
date some of the scientific and applied issues so that potential users of
polygraph tests and the public can make informed decisions about
when their applications may or may not be justified on scientific
grounds.

Accuracy of polygraph results

The first step in determining whether or not polygraph tests are
justified is an assessment of their accuracy. That involves an examination of the type of test, the purpose and context in which the
test is used, and the nature and adequacy of the research on which the
accuracy estimate is based.

Types of applications
There are several different types of polygraph tests. Commercial pre-employment screening tests attempt to assess suitability for employment by testing credibility concerning past behaviour in order to predict future behaviour. Since that is an extremely difficult task and there is no acceptable research regarding its accuracy, it is not possible to arrive at a good estimate of the accuracy of commercial screening tests. Furthermore, such tests usually incorporate no control questions, they are frequently performed hurriedly without using standard procedures required for other applications, the examiners who conduct them are often poorly trained and lacking in skill and competence, and there is relatively little concern for the welfare of the examinee. In light of those limitations it seems reasonable to assume that commercial screening tests have the lowest accuracies of any type of polygraph test.

The use of polygraph examinations in criminal investigation and judicial contexts differs substantially from commercial applications. The forensic examination concerns a past event and attempts to assess the subject's credibility in denying direct knowledge or participation in criminal acts or other specific behaviours. Most commonly, the examination employs a control question test, and considerable time (two hours or more) is required for the examination. The examiners are usually well trained and experienced, many protections for the examinee are inherent in the situation, and the negative consequences of poorly conducted examinations and errors promote a higher standard of care than is present in commercial applications.

Polygraph testing in national security programmes falls somewhere between forensic and commercial screening applications. If the test involves general assessments of lifestyle and suitability, such as many tests conducted by the US National Security Agency, then it is more akin to the commercial applications and suffers from the shortcomings inherent in that type of testing. In contrast, tests conducted for counter-intelligence purposes in which the relevant questions are directed to specific espionage activities, such as the tests employed in the US Department of Defense, are more similar to applications in criminal investigation. In either case, the government examiners are reasonably well trained and devote extensive time and effort to the careful conduct of the examinations. Such examinations typically require considerably more time than the average criminal suspect test.

Control question tests
There is much debate about the accuracy of control question tests in forensic and investigative settings. The two general sources of data

from which the accuracy of such tests may be estimated are laboratory simulations and field studies of actual cases. Each type of study has advantages and disadvantages, and both types are needed to provide an overall picture with regard to test accuracy.

The most accepted type of laboratory study simulates a real crime in which subjects are randomly assigned to guilty and innocent treatment conditions (Raskin, 1982). Guilty subjects enact a realistic crime, and innocent subjects are merely told about the nature of the crime and do not enact it. All subjects are motivated to produce a truthful outcome, usually by a substantial cash bonus for passing the test. For example, one such study used prison inmates who were offered a bonus equal to one month's wages if they could produce a truthful outcome (Raskin and Hare, 1978).

The advantages of careful laboratory simulations include total control over the issues that are investigated and the types of tests which are used, consistency in their administration and interpretation, specification of the subject populations that are studied, control over the skill and training of the examiners, and absolute verification of the accuracy of the test results. Careful studies that closely approximate the methods and conditions characteristic of the highest quality of practice by polygraph professionals produce results such as those shown in Table 8.2. Those polygraph examinations produced decisions that were 97 percent accurate on guilty subjects and 92 percent accurate on innocent subjects. However, it should be noted that there were more errors which indicated deception by innocent subjects (8 percent false positive errors) than truthfulness by guilty subjects (3 percent false negative errors).

The major disadvantage of laboratory simulations is that one cannot completely simulate the real-life situation in which a person is a suspect in a crime and the outcome of the polygraph test has important implications for their future. In order to estimate test accuracy in that situation, it is necessary to use tests conducted on actual criminal suspects. However, that type of field study creates new problems. The major problem is the need to obtain verification of the accuracy of the test outcomes, and that can be very difficult in real cases.

There are two general methods for developing a criterion of guilt and innocence against which to assess the accuracy of field polygraph tests. The best and most common method utilizes confessions to verify the guilt and innocence of those who have taken the tests. Law enforcement cases that involve polygraph tests produce rates of confessions in the range of 30 to 80 percent (Office of Technology Assessment [OTA], 1983), but we do not know how the characteristics of those cases compare to cases that do not produce confessions.

The other method relies on a panel of legal experts who review the

Table 8.2   *Laboratory accuracy of control question polygraph tests (in percent)*

	Raskin and Hare (1978)	Podlesny and Raskin (1978)	Rovner, Raskin and Kircher (1979)	Dawson (1980)	Kircher and Raskin (1982)	Combined results
All subjects	n = 48	n = 20	n = 48	n = 24	n = 100	n = 240
Correct	88	85	88	88	87	87
Wrong	4	5	4	8	5	5
Inconclusive	8	10	8	4	8	8
Decisions correct	96	94	96	91	95	95
Guilty subjects	n = 24	n = 10	n = 24	n = 12	n = 50	n = 120
Correct	88	80	88	100	88	88
Wrong	0	10	0	0	4	3
Inconclusive	12	10	12	0	8	9
Decisions correct	100	89	100	100	96	97
Innocent subjects	n = 24	n = 10	n = 24	n = 12	n = 50	n = 120
Correct	88	90	88	75	86	86
Wrong	8	0	8	17	6	7
Inconclusive	4	10	4	8	8	7
Decisions correct	91	100	91	82	93	92

The column group "Rovner, Raskin and Kircher (1979)", "Dawson (1980)", "Kircher and Raskin (1982)" falls under the spanning header "Mock-crime experiments".

'Decisions correct' was obtained by excluding the inconclusive outcomes and calculating the percentage correct using only those subjects for whom a definite decision was obtained, i.e., Correct/(Correct + Wrong).

case facts in order to provide judgements concerning the guilt or innocence of individual suspects. The use of panel decisions has much greater problems than a criterion based on confessions. Since the panel criterion for guilt and innocence is merely an educated guess, it is subject to error. Furthermore, our legal standard of guilt requires conviction 'beyond a reasonable doubt', and the panel is more likely to say 'not guilty' for suspects who are actually guilty than it is to say 'guilty' for suspects who are actually innocent. Whenever the polygraph result differs from the judgement of the panel, we do not know which is wrong. If the panel decides that the suspect is innocent and the polygraph result indicated deception, the panel may be correct and there is a false positive error by the polygraph. It is just as likely that the polygraph was correct and the panel made a false negative error. Therefore, we cannot place a great deal of confidence in the results of panel studies such as those reported by Bersh (1969) and Barland and Raskin (1976).

The other major problems with field studies concern the representativeness of the cases selected, the training and skill of the polygraph examiners who conducted the tests, and the adequacy of the test methods and diagnostic procedures employed. If we wish to estimate the accuracy of polygraph tests on criminal suspects, it is necessary to select cases in which the subjects were suspects, not victims or witnesses. Although it is generally recognized that polygraph tests are most likely to produce false positive errors on victims of serious crimes (American Psychological Association, 1987; Raskin, 1986a), at least one major field study (Horvath, 1977) used a large number of tests in which verified innocent victims had been tested (see Raskin, 1986a).

It is important that field studies select cases according to scientifically acceptable sampling procedures and use only cases in which properly trained polygraph examiners employed standard field methods for conducting the tests and interpreting their outcomes. Several of the frequently cited studies (Horvath and Reid, 1971; Hunter and Ash, 1973; Kleinmuntz and Szucko, 1984a; Slowik and Buckley, 1975; Wicklander and Hunter, 1975) failed to adhere to those principles. As a result, those studies provide limited information concerning the accuracy of properly conducted and interpreted polygraph tests.

The Kleinmuntz and Szucko study (1984a) stands out because it embodied all of the serious methodological errors. They used only cases in which persons who were suspected of theft were ordered by their employers to take tests from a commercial polygraph firm, and they provided no specification of the method for selecting the cases from the files of the commercial polygraph firm. In addition, they based the results on interpretations made by students in a commercial polygraph training course who were not trained in the proper methods of test interpretation, and they required the student examiners to make definite judgements of guilt or innocence on the basis of reactions to a single relevant question. It is not surprising that their study produced low rates of accuracy for the polygraph judgements made by the students. Gross violations of acceptable scientific methodology and polygraph procedures render their study totally meaningless for estimating the accuracy of standard field polygraph examinations conducted by competent examiners under appropriate conditions.

Unfortunately, there are few field studies from which we can estimate the accuracy of properly conducted control question tests. The OTA (1983) selected ten field studies that they felt had at least some degree of scientific merit. Those studies included all of the field studies mentioned above and two others (Davidson, 1979; Raskin, 1976). The overall accuracy of the polygraph decisions was 90 percent on criterion guilty suspects and 80 percent on criterion innocent suspects. In spite of the inclusion of many studies which have serious methodological problems, the accuracy in field cases was higher than is claimed by some of the most vocal critics (Lykken, 1987).

Given the range of training and quality of performance by field polygraph examiners, it is reasonable to assume that the results obtained by some agencies and examiners are generally more accurate than the average of 85 percent that was reported by the OTA, and some are probably lower. It should be pointed out that the field data also indicate that the rate of false positive errors (20 percent) is generally higher than the rate of false negative errors (10 percent). The implications of those findings are explored more fully in a later section of this chapter.

Concealed information tests

Another type of polygraph test is known as the concealed information or guilty knowledge test (Lykken, 1981; Raskin, 1982). It presents a series of multiple-choice questions concerning salient aspects of the crime, the correct answers to which would be known only by a person involved in the crime. Each question contains only one correct alternative, and relatively strong and consistent physiological reactions to the correct alternatives indicate that the suspect is attempting to conceal knowledge of the crime.

Proponents of the concealed information test claim that it is superior to the control question test because it can be constructed and evaluated in such a way as to eliminate false positive errors that are inherent in all other polygraph tests (Lykken, 1981). There are serious problems with that claim. If the scoring is done so as to minimize the occurrence of false positive errors, the criterion for failing the test becomes so high that it produces an unacceptable level of false negative errors. Even if the scoring is designed to produce a maximum of 5 percent false positive errors, the false negative rate has been shown to exceed 10 percent in carefully conducted laboratory studies (Raskin, 1982). The problem of false negatives is probably greater in field applications because perpetrators of crimes frequently fail to notice or remember details due to intoxication, stress, and the complex, fast-moving and confusing nature of many crimes.

The greatest problem with the concealed information test is its lack of usefulness for the majority of criminal cases. The basic premise of the test requires protected information known only by the perpetrator and the investigators, but such information does not exist for most cases. In the majority of cases the salient details of the crime are made available to the suspects by the investigators, the media and defence attorneys. That eliminates the possibility of using the test. Also, many types of cases cannot employ the concealed information test because the suspect admits being present but denies the specific alleged acts. The most common example is an alleged sexual assault in which the witness claims that force was used and the suspect admits the sexual acts but claims that they were consensual. Similar problems arise in cases where there are several suspects who were involved in the crime and all deny having been the principal actor.

Although the concealed information test is theoretically appealing, its practical utility is severely limited. Its high rate of false negative results poses problems for law enforcement and evidentiary uses, although that problem has not been acknowledged by its proponents. Because of the severe limitations on its applications, it is not frequently employed in criminal investigations, and there has never been a study of its accuracy in the field. Those who propose that the concealed information test be substituted for the control question test ignore the substantial problems with false negative errors and the practical barriers to its implementation. It is unlikely that it will replace the control question test in the foreseeable future.

Base rates and confidence in polygraph test results

Whenever we are faced with the problem of deciding if a particular application of polygraphs is justified or how much weight should be given to the results of such tests, it is necessary to consider a number of factors in combination with the overall accuracy of the test. Those would include the context of the particular application, the nature of the subject population, the issues to be resolved, the actions that will follow from particular test outcomes, and the base rate or prevalence of deception among those who are tested.

The base rate problem often exerts the most influence over the confidence we have in test outcomes, but frequently it is not understood by proponents and critics of polygraph applications. It cannot be assumed that the overall accuracy of any test is a direct indication of the confidence that can be placed in the outcome of that test in any particular application. Confidence in test results depends heavily on the base rate in the population, whether it be a medical test for cancer, a breathalyser test for intoxication or a polygraph test for deception.

To illustrate the problem of base rates, let us assume that we have a test for cancer which is 95 percent accurate in detecting the presence of cancer. Our confidence in positive or negative test outcomes is 95 percent only when half of the people who take the test actually have cancer and half do not. If that base rate departs substantially from 50 percent, then our confidence in the two types of test outcomes will vary considerably. If only 10 percent of the people who take the test actually have cancer, then 99 percent of negative test outcomes are correct. However, with that low base rate of cancer, only 68 percent of those whose tests indicate the presence of cancer actually will have cancer. Obviously, we cannot assume that a test which produces 95 percent overall accuracy always produces results in which we can have 95 percent confidence.

Pre-employment screening

Confidence in test outcomes is calculated by a conditional probability analysis. The analysis requires that we make assumptions concerning the accuracy of the test and the base rate in the population. Let us assume that we have a polygraph test for screening employees for ordinary jobs in retail stores in New York City. Let us also assume that one of every five people applying for such jobs has withheld something about their past employment or their honesty, disclosure of that information would disqualify them, and they lie about it on the polygraph test. That is a base rate of dishonesty of 20 percent. Furthermore, let us grant the proponents of polygraph screening the benefit of the doubt by assuming that such tests are 90 percent accurate in detecting deception and 80 percent accurate in verifying truthfulness. For every thousand people who are tested, the results would be as shown in Table 8.3.

Table 8.3   *Example of confidence in pre-employment polygraph outcomes*

| Test outcome | Actual status | | Confidence |
	Dishonest ($n = 200$)	Honest ($n = 800$)	Proportion correct
Deceptive	200 (0.90) = 180	800 (0.20) = 160	180/(180 + 160) = 0.53
Truthful	200 (0.10) = 20	800 (0.80) = 640	640/(640 + 20) = 0.97

The analysis indicates that 97 percent of the results indicating truthfulness would be accurate, and we could have very high confidence in assuming that people who passed the test are honest. However, only 53 percent of the results indicating deception would be correct, and approximately half of the people who failed the test would be wrongly denied employment on the basis of the polygraph result. It is estimated that approximately two million people each year are given employment polygraph tests in the United States. The example indicates that even with the generous assumption of 85 percent average accuracy of such tests, approximately 320,000 honest people would be denied employment because of false positive errors. If the true accuracy of polygraphs in the commercial employment context is closer to 70 percent, then 92 percent of the truthful test results would be correct, but only 33 percent of the deceptive results would be correct. That would translate into 640,000 false positives per year.

It should now be clear why the confidence that we can place in a polygraph-test outcome is greatly affected by the base rate in the population tested, the particular type of test that is conducted, and the accuracy of the test. Pre-employment polygraph screening in the private sector represents the worst case in terms of accuracy and the problems inherent in that type of testing. The problems are compounded by substandard administration of the tests and final actions based solely on results that have a low degree of accuracy. The situation is quite different in criminal investigation and forensic applications of polygraph tests, as well as national security applications.

Criminal investigation and forensic tests

Polygraph tests in criminal investigation and forensic applications probably have the highest accuracy of all applications. Although the existing data do not provide a definitive estimate of accuracy, it most likely falls somewhere between the accuracy obtained in careful laboratory studies (95 percent) and the field studies reviewed by the OTA (85 percent). My laboratory is in the process of conducting a major study using confirmed polygraph tests from a federal law enforcement agency, and the preliminary results indicate accuracies in that range. It seems reasonable to assume that carefully conducted tests by trained and experienced examiners in criminal contexts produce accuracies on the order of 95 percent with guilty suspects and 85 percent with innocent suspects.

In order to estimate confidence in polygraph-test results in criminal contexts, it is necessary to estimate the base rate of guilt in the population tested. I have previously described a simple method for estimating base rate using data concerning test outcomes obtained in a specific context (Raskin, 1986a). The data (OTA, 1983) indicate that high-quality investigative polygraph programmes obtain approximately 50 percent deceptive outcomes on criminal suspects. If those results are combined with the accuracy rates of 95 and 85 percent for guilty and innocent suspects, the base rate of guilt in the criminal investigation context is approximately 44 percent.

Using a conditional probability analysis in the criminal investigation context, the confidence in deceptive outcomes is 83 percent for deceptive test outcomes and 96 percent for truthful outcomes. Suspects who pass the test are very likely to be telling the truth, but approximately one out of six suspects who fail the test are also telling the truth. Therefore, we can act with great confidence in discontinuing the investigation on those who pass the test, but we must proceed with caution when a suspect fails the test. Obviously, additional inculpatory evidence is needed before charging or prosecuting that person. Similar approaches should be taken when the results of investigative polygraph tests are offered as evidence in court. In the absence of compelling evidence of guilt, an exculpatory polygraph result should be sufficient to cast a reasonable doubt. On the other hand, an inculpatory polygraph result must be accompanied by other evidence before one could be found guilty beyond a reasonable doubt.

Some have argued that polygraph tests which are conducted confidentially by the defence should not be allowed as evidence in court (Orne, 1983). He calls that the 'friendly polygraph' situation. Orne has claimed that under such circumstances guilty persons can more readily pass the test because he feels that they have nothing to lose. That position is based on a lack of understanding of the nature of the control question test and the substantial stakes which actually exist for the subject in that situation. Arguments against that hypothesis are described in detail elsewhere (Raskin, 1986a).

Orne also stated that the base rate of guilt among defendants who take confidential tests is at least 80 percent, leading to a confidence of only 50 percent in truthful outcomes. That argument is based on the assumption that approximately 80 percent of criminal defendants are guilty, which means that 80 percent of those who volunteer for polygraph tests are guilty. However, there is a fatal flaw in that logic because it assumes that guilty defendants volunteer to take tests in the same proportion as do innocent defendants. That hypothesis can be evaluated empirically.

During a twelve-year period I administered 446 polygraph examinations to criminal suspects, and 292 of those were tested on a confidential basis at the request of their defence attorneys. Only 34 percent of the confidential defence tests produced truthful test results. Using estimates of 95 and 85 percent accuracy for guilty and innocent suspects, respectively, that translates into a base rate of guilt of 58 percent. Obviously, if at least 80 percent of defendants are guilty, they do not volunteer for tests in the same proportion as do innocent defendants, even when the tests are conducted confidentially for their defence attorneys. Furthermore, the conditional probability analysis indicates that confidence in deceptive outcomes is 90 percent, and confidence in truthful outcomes is 92 percent. Given those results, there seems to be no problem regarding confidence in the results of properly conducted tests that are presented in court.

National security tests

Polygraph tests for national security purposes raise the most complex issues because they include elements present in tests used for employment screening and for criminal investigation. There are different types of national security polygraph applications. One type is for employment screening, such as those tests conducted by the National Security Agency (Ansley, 1984). Such tests often include an assessment of lifestyle in an attempt to establish whether or not the person might be vulnerable to blackmail or pressure to assist hostile intelligence organizations or governments. Questions inquire about sexual preferences, drug usage, financial condition, undetected crimes and other factors that are considered as possibly compromising the individual. In those applications, national security tests suffer from the general problems of vagueness of relevant questions and low validity which plague the commercial screening applications. However, some of the difficulties are mitigated by the amount of time devoted to such testing in order to increase the comprehensiveness and accuracy of the tests. Retesting is frequently performed in order to resolve problems.

A second type of national security testing is known as counter-intelligence scope examinations (Department of Defense, 1986). They attempt to assess credibility regarding espionage plans or activities of persons requiring clearance for top secret or special access programmes. As such, those tests are very similar to polygraph applications in criminal investigations. They assess credibility regarding behaviours which are clearly specified, and where subjects would be certain about their truthfulness in answering the relevant questions. The nature of those tests and the care with which they are administered should result in accuracies that are in the same range as those performed in criminal investigations. Similar conclusions can be drawn concerning the nature and accuracy of the third type of test which is used to investigate specific incidents of unauthorized disclosures of sensitive information.

The critical problem in national security testing of large numbers of people is the very low base rate of people who are engaged in espionage activities. Certainly, there are few spies among those who apply for government positions that require access to classified and sensitive national security information. Based on the available information, it is reasonable to assume that the base rate is no more than 1 in 1,000. That poses serious problems when large numbers of people are tested.

The magnitude of the problem caused by low base rates is revealed by a conditional probability analysis which assumes that counter-intelligence security tests have an accuracy of 95 percent in detecting spies and 85 percent in verifying the honesty of non-spies. Using a base rate of 0.1 percent spies among those tested, the confidence in truthful outcomes would exceed 99.99 percent. However, confidence in deceptive outcomes would be only 0.6 percent. In other words, we could be virtually certain of the truthfulness of those who pass the test, but we would have almost no confidence in the results of tests which indicated deception.

At first glance, the use of counter-intelligence tests seems unacceptable because of the high proportion of false positives among tests that are failed. However, there are counter-arguments to that conclusion. First, the US Department of Defense reported (Department of Defense, 1986) that of the 2,976 such examinations conducted in the preceding fiscal year no more than sixteen showed indications of deception. Many of the examinations required multiple tests to arrive at a final decision of lack of deception. Thus, the number of false positive outcomes was considerably lower than predicted by the conditional probability analysis. That was undoubtedly due in part to the amount of effort devoted to resolving disputed deceptive outcomes. It should be pointed out that such efforts rarely occur in the private sector.

Another safeguard in the government security applications of polygraph testing is the principle that adverse action is seldom taken on the basis of a polygraph result alone. Following a deceptive outcome there may be additional testing. Unresolved deceptive outcomes are followed by further interviews and investigations that attempt to resolve the situation. If no further adverse information is developed, then there frequently is no further action. The polygraph test is used mainly as an investigative tool and not as a final answer.

Even if counter-intelligence tests produce a high rate of false positives due to the low base rate, that does not mean that they are useless. On the contrary, they can be of great value in narrowing the field of investigation when the stakes are as high as they are in national security. If 10,000 people are tested, the conditional probability analysis described above shows that approximately 1,510 would fail the test. Instead of requiring full background and field investigations of the initial 10,000 applicants, a maximum of 1,510 such efforts would be required, and some spies might confess in the process.

Even with the highest predictable number of false positives, polygraph tests would produce a substantial savings for 85 percent of the initial applicant pool, and the pool containing the spies would be decreased by almost an order of magnitude. Given the importance of the issues and the tremendous cost and delays required by full investigations of every applicant, the rapid reduction of effort due to the use of polygraph tests seems to justify their use. Also, the fact that these are special positions of public trust distinguishes them from ordinary commercial jobs where employment screening is most often used.

Counter-measures raise a strong caution in the use of polygraphs for counter-intelligence purposes. Our research (for example, Honts, Raskin and Kircher, 1986) has shown that it is possible to train laboratory subjects to use physical and mental manoeuvres to defeat control question polygraph tests. Although our data show that individuals are not successful without special training from an expert, that possibility is most likely to occur in the espionage situation. Anecdotal reports indicate that such training may already be given to such agents and operatives. However, there is not yet any scientific or field evidence that such techniques are actually effective in real-life polygraph testing, but we must consider that possibility. Solid data are needed to resolve that question, and special types of ecologically valid studies are required for that purpose.

Conclusions

Careful consideration of the available evidence seems to indicate that there is scientific support for certain applications of polygraph techniques. Appropriate use of those techniques by qualified professionals in criminal investigation and forensic applications can achieve rates of accuracy that compare favourably with other forms of evidence, such as criminalistics (Peterson, Fabricant and Field, 1978; Widacki and Horvath, 1978), and are higher than common forms of evidence, such as eyewitness identification.

Polygraph testing can have serious problems of inaccuracy in the most common application, commercial pre-employment screening. That application most likely produces such high rates of error that tremendous social and personal damage results from its widespread use. There seems to be little scientific support for such uses of polygraphs.

Polygraph examinations in the context of national security programmes raise the most complex issues. Assessments of lifestyle and prior history produce problems similar to those that arise in commercial employment screening. The problems associated with low base rates of espionage in counter-intelligence contexts must be balanced against the need to identify spies because of the great security and monetary costs of failing to do so. Often, national security needs are pitted against the social and ethical needs of protecting individuals. Only the most careful programmes and techniques, coupled with research and development to minimize the errors, can help to reduce those problems. Ultimately, the future of government uses of polygraph methods will be determined by political and social considerations, hopefully enlightened by objective and thorough scientific evaluations.

9

The case against polygraph testing

David T. Lykken

Early in 1986 a major US television network, CBS, conducted its own test of the polygraph. CBS owns the magazine *Popular Photography* and arranged for that subsidiary's office manager to contact four different polygraph firms in New York City, engaging their help in determining which of four employees had stolen a valuable camera. As the polygraphers arrived (on different days) to do the testing, each one was advised that, while all four employees had had access to the camera, the manager's suspicions were focused on one individual; a different individual was specified for each polygrapher.

No camera was missing, in fact, and the four employees, who were privy to the scheme, were instructed merely to truthfully deny that they had stolen any camera. They were each offered $50 if they succeeded in passing the polygraph test. Each of the four polygraphers positively identified a culprit; in each case the innocent employee thus stigmatized as a thief and a liar was the person whom that polygrapher had been told was especially suspect. All four polygraphers expressed total confidence in their diagnoses and one of them was filmed, covertly, explaining to the manager that he should 'find some other excuse for firing this person; it's illegal in New York State to fire somebody solely because of a polygraph test'.

In some thirty of the United States employers can legally require employees or job applicants to submit to polygraph testing; this example shows how the process can malfunction in real life. Proponents of polygraphy (e.g. Inbau, 1965; Raskin, 1984a) shrug off such examples by acknowledging that '80 percent' of practising polygraphers are 'incompetent' (Inbau, 1965: 857) or that much polygraphy instruction is 'grossly deficient' (Raskin, 1984a: 3). Advocates insist that their own techniques, in contrast, are extremely accurate and they urge passage of licensure laws that would help ensure that practitioners use these allegedly accurate methods. (Such laws, of course, would also help to legitimate and institutionalize the practice of polygraphy.)

The case against polygraphy must be predicated, therefore, not on the egregious errors and abuses of typical practitioners, but on the theory and evidence pertaining to the 'correct' methods used by the most skilful and conscientious examiners. As explained elsewhere in this volume, there are two basic techniques or test formats used in the polygraphic detection of deception. The control question test (CQT) can be used only in specific issue situations as in criminal investigation because the several relevant questions in a CQT all refer to the same issue and are alternative ways of asking, 'Did you do it?' In pre- or post-employment screening situations, a different question format is employed, a format I have labelled the relevant control test or RCT (Lykken, 1981: 139–44). I shall employ this usage below.

The lie detector is stressful and intrusive. There is no doubt that a polygraphic lie test is intrusive, an invasion of privacy. Nor can there be any question that the experience of submitting to a polygraph test is emotionally stressful to most subjects (and extremely stressful to some), whether one is truthful or deceptive. The CQT is *intended* to be stressful; if a truthful subject is not disturbed by the control questions, the theory of the test indicates that the result will be erroneous or, at best, inconclusive. Only someone who has actually had the polygraph attachments applied to one's body, and then been asked a series of intrusive questions by a stranger, can fully appreciate how vulnerable one feels in that situation.

The CQT is predicated on deceit. Administration of the CQT requires the examiner to deceive the person tested in several ways. First, the examinee must be persuaded that the technique is highly accurate, thus augmenting fear of detection in the guilty suspect or increasing the confidence of an innocent person that he will be exonerated. He is therefore

> assured that if he knows in his own mind that he is being truthful, then there will not be any substantial reactions to [the relevant] questions on the polygraph instrument. [This explanation is] further reinforced by presenting a number test in which the subject is instructed to lie about the number that he has chosen and recordings are made on the polygraph instrument while he denies having chosen that number. He is then told that the charts show what his pattern of reaction looks like when he is telling the truth and when he is lying and there should be no problem on the actual test if he is truthful to all of the questions. (Raskin, 1982)

There are two deceptions here. The first is the assurance that a truthful answer will not be accompanied by 'any substantial reactions'. Many innocent persons respond emotionally to the allegations contained in the relevant questions, and every examiner knows this. Secondly, the charts obtained during the number or pick-a-card test do not show the subject's 'pattern of reaction' when lying or truth-telling. Every competent polygrapher knows that people do not have distinctive patterns of reaction for lying or truth-telling. Indeed, in the usual card test, where the polygrapher pretends to discover the chosen card from an examination of the polygraph record, it is necessary to cheat by employing a marked deck or some similar ruse, since the 'lie' about the chosen card cannot be reliably determined from the charts.

A fundamental deception involved in the CQT is that 'The control questions are presented to the subject in a manner designed to lead him to believe that admissions would negatively influence the examiner's opinion and that strong reactions to those questions during the test would produce a deceptive result' (Raskin, 1986a). The truth is the opposite of this; only by giving strong reactions to the control questions can the subject hope to pass the test. For this reason, no sensible polygraph examiner would agree to submit to a lie-detector test himself in any consequential matter because he knows that he could not be deceived in these essential ways. (A polygrapher might, of course, submit to testing with the intention of assuring a 'truthful' verdict by artificially augmenting his reactions to the control questions; see the discussion of counter-measures below.)

These essential deceptions pose at least two problems, one ethical and one practical. Experimental psychologists sometimes deceive research subjects in order to produce a state of mind necessary to test some hypothesis; this practice is routinely followed by immediate debriefing including at least an implicit apology for the deception employed. For a technique of applied psychology, involving non-volunteers and issues of considerable personal concern to them, to be predicated on deliberate deception seems to raise more serious ethical concerns. As a practical matter, a test whose validity depends upon successful deception of each subject is vulnerable, not only to the likelihood that not all examiners will successfully hoodwink every subject, but also to the probability that the truth about the test will become more and more widely known. There are now dozens of articles and books in print (including this one) each of which has inoculated all of its readers against the very deceptions upon which the CQT depends.

If it works, use it. Yet, in spite of its stressful character, its dehumanizing intrusiveness, its repudiation of cherished principles of law and justice, even the ethical concerns which it raises – if polygraphic lie detection really worked, if it were as accurate as its proponents claim, who can doubt that it would (and perhaps should) be used even more widely than it is now in the United States? A searching background investigation also is an invasion of privacy; a criminal trial is both intrusive and stressful for the defendant. If, in an hour or two, we could determine with 95 percent confidence whether a defendant was guilty, or whether a job applicant was a thief or a spy, might it not then be more humane, more just, as well as more efficient, to substitute the polygraph for alternative or traditional methods of decision-making, methods which are vastly more cumbersome and costly and yet which seldom justify such high confidence?

It is for this reason that I think the validity issue is paramount, not only for purposes of scientific inquiry but also as the principal basis for public policy decisions.

The accuracy of polygraphic lie detection

The easiest way to assess polygraph accuracy is in the laboratory where one can be certain about the criterion – which persons are in fact lying. The problem with laboratory or analogue studies is the difficulty of inducing in the subjects the degree and type of emotional concern experienced by guilty or by innocent suspects being tested in real life. This is important because the polygraph lie test depends upon fear of detection, it assumes that the guilty person will be relatively more disturbed by the relevant questions while the innocent person will be more disturbed by the control questions. We can generalize the findings from the laboratory to the real world only if we succeed somehow in simulating the consequences that are associated with polygraph testing in the real world. (These strictures may not apply to the guilty knowledge technique.)

In the mock crime paradigm employed by Raskin and his students (see Chapter 8 above), for example, it is likely that volunteer subjects regard the experience as a kind of interesting game. Those persons instructed to commit the mock crime and to lie during the test no doubt feel a certain excitement, but not the guilt or fear of exposure that a real thief feels when tested for the police. Volunteers assigned to the innocent group have no reason at all to fear the relevant questions; they are not suspected of any wrongdoing and they will not be punished or defamed even if the test goes awry. On the other hand, the control questions used in laboratory studies – 'Between the ages of 18 and 20, did you ever take anything of value that didn't belong to you?' – unlike the relevant questions, do refer to real-world events and, presumably, have the same embarrassing or disturbing effect on volunteer subjects that they have on criminal suspects. This is probably the reason why mock crime studies typically show a much lower rate of false positive errors than do studies of actual criminal interrogation in the field. Innocent suspects often fail police-administered tests (see below) because they find the relevant questions more disturbing than the control questions, since they know they are in real jeopardy in respect to the accusations contained in the relevant questions while the controls involve no comparable risk. For the volunteer laboratory subject, this imbalance is reversed.

Laboratory studies

Two laboratory investigations have been reported which appear to have succeeded in eliciting genuine concern in both the 'guilty' and 'innocent' examinees. Iacono and Patrick (1987) had forty-eight prison inmates tested in a mock crime situation. It was understood that each participant's bonus of $20 would be withheld if more than ten of the forty-eight subjects failed the polygraph test. Moreover, the names of inmates failing the test would be posted in the prison for all to see. The intent was to make both 'guilty' and 'innocent' subjects believe that, if they failed the test, they might be blamed by their fellow inmates for the loss of the $20, a considerable sum by prison standards. That this manipulation was successful is suggested by the fact that several inmates expressed their concern about the consequences of failing and a few actually declined to participate for that reason. Two skilled and experienced examiners administered control question tests and all charts were independently scored by both examiners. Although the inter-scorer reliability was very high, only thirty of the forty-eight subjects were correctly classified. Excluding inconclusive tests, there were 13 percent false negative errors and 44 percent of the 'innocent' inmates were misclassified as deceptive.

Forman and McCauley (1986) permitted subjects to decide for themselves whether to be 'innocent' or 'guilty'. Each of their thirty-eight subject volunteers was told that he or she could choose an envelope likely to contain the standard $2 participation payment or he or she could elect instead to risk opening the envelope to obtain $10. All subjects were to be given polygraph tests to determine whether they had opened the envelope. Any person who failed the test, guilty or innocent, was to forfeit whichever envelope was chosen. Twenty-two of the subjects elected to risk being deceptive on the test. A CQT was administered and the charts scored both by the examiner and by a 'blind' judge. Their average accuracy on the subjects who elected to be deceptive (that is, the sensitivity) was 85.5 percent. On the innocent, truthful subjects, the average accuracy (the specificity) was only 52.5 percent; nearly half the test results were false positives.

These two studies suggest that when a mock crime experiment is designed in such a way as to make the 'innocent' participants genuinely concerned about failing the test, the result will be as commonsense would predict from the assumptions of the CQT (and as is found in the better field studies described below) – an unacceptably high rate of false positive errors.

Field studies
The best way of assessing the accuracy of the polygraph test involves selecting a *representative sample* of polygraph tests administered under *real-life circumstances*, having the charts independently scored by polygraphers who have only the charts to guide their decisions – *blind scoring* – and then comparing these scores with 'ground truth' (which subjects really lied and which were truthful) established by some *criterion that is independent of the polygraph findings*. The four features emphasized in the preceding sentence comprise the essential criteria for a scientifically credible assessment. They rule out of serious consideration several studies included in the meta-analysis conducted by the Office of Technology Assessment (1983; the OTA is an agency of the US Congress). In Bersh (1969), for example, the polygraphers based their judgements in part upon their knowledge of the evidence and their subjective appraisal of the statements and demeanour of the suspects tested; thus this study fails to meet the blind scoring requirement. Bersh himself acknowledges that his data do not provide an estimate of the validity of the polygraph findings themselves (1969: 402.) Several studies conducted by personnel of the Reid polygraph firm in Chicago (Horvath and Reid, 1971; Hunter and Ash, 1973; Slowik and Buckley, 1975; Wicklander and Hunter, 1975) must also be rejected from consideration because, as Brett, Phillips and Beary (1986) have pointed out, they involved 'non-random selection of files [charts] and lack of explicit statements as to how truth or falsehood was established'.

In a study by Barland and Raskin (1976), which does meet the four criteria, 109 criminal suspects were tested by Barland and the charts scored blindly by Raskin who classified all but one of the guilty subjects as deceptive but who classified more than half of the truthful subjects also as deceptive. Raskin later asked twenty-five polygraphers to independently score just sixteen of these charts, charts on which Raskin's original scoring had been either correct (fourteen) or inconclusive (two) (Raskin, Barland and Podlesny, 1977). Ignoring inconclusives, as is the usual procedure, most of the rescorings of these sixteen charts were correct. Since this ex post facto study did not employ a representative sample of charts (charts which one polygrapher scores correctly are likely to be scored correctly by others trained in the same system), it seems reasonable to discard these findings from consideration also.

We are left with only three acceptable field studies (Barland and Raskin, 1976; Horvath, 1977; Kleinmuntz and Szucko, 1984a) which

I have analysed in detail elsewhere (e.g., Lykken, 1985). The results of these studies are summarized in Table 9.1.

Table 9.1 *The three scientifically credible studies of polygraph accuracy*

	Barland and Raskin (1976)	Horvath (1977)	Kleinmuntz and Szucko (1984a)	Totals
Sensitivity (guilty called deceptive)	98%	79%	76%	84%
Specificity (innocent called truthful)	45%	50%	64%	53%
Overall validity (mean of above)	72%	65%	70%	70%

No single field study of polygraph accuracy can be regarded as definitive. The charts employed, even if unselected with respect to the criterion, can never be wholly representative of polygraph tests in general. The criteria of ground truth that are available in field studies are necessarily imperfect; persons who confess, for example, may not be representative of guilty persons generally. Moreover, as Iacono and Patrick (1987) have pointed out, the confessions in these field studies mostly occurred pursuant to vigorous interrogation by the examiner, motivated by his impression that the subject had failed the polygraph test. Inevitably, therefore, guilty persons who did not produce deceptive-looking charts, in other words persons who are likely to yield false negative errors, must be underrepresented in field studies using confession criteria.

Yet these three studies agree very well with one another, in spite of their differences in locale, design and criteria. They also agree with the findings of the better analogue field studies, described above, in which the criterion was unimpeachable. Another field study which meets the four criteria was only recently completed in British Columbia with the co-operation of the Royal Canadian Mounted Police and using the RCMP's excellent record system. This study, by Iacono and Patrick and not yet published, also yielded a high rate of false positive errors. This agreement among the better studies suggests that these results are all estimates of the same basic finding, one that can reasonably be generalized to specific-issue, control question polygraph tests administered under adversarial conditions to persons suspected of specific criminal conduct. We can conclude, therefore, that the CQT, while reasonably accurate (about 84 percent on guilty suspects) in detecting lying in persons not specifically trained in counter-measures, is exceedingly inaccurate in detecting truthfulness (about 53 percent accuracy, versus a chance accuracy of 50 percent).

Counter-measures

Techniques with which a deceptive person can defeat the polygraphic lie test and produce a diagnosis of 'no deception indicated' or, at the least, an inconclusive result are discussed in detail elsewhere in Chapter 10 below by Gudjonsson. Augmenting one's responses to the control questions by means of covert self-stimulation seems to be the most reliable method. In the case of screening tests, one should either self-stimulate after all of the relevant questions that one can answer truthfully or at least to some of them on the first presentation of the list and to a different set on the next. We know that, in mock crime situations, this method reduces the sensitivity of the CQT to about chance levels (Honts, Hodes and Raskin, 1985).

It is important to remember, in evaluating the data on polygraph accuracy as summarized in Table 9.1, that none of the guilty suspects in these studies were taught effective counter-measures. Since the attempts usually made by unsophisticated persons to 'beat the polygraph' are probably not effective – there is no way to be certain, of course, since the only attempts detected by polygraphers are the unsuccessful ones – it is likely that the estimates of the ability of the lie test to detect lying shown in Table 9.1 overestimate the sensitivity that the CQT can be expected to have in future work where the persons tested are trained spies or sophisticated criminals.

The accuracy of screening tests

It will be noted that all of the studies discussed above employed the CQT format in the specific-issue context of criminal investigation. The widest use of polygraphic interrogation in the United States is in pre-employment (or in post-employment, periodic) screening. The typical screening test employs the 'relevant control' format. In spite of its wide utilization, the accuracy of the RCT screening test has never been studied with acceptable scientific controls under field conditions. Some commentators (e.g., Raskin, in Chapter 8 above) regard the assumptions of the screening test as less plausible (even) than those on which the CQT is based and conclude, therefore, that the evidence, if it existed, would show it to be less accurate than the CQT. This judgement is based on identifying the screening test with the old relevant–irrelevant (RI) format still used by some examiners in criminal interrogation.

I believe that this identification is erroneous and that the assumptions of the RCT are no more implausible than those on which the CQT depends. When an applicant for a position with the CIA responds consistently more strongly to a question about possible homosexual activities than to other 'relevant' questions pertaining to his loyalty or honesty, his financial affairs or his previous employment, then it seems reasonable to infer that this question has special significance for him – more reasonable than it would be to draw the same inference merely from the fact that he was more responsive to a question about his sexual practices than he was to irrelevant questions about his name or the day of the week, the types of filler questions used in the RI test.

One possible explanation for his relative disturbance would be that he has been involved in unrevealed homosexual relationships. But any competent psychologist could adduce a dozen equally plausible explanations such as: the applicant is sexually incompatible with his wife and thinks others might attribute this to homosexuality; he suspects that others see him as effeminate; he is himself homophobic so that this implied accusation is especially disturbing; the question calls to mind his heterosexual infidelities and he is reacting to that; he has a friend who is homosexual but is not himself; he thinks that this question is intrusive and not job-related and reacts differently to it for that reason; the examiner seemed to give this question a peculiar inflection on first asking; and so on and on.

Thus, while perhaps granting that the theory of the screening test is not quite so fatuous as that of the RI technique, there seems to be no reason for supposing that research on the RCT, if any credible research ever appears, will show it to be any more accurate than the CQT. Moreover, in the employee screening application, it is usually only a minority – sometimes a very tiny minority – of the persons tested who are actually offenders. This low 'base rate' of offenders greatly attenuates the utility, the 'predictive value' (Brett, Phillips and Beary, 1986) of even a relatively accurate test.

Brett, Phillips and Beary (1986) have shown that, even if the RCT were much more accurate than we have reason to expect, its use in employment screening *must* lead to the unacceptable result that most of the rejected applicants will be honest and innocent persons. We can use Brett, Phillips and Beary's formula to evaluate the polygraph screening programmes now in place, both in Britain and the United States, for vetting government employees. We shall assume that not more than one in 1,000 employees holding security clearances are actually spies. On this reasonable assumption, and using the average values of Table 9.1 to estimate the sensitivity and specificity of the polygraph screening test, we find that, for every employee who 'fails' the polygraph, the odds that he is nonetheless an honest, loyal citizen are more than 560 to one!

How accurate is 'accurate enough'?
But many criminal situations involve only one suspect whose prior probability of guilt is essentially impossible to quantify. A recently

common example in the US is the adult or parent against whom an allegation has been made of the sexual abuse of a child. We have known, at least since the Salem witch trials of the eighteenth century, that children can and do lie about such matters. On the other hand, it is plainly important to protect children from real abuse and to apprehend and punish the real offenders. Given such an accused, there may be no reason to set the prior probability (the base rate) of guilt higher or lower than $p = 0.50$. If the suspect fails the CQT, Brett, Phillips and Beary's equation tells us that the odds in favour of his guilt rise from 50:50 to 64:36. It might be argued that such a finding would justify removing the child from this parent's custody and proceeding with criminal prosecution; moreover, some might think it appropriate to permit the jury also to learn of these results.

The essential uniqueness of the individual case. At this point, one hopes the reader has begun to get a little nervous. Your estranged spouse has taken your four-year-old daughter to the police, alleging that the child complained of vaginal soreness after her last visitation with you. Asked, 'Did Daddy (Mommy) put his finger in there?' she nods assent. You are asked to take a polygraph test; what will they think if you refuse? The relevant questions are various forms of: 'Last Sunday, did you put your finger in your little daughter's vagina?' The control questions include: 'Prior to two years ago, did you ever commit an unusual sex act?' If the questions about sexually abusing your daughter make your palms sweat more, your heart beat harder, than such 'control' questions do, you will fail the test. You know, of course, that you are innocent of these scurrilous charges. Are you prepared to proceed?

Now let us look at the other side of the same coin. Suppose you are the accusing spouse in this case; you know that the child was in pain when she came home; you know that you did not suggest to her that 'Daddy (Mommy) did it' – she volunteered that information. But you also know that your spouse once read a book on lie detection and commented on how easy it is supposed to be to 'beat' the test by biting one's tongue at the right times. If you agree to a trial-by-polygraph and the test is passed, you must deliver little Sally to your spouse again next week as usual. Are you ready to agree?

The problem is, of course, that the statistics we were considering above often do not fit the facts of the individual case. The studies on which they were based did not involve guilty persons using sophisticated counter-measures; if they had, the sensitivity obtained would have been much less than 0.84. The validity studies did not involve innocent parents accused of awful crimes against their own children; had they done so, the proportion of innocent persons who fail might have been even higher than 43 percent – and what sensible, innocent accused would commit his fate to a test that is almost as likely to condemn as to exonerate him?

When one is contemplating the cost/benefit of polygraphing the Pentagon or the merits of legislation prohibiting polygraph screening by private employers, utility functions or base-rate calculations seem pertinent and useful. When one is considering the pros and cons of relying upon (or even permitting) polygraph testing in the particular case, however, especially as it arises within the context of criminal investigation, one is impressed by the uniqueness of that case, by the important ways in which it seems to differ from the small samples of other cases from which the available statistics were derived. It is perhaps for this reason that the criminal courts traditionally depend upon the specifics of the case, rather than upon base rates and statistics, evaluated by the human judgement – not of some poly-grapher – but of a jury.

The guilty knowledge test

It is a relief to turn now to a method of polygraphic interrogation for which the theory and assumptions have a ring of plausibility and the data appear to be relatively consistent and encouraging. The guilty knowledge test or GKT, first described some thirty years ago (Lykken, 1959; see also Lykken, 1981), does not attempt to determine whether the respondent is lying but, rather, whether he or she posses-ses guilty knowledge, that is, whether the respondent recognizes the correct answers, from among several equally plausible but incorrect alternatives, to certain questions relating to a crime. For example, escaping through an alley a bank robber drops and leaves behind his hat. A likely suspect is later apprehended and, while attached to the polygraph, he is interrogated as follows:

1 'The robber in this case dropped something while escaping. If you are that robber, you will know what he dropped. Was it: a weapon? a face mask? a sack of money? his hat? his car keys?'

2 'Where did he drop his hat? Was it: in the bank? on the bank steps? on the sidewalk? in the parking lot? in an alley?'

3 'What colour was the hat? Was it: brown? red? black? green? blue?'

4 'I'm going to show you five red hats or caps, one at a time. If one of them is your hat, you will recognize it. Which of these hats is yours? Is it: this one? this one? ... etc.'

An innocent suspect has about one chance in five of reacting differentially (perhaps most strongly) to the correct alternative in any one of these questions. He has only about two chances in a thousand of reacting differentially to the correct alternative in all four questions. If the case facts permit the development of ten questions of this type, an innocent suspect's lack of guilty knowledge can be demonstrated with great confidence. The *specificity* of the GKT is its cardinal virtue.

The *sensitivity* of the GKT depends upon whether it is possible to generate enough items pertaining to matters which a guilty suspect will remember, items for which a guilty suspect is likely to be able at once to identify the correct alternative. The case facts thus employed must not involve matters discussed in press reports or about which the suspect has previously been interrogated. The above example illustrates how, with a little ingenuity, a single innocuous-seeming fact can be used to generate several GKT items.

It will be obvious that ingenuity is also required in the formulation of the foils or incorrect alternatives; all of the alternatives must each seem about equally plausible to someone lacking guilty knowledge. When this is accomplished, the incorrect alternatives serve as genuine control questions, in contrast to misnamed 'control questions' used in lie detection. That is, the subject's responses to the incorrect alternatives provide an estimate of how that subject would be expected to respond to the correct alternative if he does not have guilty knowledge.

The GKT is obviously susceptible to the counter-measure of self-stimulation, for example, to the subject's biting his tongue after some or all of the foils. The guilty suspect's task is perhaps more difficult than in lie detection, however, where it is necessary merely to augment one's responses to all of the control questions. If this is done on a GKT, then one will betray one's guilty knowledge by the fact that one's responses to the correct alternatives tend to be consistently the smallest in each set. Perhaps a greater weakness of the GKT is its sensitivity to manipulation, deliberately or unconsciously, by the examiner. By choosing implausible foils, or by accenting the correct alternative as the questions are asked, it might be easy to produce a false positive outcome. These problems could be minimized by, for example, testing the set of alternatives on known innocent persons, having the questions spoken by someone ignorant of the correct alternative, and so on.

The accuracy of the GKT

Unlike lie detection, the accuracy of the guilty knowledge test does not depend upon the nature or degree of the subject's emotional concern. The physiological variables employed are not intended to measure emotional response but, rather, to signal the cognitive processes involved in the recognition of the correct alternative. For this reason one avoids cardiovascular and respiratory variables, which are noisy and cumbersome, and one uses instead variables that are more sensitive to higher-level processes. Most researchers have employed electrodermal activity exclusively but one recent and promising study made use of the electrical activity of the brain evoked by the test stimuli.

Farwell and Donchin (1986) adapted for GKT use the 'odd ball' paradigm widely used in research on the cognitive significance of slow-wave components of the event-related brain potential (ERP). In this paradigm a large number of stimuli are presented, of which some small fraction have special significance. The averaged ERP to the 'odd ball' or target stimuli reliably shows a late-appearing positive slow wave, the P300 response, which seems to signal special cognitive processing of these stimuli. Farwell and Donchin found that 'guilty' subjects produce P300 responses to stimuli recognized as guilty knowledge. In their small pilot study they were able to achieve perfect detection both of 'guilty' and 'innocent' subjects.

Because the GKT depends upon cognitive rather than emotional responses, it can be argued that laboratory studies can provide reasonable estimates of how accurate the technique might be in real life. In any case, laboratory studies are all we have presently on which to base a judgement. The results of eight such studies, involving a total of 313 volunteer subjects, about half of them 'guilty' of some mock crime, are summarized in Table 9.2. All of these studies used the EDR as the dependent variable.

Table 9.2   *Aggregated results of eight analogue studies of the accuracy of the guilty knowledge test*

Status of subject	GKT diagnosis		Totals	
	Innocent	Guilty	*n*	Accuracy[a]
Guilty	19	142	161	88.2%
Innocent	147	5	152	96.7%
Totals	89%	97%	313	93%

[a] For comparison with Table 9.1, the *sensitivity* (proportion of guilty suspects identified) of the GKT averaged 88.2 percent in these studies, while the *specificity* (proportion of innocent suspects cleared) averaged 96.7 percent.

Sources: The studies summarized in this table were: Balloun and Holmes (1979); Bradley and Warfield (1984); Davidson (1968); Giesen and Rollison (1980); Iacono, Boisvenu and Fleming (1984); Lykken (1959); Podlesny and Raskin (1978); and Stern et al. (1981)

With the GKT, unlike lie-detection methods, it is possible to estimate the sensitivity and specificity of any particular test given only the number of items used, the number of scored alternatives per item, and an estimate (testable in the laboratory situation) of the probability that a guilty person will give his or her largest response to the correct alternative of any given item. Five of the eight studies summarized in Table 9.2 used six items with four scored alternatives (one used ten items and two only four items). For a good GKT item with four alternatives, the probability that an innocent suspect will give the largest response to the correct alternative is about 0.25. We shall assume that this probability rises to 0.80 if the suspect is guilty.

It is then possible to calculate what proportion of guilty or innocent subjects will pass or fail the GKT with any specified cutting score. Let us agree to classify a subject as passing the test if he or she gives the largest electrodermal response (EDR) to the correct alternative on no more than three of the six items; subjects who 'hit' on four or more items will be said to fail. One can calculate that 96.2 percent of innocent subjects should, in the long run, pass such a GKT; Table 9.2 shows that 96.7 percent of the 152 innocent subjects did in fact pass. Similarly, 89.1 percent of guilty suspects should exceed the cutting score and fail the test; Table 9.2 shows that 88.2 percent of 161 'guilty' subjects failed.

Conclusions

Unlike the fictional Pinnochio, we are not equipped with a distinctive physiological response that we emit involuntarily when, and only when, we lie. There are many reasons other than deception why a truthful person might show physiological disturbance in response to an accusatory question. Polygraphers cannot delude each innocent suspect into the belief that he or she has nothing to fear from the relevant questions but something important to fear from the 'controls'. The fact that one of several accusatory questions causes my heart to beat harder, my palms to sweat more, than the other questions do does not necessarily mean that I am guilty of that accusation. The assumptions on which the various forms of lie-detector test are based have only to be articulated to be seen to be implausible.

Many poorly designed, badly controlled studies are to be found in the polygraph literature. The few relatively competent studies agree with each other and with what one might expect from the theory: polygraphic lie detection is wrong about one third of the time overall; it is seriously biased against the truthful subject; deceptive subjects with minimal coaching can deliberately produce augmented responses, undetected by the examiner, which will allow them to defeat at least one common type of lie test.

It seems to me that we must now acknowledge that this application of psychophysiology has been a failure, that polygraph lie detection does not and, in the foreseeable future, probably cannot work well enough to justify its continued use in the field. Polygraphic detection of guilty knowledge, based on entirely different and more plausible assumptions, has proved itself in the laboratory and deserves controlled study in the field of criminal investigation.

10

How to defeat the polygraph tests

Gisli H. Gudjonsson

One major challenge against the accuracy of the polygraph in detecting deception relates to the possibility that deceptive subjects may be able to produce false negative outcomes by employing one or more 'counter-measures' during a polygraph examination. Counter-measures are deliberate techniques that some subjects use to appear truthful when their physiological responses are being monitored during a polygraph examination. Counter-measures should not be confused with 'accidental' false negatives or with psychological factors other than specific attempts to defeat the polygraph. Indeed, a number of factors other than counter-measures may affect the accuracy of the polygraph in detecting deception. These may relate to such variables as the type of polygraph technique used, the nature of the questions chosen, the mental state, motivation and personality of the subject, the subject's faith in the polygraph test, the competence and experience of the polygraph examiner, and the circumstances and purpose of the testing.

My aim is to describe, discuss and evaluate the effectiveness of counter-measure techniques in the physiological detection of deception. Many laboratory studies employing mock crime paradigms have been conducted into counter-measures during the last decade and some important findings have emerged. The findings will be discussed, particularly with reference to the 'control question technique' (CQT) and 'concealed information tests' (CIT). The two techniques represent respectively 'direct' and 'indirect' ways of detecting deception. The most commonly used and researched CIT is the 'guilty knowledge test' (GKT) of Lykken (1959). The two techniques – CQT and CIT – are based on different theoretical assumptions (Lykken, 1981) and some differences may therefore exist between them with respect to counter-measures.

These two techniques are most frequently used within the context of a criminal investigation and are the only techniques that have some scientific credibility. The 'relevant–irrelevant technique', which was the first standard polygraph technique developed, has failed to be accepted within scientific circles and will therefore not be broached in this paper. It is mainly used for pre-employment screening and lacks theoretical and empirical support (Office of Technology Assessment, 1983).

The two polygraph techniques

The control question technique employs specially designed 'control' questions and the physiological responses to these are compared with those obtained for the 'relevant' or crime-related questions. If subjects give stronger reactions to the control as compared to the relevant questions, then their answers are considered to be truthful. In contrast, stronger reactions to the relevant questions indicate deception. The absence of a clear difference in physiological responses between the control and relevant questions in either direction gives 'inconclusive' results. This means that the examiner cannot give a definite opinion with respect to diagnosis of truthfulness or deception, which may in the field result in a further test being constructed and administered. Clearly, deceptive subjects who wish to beat a CQT need to appear truthful on the test (thus create 'false negative' results) rather than being classified as 'inconclusive'. In order to achieve this they must successfully change the direction of the differential reactivity between the relevant and control questions and do this in such a way that their efforts are not readily detected by the polygraph examiner. Although counter-measures are undoubtedly most commonly used by deceptive subjects, innocent subjects may on occasions also employ such tactics because of the fear of failing the control question test. Therefore, it cannot automatically be assumed that all subjects who are observed to use counter-measures are 'guilty' of the crime they are being questioned about.

Unlike the CQT, concealed information tests do not rely on direct questions concerning truthfulness and deception but rather attempt to detect whether a suspect has information about a crime that only a guilty subject should have. A number of tests may be constructed, each employing one relevant item and several (usually four) control items, which are presented in a multiple-choice format. Unlike the CQT it does not utilize an 'inconclusive' category. In order to defeat the test subjects may attempt to respond equally to all items and therefore reduce to a chance level the likelihood of the relevant information being detected. This would appear to be the most convincing way of defeating a CIT since theoretically for an innocent subject all items should have approximately equal psychological significance.

Although in practice all the 'neutral' items are unlikely to have equal psychological significance for the subject, a disproportionately large reaction to one or more of the control items may make the polygraph examiner suspect that counter-measures are being applied. A disproportionately large reaction to the control questions on the CQT, on the other hand, would be less likely to arouse suspicion since it would theoretically be a 'typical' pattern of responses among genuinely truthful subjects.

Another difference between the CQT and CIT relates to arousal or anxiety level of subjects during the polygraph examination. The CQT employs accusatory, intrusive and emotionally loaded questions which require a direct denial by the subject and are deliberately constructed during a pretest interview in such a way as to increase the subject's concern and anxiety. In contrast, no manipulations or emotionally loaded questions are used with CITs and the physiological responses elicited by the items (questions) reflect the signal value of the different stimuli and the amount of attention the subject pays to the particular items. Therefore the overall level of physiological arousal during the polygraph examination is likely to be much higher when the CQT is used, which has implications for counter-measures. In view of the different nature and arousal properties of the CQT and CIT, Raskin (1979) provides an important conceptual distinction between the two techniques related to arousal values. That is, the CQT is more likely to produce physiological responses associated with 'defensive reflexes' whereas the responses obtained with CITs are more characteristic of 'orienting reflexes'.

Defensive reflexes normally occur in response to perceived threat and are best construed as a protective mechanism. Orienting reflexes, on the other hand, are more commonly elicited by the novelty and signal value of the stimuli rather than by perceived threat. A further difference is that whereas the orienting reflex represents increased attention to a stimulus, a defensive reflex represents a tendency to turn away from a painful stimulus. This implies that the discrimination between truthful and deceptive subjects on the two different types of tests is based on different physiological response characteristics. The physiological evidence for this relates to rapid heart rate deceleration and blood pressure increases reflected in responses to accusatory questions on the CQT which are not evident when CITs are used. The typical physiological responses associated with CITs are increased skin conductance and vasoconstriction.

Types of counter-measures

Many different types of counter-measures have been reported in the literature and these are commonly discussed under various headings such as physical, mental, hypnosis, biofeedback and drugs, and comprise three different ways of beating the polygraph test:

Suppressing physiological responses to relevant questions. Individuals can attempt to suppress their physiological responses to the relevant questions/items and hence make the difference in responsivity between the relevant and control questions minimal, or in the desired direction.

Augmenting physiological responses to control questions. Individuals can attempt to intentionally produce physiological responses to the control questions/items so as to reduce the discriminative power of the relevant item.

Suppressing the overall level of physiological reactivity. Individuals can attempt to reduce the overall level of anxiety during a polygraph test, for example by taking drugs, in order to make it more difficult for the examiner to differentiate between physiological responses to the control and relevant questions.

The second method is generally considered to be most effective as it is generally easier for subjects to augment responses to the control questions rather than suppress genuine responses to the relevant questions.

Physical counter-measures

Many different physical manipulations can be used to distort the polygraph record but the most common ones consist of inducing either physical pain or muscle tension. For example, biting one's tongue in response to the control questions may create sufficient pain or discomfort to elicit an artificial physiological response indistinguishable from that of a genuine one. Similarly, pressing the toes against the floor or the thighs against the chair the individual is sitting in have been shown to be effective techniques under certain circumstances.

Serious research into the effectiveness of physical counter-measures is a relatively recent endeavour and some of the findings are contradictory. For example, in one study (Kubis, 1962) asking subjects to press their toes against the floor reduced the detection rate from 75 to 10 percent, but a replication of the study (More, 1966) found no reduction in detectability caused by leg movements. One possible reason for the difference may be that the motivation and co-operation of the subjects in the two studies were different and significantly affected the outcome.

More recently laboratory studies (reviewed by Office of Technology Assessment, 1983, and Raskin, 1986b) have shown that physical counter-measures such as biting one's tongue and pressing the toes against the floor can be effectively utilized by some people in order to defeat the CQT. However, the following four factors appear important from the available evidence: (1) counter-measure efforts commonly result in 'inconclusive' rather than 'truthful' diagnosis, which indicates that in many cases they are only partly successful in defeating the CQT. In some instances the 'inconclusive' rate among deceptive subjects has been shown to be over 40 percent (Honts and Hodes, 1982a); (2) employing multiple physical counter-measures rather than relying on a single method (for example, biting the tongue and pressing the toes against the floor at the same time rather than relying on only one counter-measure) appears to improve subjects' ability to defeat the CQT (Honts and Hodes, 1982b); (3) providing subjects with information about counter-measures without special training and practice appears ineffective (Honts, Raskin and Kircher, 1984); (4) the use of some physical counter-measures by subjects is not readily detectable by visual observation and requires special electromyograph recordings (Honts, Raskin and Kircher, 1983). In the field this finding is particularly important since polygraph examiners are unlikely to have the equipment and expertise for monitoring subtle movements associated with such counter-measures as biting the tongue. Most polygraph examiners might be able to detect gross body movements and hyperventilation by close observation of the subject or the polygraph chart, but it is often not easy to determine whether such movements are due to general restlessness of the subject or deliberate counter-measures.

Mental counter-measures

Mental counter-measures comprise deliberate attempts by subjects to change their pattern of thinking during the polygraph examination in order to defeat the test. This can be conceptualized as falling into one of three broad categories:

Artificially producing responses to control questions. Subjects attempt to artificially produce responses to the control questions by eliciting emotionally arousing thoughts (for example, by reflecting back to an erotic or painful experience).

Attenuating responses to relevant questions. Subjects make an effort to attenuate their physiological responses to the relevant questions. They may do this by attempting to calm themselves down when asked the relevant questions.

Mental dissociation. Subjects may deliberately attempt to distract or dissociate themselves away from the arousing quality of the relevant questions. They may do this during a polygraph examination by trying to focus their attention upon some irrelevant object or thought and answer questions 'automatically' in a uniform way. Related to dissociation is the deliberate attempt of some subjects to 'rationalize' their offence in an attempt to minimize the emotional impact of the relevant questions.

The available evidence suggests that mental counter-measures are generally less effective in defeating polygraph tests than physical counter-measures, although some subjects can successfully apply such techniques. The most effective mental counter-measure appears to be for subjects to elicit emotionally arousing thoughts whilst asked the control questions.

The advantage of employing mental counter-measures is that they are impossible to detect by observation and at present cannot be monitored by modern equipment as some physical counter-measures can.

Hypnosis and biofeedback

The effectiveness of hypnosis as a counter-measure has been researched in a number of studies. The hypnosis typically involves inducing amnesia for the 'crime' or relevant items subjects are being interviewed about. Training in hypnosis prior to the polygraph test undoubtedly can affect physiological responses, but it appears from the available evidence that hypnosis is not a strikingly effective counter-measure.

Biofeedback with respect to counter-measures consists of providing subjects with instructions about how to defeat a polygraph test and subsequently giving them the opportunity of practising a particular counter-measure before the polygraph examination proper. There is no doubt that biofeedback, in its broadest sense, is a potentially effective way of training people to defeat a polygraph test. It is generally easier to train people to use physical rather than mental counter-measures and they are consistently more effective. The training itself appears crucial in that merely training people with information about polygraph techniques and counter-measures appears to be ineffective (Honts, Raskin and Kircher, 1984). Providing subjects with information and training, on the other hand, significantly reduces the detection rate (Rovner, Raskin and Kircher, 1979).

Drugs

The main objective of using pharmacological substances as counter-measures is to alter the person's overall physiological arousal during the polygraph examination so that deceptive answers cannot be physiologically differentiated from truthful ones. Four recent studies have been reported in the literature and the findings have been contradictory.

Waid, Orne, Cook and Orne (1981) gave subjects 400 milligrams of the tranquillizer Meprobamate and found that it significantly reduced the detection rate on a CIT.

Iacono, Boisvenu and Fleming (1984) studied the effects of the tranquillizer Valium and the stimulant Ritalin in defeating a CIT. The deceptive context involved a simulated burglary. The overall detection rate was 94 percent and the drugs did not significantly affect the validity of polygraph examination.

Bradley and Ainsworth (1984) examined the effects of alcohol on the results of polygraph examination involving both a CIT and the CQT. This study is unique in that it investigated separately the effects of alcohol consumed prior to a mock crime and prior to the polygraph examination. Subjects who were intoxicated during the mock crime had lower detection rates on the two polygraph techniques than the sober subjects, but alcohol intoxication during the polygraph examination did not significantly affect the detection rate. These findings have implications for polygraph validity concerning individuals who were intoxicated at the time of the alleged offence. It is possible that alcohol consumed prior to a criminal act affects people's memory and emotional processes and therefore makes deception more difficult to detect during a polygraph examination. Replication of the findings and further research into the mechanisms involved are needed before one can draw generalizations from the findings.

According to the Office of Technology Assessment (1983), an unpublished study by Gatchel and his colleagues has shown that the beta-blocker propranolol, which is an effective drug in reducing cardiovascular output, is not an effective counter-measure for defeating the CQT.

A major concern about the use of drugs as counter-measures is that their use may be difficult to detect by the polygraph examiner. However, the evidence to date suggests that drugs are not a particularly effective counter-measure and are unlikely to pose a great threat to the validity of the CQT. Drugs may on occasions be effective in defeating CITs in situations where the overall level of arousal and concern are low. In this respect it is worth noting that the study by Waid, Orne, Cook and Orne (1981), where Meprobamate was found to be an effective counter-measure, suffered from a major methodological limitation in that the experimental paradigm did not employ a realistic mock crime but rather relied on making subjects sensitized to six common words they had to memorize. Had the deceptive context been more realistic Meprobamate might not have proved to be such an effective counter-measure. Finally, in view of the fact that drugs are unlikely to differentially affect the control and relevant questions on the CQT, such counter-measures would be likely to lead to inconclusive diagnosis rather than false negative results.

Counter-counter-measures

Counter-counter-measures are special techniques employed by polygraph examiners in order to detect subjects who are trying to make deliberate attempts to defeat the polygraph test. Many counter-measures are not immediately visible to the human eye and the evidence suggests that even experienced polygraph examiners may be unable to detect the spontaneous use of physical counter-measures. The use of drugs and mental counter-measures is even more difficult to observe but it is some compensation that they are much less effective in defeating the polygraph techniques than physical counter-measures. It is therefore the use of physical counter-measures which most urgently needs to be detected.

In an early study Reid (1945) developed an objective way of recording certain body movements by means of pneumatic sensors built into the back and seat of the subject's chair. The procedure allowed the polygraph examiner to monitor gross movements but more subtle physical counter-measures, such as biting one's tongue and pressing the toes against the floor, clearly require more sophisticated equipment. With increased technology this has proved possible. For example, in one study plectromyographic recordings obtained from the temporalis and gastrocnemius muscle areas detected 80 percent of subjects using physical counter-measures (Honts, Raskin and Kircher, 1983). However, from the point of real-life polygraph examinations carried out in the field, few polygraph examiners are likely in the near future to have the expertise or equipment to utilize electromyographic recordings, regardless of their effectiveness in detecting physical counter-measures. Most polygraph examiners will therefore have to rely on more simple ways of detecting subjects using counter-measures. This will probably mainly consist of close observation of behavioural signs indicative that counter-measures are being used, or careful inspection of the polygraph record itself. Some physiological responses are easier to augment by self-stimulation than others; electrodermal or 'galvanic skin responses' are more sensitive than cardiovascular responses to minor stimulation although it seems that most physiological modalities can be affected by counter-measures. The simultaneous use of more than one type of physiological response makes it easier to 'identify' a distorted polygraph chart resulting from the use of counter-measures. In future research cardiovascular responses associated with specific 'defensive reflexes' may prove particularly useful in distinguishing between genuine and faked responses. Indeed, in certain circumstances cardiovascular responses may be very idiosyncratic and difficult to fake (Gudjonsson and Sartory, 1983).

Lykken (1981) argues that subjects using counter-measures during a GKT could theoretically be detected by scoring the test according to 'expected ranks'. Any significant deviation from equal rank frequencies of the items suggests that the subject had been able to identify the relevant alternative and was deliberately attempting to distort the polygraph record. Such a scoring system cannot be used on the CQT.

With respect to counter-measures there is one further important difference between polygraph techniques. On CITs innocent subjects have no reason to attempt to defeat the test. They are unaware of the relevant alternatives and there would be no advantage in their attempting to react to a particular item. When the CQT is used subjects can readily differentiate between the relevant and control items. This means that on occasions it may be tempting for innocent subjects to use counter-measures out of fear that they could be wrongly classified as deceptive. The problem is that for innocent subjects an attempt to use counter-measures to establish their innocence can actually improve their chances of appearing deceptive on the test (Dawson, 1980). It is also interesting to note that on CITs attempts to use mental counter-measures actually increase subjects' chances of their deception being detected (Gudjonsson, 1983). This is probably due to the fact that employing counter-measures on non-threatening tasks increases the subject's involvement in the test and makes them more sensitized to the relevant items.

Conclusions

I have evaluated the scientific evidence with respect to counter-measures. Unfortunately, all the scientifically acceptable studies have been carried out under controlled laboratory conditions and the use of field studies is lacking. Bearing in mind that one must be cautious in drawing sweeping inferences and generalizations from 'mock crime' experiments, the following conclusions are tentative with respect to field examinations.

1   Lies differ in their importance to the individual. The more significant the lie is and the greater the perceived consequences of detection, the stronger the individual's physiological responses during a polygraph test tend to be.

2   There are several different polygraph techniques available based on different principles and operation. The two most scientifically acceptable techniques are the control question technique and the concealed information test. These two techniques differ markedly with respect to counter-measures. The former technique generally elicits far greater physiological arousal than the latter and relies on cardiovascular and respiratory modalities, in addition to the more sensitive electrodermal modality for chart evaluation.

3   For counter-measures to be effective with the control question technique, individuals have to produce responses to the control questions that are substantially larger than the responses they give to the relevant questions. On concealed information tests, on the other hand, subjects have to give approximately equal responses to all items. In addition, the counter-measures must be implemented surreptitiously in such a way that they are not readily detected by the polygraph examiner who could otherwise not give a valid diagnosis.

4   The use of different classes of counter-measures has been reported in the literature. The available evidence shows that mental counter-measures and the use of pharmacological substances (such as tranquillizers) are only moderately effective at best, whereas physical counter-measures can be highly effective under certain conditions. Two conditions appear important to the effective use of physical counter-measures. First, employing multiple counter-measures simultaneously improves the person's chances of defeating a polygraph test, at least as far as the control question technique is concerned. Second, physical counter-measures appear relatively ineffective unless people are given special training in their use. It is generally not sufficient merely to provide people with instructions about polygraph techniques and counter-measures.

5   Although there are clear individual differences in the ability to apply counter-measures effectively, training by experts in the use of physical counter-measures poses a potentially serious threat to the validity of polygraph techniques. For this reason it becomes

very important that the use of counter-measures is readily identified by polygraph examiners. Unfortunately subtle and effective physical counter-measures are not readily observable without special expertise and equipment which are not generally available to field examiners.

PART FOUR

Legal Issues and Civil Rights

11
Lie detection and the British legal system

Robert Grime

British lawyers are forced to confess that they are years behind their American colleagues in using the polygraph, or any other scientifically based form of truth-testing, and consequently in facing the problems that such use may bring with it. The first official British reference to the polygraph in a legal context is to be found in the report in 1981 of the Royal Commission on Criminal Procedure. The Commission examined the United States' experience with the polygraph, both as presented in the literature and at first hand, commissioned a study of the polygraph and its uses and came to the unenthusiastic conclusion that 'although it [the polygraph] may be useful as an aid to investigation, its lack of certainty from an evidential point of view tells against its introduction in this country for the purpose of court proceedings' (HMSO, 1981: para. 4.76).

Against the background of over sixty years of admittedly hesitant development of the forensic use of the polygraph in the United States, such an attitude is extremely restrained. The device has not, however, been utterly cast aside in the United Kingdom. It is thought to be in use in connection with security clearance procedures and possibly also in ordinary employment recruitment. It is not presently used in criminal trials.

The problems for lawyers that are raised by the use of the polygraph are essentially similar in every context. In essence they are, first, how far the polygraph can be relied upon as probative of the truth of the evidence tested by polygraphy and, second and quite separately from the issue of reliability, whether a polygraph test infringes some legal right of the polygraph subject, such as the right of silence in a criminal trial, or offends some rule of evidence or other legal provision excluding any matter from consideration. At present, the use of the polygraph is not legally controlled or officially licensed in any way in the United Kingdom, so the legal problems arise indirectly – how far and in what contexts its results may be significant.

The establishment of truth

Were a machine invented which regularly produced an acceptable measure of truthfulness, there could be no reason in principle why the information derived from that machine should not be presented to courts to assist them in their traditional task of deciding whether witnesses are lying, nor used by employers or others, if and when called upon by the law so to do, to justify their decisions to hire, fire, transfer or promote. Such a measure of 'truth' might remain acceptable despite the machine being less than perfectly accurate. The definition of acceptability would be pragmatic rather than scientific, a process more easily understood in a political context.

If there were sufficient support for the use of polygraphy as a test of truthfulness, there is no reason in principle why this could not be done. English law, like other systems, already has mechanisms designed to test the veracity of evidence, some of them not obviously more reliable than polygraphy. There is the requirement that evidence be given on oath, the practice of cross-examination, as well as rules requiring corroboration of certain types of testimony, and the general exclusion of hearsay evidence. Many of these mechanisms are difficult to justify in scientific terms (for example, is evidence given on oath really more reliable than unsworn statements?) or indeed explicable otherwise than by reference to the complex history of our legal system. The insertion of the polygraph into this complexity would certainly be possible and need be as little affected by arguments as to its reliability than is the oath, provided that political agreement was first achieved. Were that ever to be done, then the results of the chosen test itself would become the legal measure of accuracy in the circumstances governed by such rules. Every legal system must contain compromises between efficiency and justice: under such rules the test would be, as a matter of law, unarguably correct.

An instructive analogy might be drawn from the successive attempts made to use the criminal law to deal with the serious social problem of drunken driving. To identify that problem is relatively easy. When drunk, drivers are more likely to drive too fast or in some other way dangerously and further that because both their perception and motor abilities are dulled by alcohol, they become less skilful. To define effectively the points that a law against drunken drivers must raise is rather more complicated. 'Drunk' in this context must mean a drunkenness likely to have these undesirable effects. It cannot be denied that individuals vary in their tolerance of or response to alcohol. Presenting evidence that an individual charged under Section 11 of the Road Traffic Act 1930 was 'driving a motor vehicle while under the influence of drink to such an extent as to be incapable of having proper control of the vehicle' inevitably led to unedifying and expensive debate about the validity and basis of the arresting officer's, or the police surgeon's, 'evidence' that the accused was 'drunk'. Erratic steering, lurching gait, slurred speech, malodorous breath, sometimes supplemented by reported failure to repeat simple tongue-twisters or march without deviation along a painted straight line were argued over, seemingly without clear end.

There were various statutory attempts to narrow the question to be investigated so as to avoid the vagueness of the law. These attempts logically led to the introduction by the Road Safety Act 1967 of breath, blood or urine analysis as an alternative method of settling the question of whether an individual was 'drunk'. Now if a police officer sights a driver who seems to be drunk, he or she stops the vehicle and, subject to a large number of safeguards designed to protect individual liberties, administers two of four standard defined tests which give an indication of the amount of alcohol present in the subject's blood. If that indication shows more than 80 milligrams per 100 millilitres of blood, then, provided the safeguards have been properly observed, provided that the tests have been carried out according to the procedures specified by the law, the accused is guilty of an offence. It is irrelevant that he or she may be able persuasively to argue that his or her ability to drive was not seriously impaired. A driver who 'fails' the test is 'drunk'.

There can be no doubt that exactly the same process might be adopted with the polygraph, or any other procedure designed to give an objective index of truthfulness. A future Public Honesty Act might simply specify that any person giving evidence under oath or making statements in circumstances where the truthfulness of any such statement was required by statute, contract or other legal instrument, might be requested to submit to a polygraph test in accordance with the procedure set out in the regulations accompanying the Act and that, if such request was refused, or if, when tested in accordance with the specified procedure, the subject's responses should show a deviation from the normal responses (as defined) of more than a specified percentage, then the evidence or statements made by the subject and so tested should be conclusively presumed to be untrue, and the subject of the test be thereupon liable to conviction for perjury, or suffer such other relevant legal consequence. Were such legislative action taken, the lawyer would cease to be concerned with whether a polygraph test was reliable: lying and failing the test would have been equated by statute, just as failing another test and drunken driving have been equated.

It is not suggested that such a development is likely or desirable: it is merely intended to demonstrate that for a lawyer truth is necessarily circumscribed, maybe even defined, by procedural necessities. Nor is it suggested that the only way in which a polygraph could enter the legal system would be through a statute, whether or not it bore the fanciful title of the Public Honesty Act. Persons accused of a crime might offer polygraph evidence in support of their own statements of self-exoneration, or at a lower level offer as evidence (also supportive) that they had offered to undergo a 'lie-detector test'. An employer, justifying a dismissal in an industrial tribunal might offer as evidence of the ex-employee's dishonesty a 'failure' of the polygraph test. The court or tribunal might decide to accept or to reject such evidence. Whether the decision is made in a judicial or in a legislative context, however, similar issues are raised: how far is polygraph evidence probative of the truth of the statement tested and what compromise is acceptable in the interests of the proper and efficient administration of justice? This issue is likely to be more overtly raised in a legislative than a judicial context, but in either case it might be instructive to examine in brief the range of matters which might be thought to have a bearing upon the question of whether the polygraph meets the likely minimum standards of acceptability.

To oversimplify, a polygraph is a machine for measuring various bodily reactions which are asserted as indexes of stress. To the extent that those bodily reactions are so accepted, the results of a polygraph test may be regarded as an index of stress. It is of course agreed that bodily responses to stress are not constant among all individuals, so the reliability of the test as an index of stress depends upon the skill of the polygraph operator in tuning the machine to the responses of the subject to be measured, by reference to some standard base line. Such a process may be rather more complex than the specification of a standard test procedure for, say, the administration of the 'Alcotest' breath test equipment. Unavoidably, as any procedure becomes complex, more variations must be expected in the results received from expert practitioners of differing experience, skill and native intelligence. Thus, the extent to which polygraph results may be accepted as evidence of stress is not simple.

Whether and how far an index of stress can be offered as probative of truthfulness is a further, and greater, step. It would require a measure of agreement upon the relationship between stress and lying as well as acceptance of a technique which would exclude stress arising from other sources to a satisfactorily reliable degree. To repeat, absolute certainty is not necessary: merely enough to support agreement.

The polygraphist need not, of course, appear as a Truthfinder-General. He or she might be accepted as expert witness of stress, able and qualified to give evidence to the effect that when X made the statement that on the 23rd of the month he was nowhere near the bank that was robbed on that day, he exhibited exceptional stress. As such, the polygraphist's qualifications and skill as an expert would be subjected to (admittedly unscientific) tests similar to those applied to a fingerprint or ballistics expert. In short, he or she would be examined as to his or her qualifications and experience and would be subjected to the process of cross-examination which (like the medieval ordeal) lawyers believe to establish the personal reliability of witness. Having survived, his or her expert evidence might be accepted. The court or tribunal might then further deduce that therefore the evidence of X was to an extent unreliable (or reliable).

Such a process might not obviously violate any principle of law but it would hardly satisfy either the proponents of the polygraph or its doubters. It evades the central question of whether polygraph evidence should be accepted as probative of the falsity of statements by leaving it to untraceable ad hoc decisions in each case. Certainly it is not a simple proposition that a polygraphist's conclusions as to stress should immediately be accepted as evidence of the truth or falsity of a statement. It may be a long time before the relationship between stress and truth-telling can be clearly and satisfactorily established. In the meantime the courts at least, as the formal part of the legal system, might be expected to take *their* time. Meanwhile, if we are to see a development, it is likely to follow the path of this not very satisfactory compromise.

The experience of the United States of America may be of interest. Polygraphs had been in use, substantially on a voluntary basis for non-forensic purposes such as employee screening and selection, for sixty years when, in 1972, the results of the polygraph tests were first accepted in criminal trials in America. The courts' wariness was based upon scientific doubt; and there was hardly a rush to judgement. It is possible to hold several views about the present position of the polygraph in US courts, but it seems easier to admit polygraph evidence to sustain or attack statements (whether confessions or exonerations) whose voluntariness is under attack than it is to have polygraph evidence accepted as 'free-standing' evidence of the truth or falsity of the statements themselves. An involuntary statement (one made under threat or extracted by promise of favour or benefit) is not acceptable as evidence. Stress is clearly often relevant to the issue of whether the statement was obtained by threat or inducement.

It would seem that US courts are more ready to accept the polygraph as evidence of stress than to take the next step, with its greater philosophical difficulty.

It might therefore be concluded that the practical likelihood of wholesale introduction of polygraphy into the British court system as an index of truthfulness is not at present high. However, were such a course followed, certain problems would be encountered.

The right to silence and evidence of previous convictions

Perhaps the simplest way in which a polygraph might be used as an index of truth would be to test the truthfulness of denial of the charge by an accused person. The first problem for the lawyers would be the apparent infringement of the right to silence. This assumes that in some circumstances a person is entitled to keep quiet, may not be required to give evidence and that adverse inferences from his assertion of that right may not be drawn. In a criminal trial the accused retains this right in its simplest form. An accused man may not be required to speak against himself.

English law has never known an *absolute* right to silence; nor has it the same significance as it has in the United States, where it is a *constitutional* right, protected by the Fifth Amendment. There have always been exceptions to the rule and the rule itself has been less than universal in its application.

Closely allied to this rule, but sharply distinguishable from it, is a more diffuse notion that certain types of prejudicial information are excluded from consideration in various legal processes. So, in general, the previous convictions of an accused person may not be presented to a criminal trial. More generally, under the provisions of the Rehabilitation of Offenders Act 1974 (c. 53) convictions which are 'spent' because of the time that has passed since sentence was served may not be used in any legal process.

Polygraph evidence clearly cannot be used indirectly to establish facts which may not be established at all. If a conviction is spent, the convict is legally permitted to assert that there never was a conviction, and polygraph evidence legitimately casting doubt on such a statement cannot be admitted. The position in respect of the true right to silence is more complex. An accused murderer may refuse to give evidence, but the prosecution is at liberty to establish by other, less direct means that he did the killing. Polygraph evidence as to his reactions, and the expert conclusions to be drawn therefrom, is clearly inadmissible if it is considered as a statement *by* the accused. If, however, it is thought of as evidence *about* the accused, then there is no clear objection. The matter has not yet been tested in the United

Kingdom. It may be that the trial judge's discretion to exclude evidence on the ground that its prejudicial effect outweighs its probative value could be used to prevent the use of a polygraph in these circumstances.

The hearsay rule

The test of truthfulness most favoured by traditional lawyers is cross-examination. The hearsay rule buttresses that test. Evidence given by an eavesdropper of what the soldier said is not evidence of the truth of the soldier's statement: that must be tested by cross-examining the soldier, not the eavesdropper. (Such testimony is, of course, good evidence of the fact that the statement, true or false, *was made by the soldier*.)

Polygraph evidence may easily fall into the hearsay trap. It depends upon the purpose for which it is tendered. If the polygraphist's evidence that the witness 'passed' the test is offered as proof of the truth of the contents of the statement the witness made, that is clearly hearsay. Similarly, if evidence that the witness 'failed' is offered to establish the converse of what the witness said, that is, slightly less obviously, hearsay in respect of that implicit converse statement.

However, that a polygraph test was 'passed' or 'failed' is a fact. It is a fact *about* the making of a statement, and as such of some (variable) probative value. For example, the fact that the accused made a statement may be offered as consistent with innocence: the fact that an accused person underwent polygraphy might, subject to questions about 'self-serving evidence', be offered as consistent with innocence. That a witness made a previous inconsistent statement is clearly relevant to the weight of his present evidence; the results of polygraphy may be considered as relevant to his consistency. Evidence tendered merely to establish such facts which help to explain the circumstances of admissions or statements made by witnesses or accused persons cannot run foul of hearsay – although it may be excluded on other grounds, as, for example, being more prejudicial than probative.

Expert opinion and credibility

Thus far it appears that the operation of the rules of evidence, as well as doubts as to the function of polygraphy, may mean that polygraph evidence will be more acceptable as expert evidence about the witness than as to his statements. It is, of course, commonplace that character evidence may be given and may be weighed by the judge or jury in deciding whether the accused was guilty as charged – which includes believing or disbelieving the stories told by or about him or her. Are there, then, any difficulties in treating the polygraphist as a sort of expert character witness?

The first question is what such a witness would give evidence of. The courts have accepted, albeit with some doubt and reluctance, on the part both of lawyers and scientists, that psychologists and psychiatrists might give evidence as to the condition of a person's mind in a regard that has a bearing upon his or her legal responsibility. But in that case what such experts give evidence of is the accused's psychological condition – that he or she is suffering from a 'disease of the mind' – regarded as such as likely to have impaired his or her responsibility. It is unlikely that we can reach a ready and wide agreement to the proposition that veracity or mendacity is a psychological condition which can be tested (by polygraphy or in any other way) and made the subject of expert evidence on oath.

If polygraph evidence is not evidence of a psychological condition of mendacity in the polygraph subject, the polygraphist must be considered to be an expert on the perhaps non-psychological question of whether the evidence offered by the subject can or cannot be believed. But deciding who is to be believed is a central function of the trial process. It is a very healthy rule of evidence that experts may not be called to settle the very question to be decided by the court. Or, to put it another way, truth is tested by cross-examination, oaths, and so on, and not by experts. Which may beg the very question with which we began.

The problem only has to be stated to demonstrate the complex confusion in this area of the law. For a polygraphist to give evidence that the subject is, in his or her expert opinion, a liar may not be scientifically acceptable, but would seem to raise a few legal problems. For a polygraphist to offer the results of polygraphy as proving the truth (or falsity) of a statement by the subject would be hearsay. For a polygraphist to offer expert evidence to the effect that in his opinion the court should not rely upon the statement made by the witness does not offend hearsay but only if we can distinguish evidence as to credibility and evidence as to the truth of the statement made. Even then, a court might be unhappy at allowing expert evidence on the matter since the credibility of the witness, and his or her evidence, is the main question to be answered by the trial process.

However, if a polygraphist is not swearing that the accused is, in general or in particular, a liar (or a truth-teller), he or she can only be treated as giving evidence of no more than the indexes of stress measured. This is an area well known to the lawyers. Admissions are in general admissible in evidence and may be regarded as an exception to the hearsay rule. It is also regularly acceptable to hear evidence of the circumstances of the statements made by the accused. A witness may be asked about the demeanour of the person under investigation: did he stammer, was he confused, excited? Polygraphy clearly fits in here – a sort of electronically measured blush. A polygraphist's evidence could therefore amount to evidence of circumstance or behaviour, tendered as relevant to the more complex question of the credibility of the evidence under investigation.

Self-serving statements

The law of evidence has a salutary if not very precisely defined rule outlawing self-serving statements. An accused person who has, perhaps, searched around and come up with some evidence which he or she then offers as evidence of his or her own veracity must be received with some suspicion. Of course, such a 'rule' could not be absolute, or then an accused person would still, as was the case before the reforms of the late nineteenth century, be prohibited from entering the witness-box at all. However, the voluntary submission to polygraphy in order to boost the value of evidence that is to be given might be excluded on this ground.

Whether such an exclusionary rule could also be applied to the circumstance, beloved of the directors of gangster films, where an accused person is believed in his protestations because he *offers* to submit to a 'lie detector', remains to be seen. Evidence of such an offer, if tendered in support of the accused's self-exoneration, is just as self-serving as the submission.

Polygraphy and accusations

The use of polygraphy by or for victims or accusers has not yet been widely discussed in this country. The practicalities of such use might first be considered in connection with 'secret' crimes such as rape where accused and victim are often the only direct witnesses and the strength of a prosecution case must depend upon the statements of the accuser.

The testing of accusations in such cases by means of the polygraph might seem to have one of two uses. First, it might be offered by the victim in support of the accusation. As such, the results of polygraphy would run the risks of being regarded as a self-serving statement by the accuser, of no probative value, or even hearsay, and again valueless, particularly since the witness is likely to be available for cross-examination anyway. In this connection, it may be that polygraphy might be seen as a mechanism appropriate for use in some procedure designed to avoid the direct giving of evidence by distressed victims of harrowing crimes like rape. But if an out-of-court statement whose veracity has been authenticated by polygraphy is to be accepted as equivalent, or even superior, to evidence from the witness-box, substantial alterations of attitude will have to be achieved. If such alterations can only be reached by legislation, as seems likely, then agreement will have to be reached on the reliability of the polygraph as an index of truth.

Another perhaps more controversial use of polygraphy in secret crimes might be as a filter used by prosecuting authorities to assist them in their decision as to whether to proceed with prosecutions. Since virtually no legal principle is applicable to the exercise of the discretion to prosecute or not, there is no specifically legal dimension to this knotty political problem.

Voluntariness

Statements made by an accused person otherwise than in the witness-box in open court are only admissible if they are voluntary. There is, naturally, a great deal of complex law relating to what in practice is the admissibility of confessions. Most of the questions that can be raised relate to whether or not the confession was extracted under threat, trick or promise: clearly polygraphy, with all its paraphernalia, designed in part to persuade the subject of the reliability and accuracy of the machine, may feature in an argument that the accused was cowed into confessing. That will depend on the circumstances. It would be unfair to offer a general conclusion, but it may be sufficient to point out that a polygraphist will need to approach his task with great care. It may be that before polygraphy can be used on anything like a widespread basis in a forensic context, acceptable guidelines, designed to protect a witness from undue pressure in the process of polygraphy, will need to be worked out.

A further point might be raised. It is perhaps possible to argue that the readings on the polygraph themselves amount to an involuntary statement. Once again, there may be little force in this argument if polygraphy is treated only as evidence of circumstance or demeanour. Evidence of a blush is not inadmissible because it was not a voluntary act. But if polygraphy results are offered as a sort of disguised contrary statement – the subject failed the test when he said he was not there = the subject in fact said he was there – the argument is stronger.

Civil cases

So far we have been primarily concerned with the use of polygraph tests in criminal trials. It is conceivable that a use might be found for polygraphy in civil claims. The specific examples of employment and unfair dismissal claims are considered in the next section, but there may be wider possibilities. However, simple issues of deciding whether a fact that has been vigorously asserted by one side and hotly denied by the other perhaps occur more commonly in criminal trials than in the more rarefied reaches of civil claims. There the courts are much more likely to be facing abstruse issues of the interpretation of documents or the proper characterization of the behaviour of the defendant by reference to some generally applicable standard.

Nevertheless, issues of fact to be decided by the truthfulness of witness do regularly arise. It may be attractive to think of introducing polygraphy into a court faced with having to decide whether the salesman is to be believed when he swears that he never guaranteed that the motorcar he sold would do better than 35 miles to the gallon; whether the loving son really did tell his elderly father that the transaction concerning his house might result in its being taken by his business creditors; whether the writer of the damning and libellous character reference was, despite his evidence to the contrary, actuated by malice when he wrote the letter. However, the rules of hearsay and principles concerning self-serving statements and the limits of expert or opinion evidence apply also in civil claims in the ordinary courts. There is, of course, no right to silence.

Non-forensic uses

Polygraphy may find its greatest use outside court proceedings. The most obvious area of activity is probably in employee screening, either for security or more generally as some part of character and suitability assessment. The law has markedly less to say in this area than in connection with evidence and the courts. There are, of course, many arguments that are relevant, both as to the scientific reliability of polygraphs as indicators of more general character traits (if they be so) as honesty, security-worthiness, or the other matters which users of polygraphs may wish to identify. Further, the introduction of polygraphs presents substantial industrial relations problems. But there are few legal problems in a jurisdiction with no Bill of Rights and no relevant guaranteed right of privacy.

If an employer introduces polygraphy to screen his or her workforce, legal issues can only arise in so far as the action may lead to legal claims or proceedings. So the effect will vary in a way which, considered from the point of view of the use of polygraphy, is quite arbitrary. The law has nothing to say of polygraphy as such.

First, an individual who is refused employment on arbitrary

grounds has no general remedy. If the refusal amounts to an act of racial or sexual discrimination, some protection is available, but this is not relevant here. So if a subject 'fails' a polygraph test or refuses to submit to one and as a result is not offered work, no claim can be made.

An employee who is dismissed has in general the right to test the fairness of that dismissal before an industrial tribunal. In most cases, a claimant must have had one, or sometimes two, years' continuous employment with the employer concerned before he or she gains that right. In an unfair dismissal claim it is for the employer to establish the reason for the dismissal and that the reason was a fair one. The legislation sets out a range of four 'good' reasons for dismissal, of which the ones most likely to be relevant in these circumstances are: a reason connected with the employee's conduct and the capability or qualifications of the employee to carry out the work he or she was employed to do.

It is, of course, arguable that failing a polygraph test might count as 'conduct' in justification of a dismissal, but the conduct required in law needs to relate closely to the duties of the work. It is best thought of primarily in terms of industrial misconduct. More mileage may be obtained from 'capability', which may be assessed by reference to any physical or mental quality. It would seem possible for an employer to argue that the failure by an employee to complete satisfactorily a set of polygraph tests renders him or her unqualified for the work. However, this must be established. It would be necessary to show more than that the employer had established a policy of using polygraphy. The employer would have to persuade the tribunal that polygraph failures were not capable of the work. This could be difficult, since there is little scientific agreement as to the extent which polygraph results can be used, say, to predict unreliability in areas of employment responsibility.

Finally, perhaps it should be said in this context that unfair dismissal claims are heard in industrial tribunals, not in the ordinary courts. Industrial tribunals are relieved of the responsibility to follow the rules of evidence. They can, and often do, happily admit hearsay evidence, secure in the commonsense understanding that hearsay evidence is often very good evidence indeed. We might therefore expect fewer technical objections to polygraphy evidence in unfair dismissal claims.

In security matters the issue is simpler since the law permits the operation of the rules of unfair dismissal to be removed from areas of security sensitivity. This appears to be the practice of government.

One final point might be reiterated. The Rehabilitation of Offenders Act 1974 protects the position of those whose convictions are 'spent' under the Act. Polygraphy may not be offered to establish that a denial of a spent conviction was false, in any court or tribunal.

Conclusions

While there is no obvious substantial objection to the use of the polygraph in English law, it seems that its introduction will need to deal with several different types of problem. The law of evidence, that monument of an era of illiterate juries and accused persons with no right to speak for themselves, contains several pitfalls for the polygraphist who wishes to use his skill in a forensic context. Outside the court, in employee screening, in security activity or even in general police work not directly intended to produce evidence for a trial, its use may be easier.

Clearly, polygraphy raises moral and political questions. It seems very close to an invasion of privacy. Yet it may offer practical advantages in difficult areas of assessment of evidence. If it is to be introduced, such problems should first be addressed. Perhaps a Polygraph Act, or at least a Code of Practice for the Use and Operation of Polygraphs, is a necessary condition precedent.

12

Lie detection and civil liberties in the UK

Peter Thornton

'Listen, I don't know anything about polygraphs and I don't know how accurate they are, but I know they'll scare the hell out of people.' Richard Nixon's endorsement of the polygraph, recorded privately on the presidential tapes on 14 July 1971, may lack the finesse of scientific elucidation, but it identifies the double weakness of lie-detector tests in a civil liberty context. There is considerable concern about both their accuracy as instruments to test veracity and their use as weapons of intimidation as a substitute for the proper investigation of the truth. Neither weakness bodes well for the individual whose job, or worse still liberty, may be at risk.

The use of the test in the UK

The threat of the polygraph cannot lightly be dismissed. Its use in the United States, and some other countries, is widespread. It has been employed for security screening by governments, for staff selection by private businesses, and in the investigation of crime. The USA has fifty years' experience of polygraph screening, now a multi-million dollar industry. Polygraph methods are used by the FBI and the Pentagon. They are taught at the US Army Polygraph School. And the results of polygraph tests are admissible in the courts in many states.

On this side of the Atlantic the polygraph has been, thus far, less favoured; but this may be changing. Major American companies, such as Polygraph Security Services, have established branch offices here. Lord Bridge's Security Commission report in 1983 on the Geoffrey Prime spy case, despite concluding that even in the USA the polygraph remained 'a subject of controversy', recommended and led to an experiment in screening at GCHQ and other security establishments. *The Times* of 16 January 1987 reported that in answer to a parliamentary question the Minister of State, Foreign and Commonwealth Affairs, Mrs Lynda Chalker, said the first phase of the pilot scheme had been completed. The government is to commission further independent research into the validity of the polygraph before deciding on a starting date for the second phase. The police, too, have shown some interest, just as some senior officers have put remarkable faith in investigation by hypnosis.

These developments are worrying. While the use of mechanical tests to detect lies gathers general credence, the stream of scientific evidence confirming their unreliability continues unabated. With hypnosis the dangers of unreliability are said to come from inaccuracy of recollection, confabulation (filling in gaps in the memory by making up details – and doing so convincingly), repetition of confabulation in the waking state, cueing (vulnerability to suggestion), and misplaced memory (see Thornton, 1984). With the polygraph there is evidence to suggest that the test fails to detect one in every four guilty people and wrongly accuses nearly half of those telling the truth. For the lay person concerned with the rights of individuals exposed to voluntary or compulsory lie-detector tests, this is indeed worrying.

The evidence against the polygraph is not insubstantial. Irving and Hilgendorf's (1981) work for the Royal Commission on Criminal Procedure concluded that 'the lack of theoretical base to the procedure makes testing its validity and reliability a scientific nightmare'. The House of Commons Employment Committee's investigation (1984–5) into the polygraph was concerned at the 'low level of accuracy' of the polygraph. American academics Barland and Raskin (1976), both supporters of the polygraph, found that, in a laboratory situation, only 53 percent of the test readings were correct, 35 percent were inconclusive and 12 percent incorrect. President Reagan has always favoured expanding the federal use of the polygraph test, despite the conclusion of the US Office of Technology Assessment in 1983 that there was no scientific evidence to support the validity of the type of test used in employment screening. Lykken, a contributor to this book and a passionate opponent of the polygraph, has deplored the American experience as 'twentieth-century witchcraft' (Lykken, 1983). A reassessment in 1986 by medical scientists in Boston, Chicago and Washington of previously published evidence for the sensitivity and specificity of the polygraph found that in some circumstances truthful persons diagnosed as liars will outnumber actual liars by a wide margin. They concluded that the implications of their findings were 'disturbing' (reported in *The Times*, 11 March 1986).

It is not difficult to conclude that the polygraph may well be an unreliable creature. The polygraph test records the heart rate, blood pressure, respiration rate and skin response of the subject. The questioning comprises key questions and control questions. But the test is based on an unproven assumption that the act of telling a lie is accompanied by a specific and reproducible set of physiological responses. And if the test itself may produce inaccurate results even under ideal conditions, a number of claims have been made that the test can be easily beaten anyway. If true, the polygraph is a dangerously unreliable creature. Foreign agents trained to beat the test would become more protected from exposure than before.

Sir Maurice Oldfield, head of the British intelligence service MI6 from 1972 to 1978, is said to have taken a lie-detector test after the Burgess and MacLean spy scandal, and to have remarked afterwards: 'However heterosexual we may be, we bachelors today are always suspected of being homosexual just because we aren't married. Maybe they will now agree I have no such problems' (*Guardian*, 24 April 1987). On 23 April 1987 Mrs Margaret Thatcher announced to a surprised House of Commons that Sir Maurice, who died in 1981, had in fact engaged in homosexual activity which had been considered in 1980 to be 'a potential risk to security', so much so that his positive vetting clearance had been withdrawn.

It is said that the use of drugs or the technique known as biofeedback or even simply clenching your toes can defeat the polygraph. Other known counter-measures include recognizing the control questions and augmenting the response to these questions so that they are stronger than the natural responses to the key questions (see Chapter 10 in this volume by Gudjonsson). Lykken believes that sophisticated liars can defeat the test with ease. Merlyn Rees, a former Home Secretary, told the House of Commons during a debate on a ten-minute rule bill that he had heard that you could beat the polygraph by holding a pen in the palm of your hand and focusing thoughts on sex. 'That leads me to observe,' he added, 'that, if an antidote is not provided, some newspaper editors will be immune for life' (*Hansard*, 28 March 1984).

No wonder then that – the security experiment apart (this is discussed elsewhere in this book) – the polygraph is not officially welcome in this country. The courts refuse to admit any evidence resulting from the administration of a mechanically or chemically or hypnotically induced test on a witness which is designed to show the veracity or otherwise of that witness (see, for example *Fennell v. Jerome Property Maintenance Ltd* [*The Times*, 20 November 1986], a civil case in which the judge ruled that as a matter of principle there was something inherently wrong in admitting evidence which could distort the normal process of trial by usurping the function of the judge in deciding who was telling the truth). Similarly the Home Office in 1984 refused Vincent Hickey's request to take a polygraph test on the ground that it would not consider the results as a possible reason for taking any action to review his conviction in the Carl Bridgewater case. (Vincent Hickey was one of three men convicted of killing a thirteen-year-old boy, Carl Bridgewater, who was delivering a newspaper to a farmhouse when he interrupted a robbery. Four weeks after the convictions another murder took place, at the farm next door. All three accused have vigorously protested their innocence and serious doubts have been cast on the convictions. Foot [1986] makes a plea for the case to be reopened.)

Civil liberty implications

Personal information
What then are the civil liberty implications for a lie-detector test which is less than reliable and which may easily be beaten? First, the recording, storing and use of unreliable information about individuals is quite simply unfair. The use of the polygraph becomes just one more source of potentially irrelevant, inaccurate, unsubstantiated or out-of-date 'information' which could affect employment prospects or employment improvement and to which the individual normally has no right of access, no right to put the record straight and no remedy in law.

Invasion of privacy
Secondly, the polygraph is capable of becoming an unwarranted intrusion into matters private and personal to the individual. The House of Commons Employment Committee expressed great concern at intrusive questioning. In the USA lie-detector experience has led to claims that unemployed workers seeking jobs have been tested on union sympathies and sexual preferences. In some states rape victims are required to submit to polygraph testing. And in the security industry full lifestyle examinations have taken place. The Central Intelligence Agency is said to probe into areas such as criminality, homosexuality, drug-taking and financial affairs. Lord Bridge's report on the Prime case had strong words to say about this.

> Full lifestyle examinations would certainly be regarded in this country, even more strongly than in the United States, as an unwarranted invasion of personal privacy. They would operate as a powerful and, in our judgement, unacceptable disincentive to recruitment. We think they clearly have no place in a pilot scheme. (HMSO, 1983: 33)

Regrettably these sentiments were not echoed by the Government in its acceptance of the report and its introduction of a pilot scheme of security screening in the intelligence and security agencies.

Bias against the innocent

Thirdly, in the criminal process the polygraph could be a dangerous tool against the innocent. Lykken claims that polygraph tests are actually biased *against* the innocent and conscientious person. This device must therefore play no part in the administration of justice. The innocent defendant would be at risk in three ways: from false evidence supplied by prosecution witnesses and supported by inaccurate polygraph test findings, from false confessions induced by the irrational fear of the threat of polygraph testing, and from being falsely classified as 'deceptive' after taking the test.

In 1978 Floyd Fay was convicted in Ohio, USA, of a crime of aggravated murder he had not committed. Because the evidence against him was so thin – the dying victim had said that the masked robber 'looked like' Fay, but the police could find no other evidence against Fay – the prosecution had offered him a deal. If he passed a lie-detector test they would offer no evidence and set him free. If he failed the test the results would be put before a jury. He failed two tests and was subsequently convicted. Two years later the real killers were caught. They confessed (without the use of polygraphs) and exonerated Fay, who was released from prison. Two of the tests which Fay failed were, according to Lykken, typical examples of tests claimed by the polygraph industry to be accurate at least 95 percent of the time (Lykken, 1984b).

But Floyd Fay had not been idle in prison. His experience of polygraphs was put to use. He tested the counter-measure theory that if control questions could be identified and interfered with by increasing the responses, normal responses to the key questions would produce false results. It seemed to work. The prison, the London Correctional Facility in Ohio, invariably used polygraph tests in the investigation and adjudication of charges of breaches of prison discipline. Fay coached twenty-seven inmates who had confessed to him that they were guilty. Twenty-three of them beat the lie detector.

These three consequences of the use of polygraph tests – the use of unreliable information, the invasion of privacy and the bias against the innocent – may produce loss of job, of status, of prospects, even wrongful conviction. It may remove the loyal from positions of trust and protect the disloyal from exposure. In the United States it also produces much litigation as well as industrial disputes. The Society of Civil and Public Servants in this country has accused the Government and the Security Commission of 'risking a serious breakdown in industrial relations at Britain's security establishments' in order to appease what they described as 'American blind faith in technological short-cuts to better security' (see Chapter 14 by Ken Jones in this volume).

What then is the answer to the ever-approaching encroachment of the polygraph on the rights of the individual? The short answer is to ban the use of polygraph tests altogether (except for harmless private use, as in courses for psychology students). Nearly half of the American states have statutes in force restricting or prohibiting the use of polygraph screening of employees in the private sector (for example the Polygraph Protection Act of 1981, State of Michigan). However, legislation is not always effective. It is suggested that in some cases, in order to avoid legal sanctions of litigation, polygraphers issue false written reports saying that the subject passed the test or that the test was inconclusive, while verbally informing the employer that the subject was lying, or at least, polygraphically speaking, 'deceptive'. Nor is it any good making polygraph tests voluntary if the refusal to take a test inevitably casts suspicion on an unco-operative subject. The House of Commons Employment Committee reviewed the workings of polygraphs in 1985, and was unimpressed. It recommended that if they were to become established in the private sector, there should be, as a minimum, a strict licensing system for polygraphers, supported by a Code of Practice approved by Parliament. There was also, the Committee said, a powerful case for considering the stronger course of legislation to ban the use of tests in the general employment field. But none of these steps has been taken.

A programme of fair information practice

The longer answer lies in the development of a comprehensive programme of fair information practice, which includes the individual's right to privacy and the protection of personal information (Hewitt, 1977, 1982). The use of the polygraph, if not directly prohibited by legislation, would be narrowly circumscribed by laws of wider application in this field.

Privacy Act

First, the law of breach of confidence, at present uncertain and confusing, should be developed into a Privacy Act. A Privacy Act would protect the individual by law against the collection and use of personal information without consent. It would provide a sanction in damages under the civil law for the individual who suffers distress or financial loss, and a corresponding sanction in the criminal law for obtaining confidential information by deception (as the Law Commission proposed in 1974). It would give the aggrieved individual a remedy in the civil law for unlawful surveillance, and would create a criminal offence of surreptitious surveillance by means of bugging devices (as the Younger Committee proposed in 1972).

A warning note rings out from the private company Polygraph Security Services in their passing reference to the ethical questions raised by the polygraph: 'Of course, an individual's right to privacy must be guarded and respected but the need for society to protect its business, its job security, its hard earned wages and its health, safety and welfare must be equally sacred' (see Judge, 1984: 20). The Data Protection Act has gone some way to protecting computer records and giving individuals access to information held about them, but it is hedged about with restrictions and limitations (Cornwell and Staunton, 1985). Manual records, for example, continue to fall outside its scope. The Act does not protect, sufficiently, for example, the transfer of confidential information collected by doctors and social workers to the police or the Inland Revenue, without the knowledge or consent of the patient or client. The Act also fails to establish an efficient system of regulation and enforcement. There are limited rights of access to credit information in the 1974 Consumer Credit Act. And the 1985 Interception of Communications Act makes up some ground towards the control of telephone tapping. But these changes in the law are token protection for the individual compared with the solid statutory protection which some other countries provide.

Freedom of Information Act
Secondly, a Freedom of Information Act should be introduced, placing a duty on government departments and agencies to disclose documents in their possession. With certain narrowly drawn exceptions, the individual should have the right to see employment records, medical records, school records, and much other collected material – the right to inspect and correct. Vetting of personnel behind their backs, such as the vetting of BBC staff appointments by the security services with a view to blacklisting those with assumed left-wing views, must be seen as backdoor censorship of the media as well as a gross invasion of privacy. Isobel Hilton, a journalist, was barred from a BBC TV post in 1976 on the basis of secret information provided by MI5 which was entirely false. MI5 had confused her membership of an organization with another organization with a similar name. Isobel Hilton had no knowledge of the existence of the file. The National Council for Civil Liberties is assisting Isobel Hilton to take her case against the Government before the European Court of Human Rights.

Repeal of the Official Secrets Act

Thirdly, no programme of fair information practice would be complete without the repeal of the 1911 and 1939 Official Secrets Acts. Although Section 1 provides a maximum sentence of fourteen years for serious breaches of national security – George Blake, the Russian spy, was given forty-two years by virtue of consecutive sentences – it is not limited to spying. It has also been used to convict members of the Committee of 100, a group of anti-nuclear protestors, who held a demonstration at Wethersfield Airfield, a prohibited place. Section 2 of the Act provides for sentences of up to two years for information leaked to the press without security implications. Clive Ponting, a senior Whitehall civil servant, leaked to a Member of Parliament two documents about events in the South Atlantic in the Falklands War which led to the sinking of the Argentinian cruiser the *General Belgrano* in May 1982. In effect, he alleged a political cover-up. Despite the Government's admission that national security was not involved, Ponting was charged and tried at the Old Bailey (Ponting, 1985). He escaped conviction, although after his acquittal the Government introduced a new loyalty code telling civil servants to obey or resign if they were given an instruction they believed to be morally wrong. Sarah Tisdall was not so lucky in the courts; her conscience brought her six months' imprisonment. A clerk in the private office of the Foreign Secretary, she sent copies of Ministry of Defence minutes on the arrangements for the arrival of US cruise missiles at the RAF base at Greenham Common to the *Guardian* newspaper. She pleaded guilty at the Old Bailey to a Section 2 (of the 1911 Act) offence.

The Official Secrets Act should be repealed and replaced in part only by criminal sanctions restricted principally to properly classified material in the realms of security, defence and foreign affairs (Dorsen, 1984). Civil servants should be allowed to appeal to a higher authority when their conscience prevents obedience to instructions which they consider immoral or unlawful.

Conclusions

It is, therefore, time to set back the progress of the polygraph. But it is also time to press forward with a radical programme of legislative reform. Unfortunately legislative programmes are not often directed at promoting the rights of individuals. The Public Order Act 1986, for example, creates more than twenty-five new criminal offences, but nowhere creates a right of assembly or a right to protest peaceably in public. Bold steps must be taken (Thornton, 1987).

The polygraph may be more a symptom of the denial of rights than the disease itself. But the obsession for absolute truth, or in security matters for absolute loyalty, should not hide the weaknesses of the polygraph and its capacity for misuse. In *Don Juan* Byron said, 'And, after all, what is a lie? 'Tis but the truth in masquerade.' The polygraph needs unmasking. If it is true that the idea originated from a tract published by Daniel Defoe in 1730 entitled *An Effectual Scheme for the Immediate Prevention of Street Robberies and Suppressing All Other Disorders of the Night*, this country might be the right place to bring about its demise (Lykken, 1984b).

Note

I would like to thank Sarah Spencer and Marie Staunton of the National Council for Civil Liberties and Sue Dalal for their helpful comments on the manuscript.

13

American individual rights and an abusive technology: the torts of polygraphing

Edgar A. Jones Jr

Throughout American history, constitutional and common law theories protective of the autonomous rights of persons have reflected the philosophical view of women and men as individuals whose integrity and dignity must be respected, regardless of social status. Practices have of course, in the human way, always fallen short of the ideal. But that fundamental acceptance has served as the premise for the judicially established duty of all in the community to refrain from unwarranted personal intrusions and of government to support and protect those interests and, assuredly, not itself to jeopardize or invade them. This commitment has often been expressed in judicial decisions in criminal proceedings that have been protective of the rights of persons suspected or accused of crime, as well as in civil litigation protective of various rights of personality or property.

The basic philosophy was given its classic expression by Justice Louis D. Brandeis in 1928:

> The makers of our Constitution . . . recognized the significance of man's spiritual nature, of his feelings and of his intellect. They knew that only a part of the pain, pleasure and satisfactions of life are to be found in material things. They sought to protect Americans in their beliefs, their thoughts, their emotions and their sensations. They conferred, as against the government, the right to be let alone – the most comprehensive of rights and the right most valued by civilized man. (*Olmstead v. United States*, 1928, Brandeis, J., dissenting: 478)

In scientific contemplation, the theory of polygraphing is remarkably simplistic. But the social costs have been extensive and complex. They have involved harmful intrusions upon the rights of uncounted thousands of persons among the several millions who have been subjected to it. The practices of polygraphers and the inadequacy of the technology have resulted in economic and psychic harm that has resulted, because of adverse actions undertaken by law enforcement officials or employers, either in reliance upon reports of deception by polygraphers whom they have hired to ferret out wrongdoers, or in reaction to refusals to submit to polygraphing.

Legal processes thus far have only sporadically protected innocent persons suspected or charged with wrongdoing from false accusations of guilt by polygraphers and consequent unwarranted terminations by employers or verdicts of guilt by courts. This legal default is becoming increasingly manifest due to the sheer numbers of those being subjected to suspicious testing by their employers. In our society, when the recognition of such a situation occurs, the time is at hand for legal accountability.

It is quite common for polygraphers to make affirmative representations about the process to suspects (and on occasion to employers), about its validity and infallibility. Yet such statements, once possible neither of confirmation nor of denial for lack of valid data, have now been disclosed in published studies to be demonstrably false in fact, as several contributions to this book attest. Must not the polygrapher today be taken to be knowledgeable of that, or at least of the evidence leading to such a conclusion? Surely he must also be presumed to possess a reasonably prudent practitioner's knowledge, acquired in keeping up to date with the state of his art, of the inadmissibility of polygraph proof in practically all courts, and of the widespread publicity that has swirled around polygraphing in the course of the growing validity controversy? It is a serious matter to withhold information of such relevance and critical import from an innocent person who is in the process of deciding whether to submit to polygraphing in order to be cleared of suspicion. But, worst of all, polygraphers are taught routinely to make knowingly deceptive statements – lies – to suspects about to be polygraphed, in order to create in their minds the belief that the process will infallibly accuse them if they are liars and clear them if they tell the truth. They are even taught to use rigged card tricks to induce that false belief in the suspect. They justify the telling of those lies on the ground that they are unmasking liars guilty of wrongdoing. But public policy surely should not ratify the calculated use of deception in order to entrap deception.

The circumstances are recurrent, and they form a pattern of typical conduct which summons a wide range of theories exposing to liability the polygraphers, those who commission them, and the polygraph manufacturers. Because concepts of law are situation-specific, the existence and extent of that exposure is always dependent upon the circumstances involved in particular cases.

This chapter is not intended to be an exhaustive legal survey of American court decisions on polygraphing. It should, however, enable a realistic appraisal of the current state of the art of polygraphing, and the conduct of its practitioners, as seen through a legally focused lens. It is primarily aimed at alerting the reader to the emergence of a significant new phase in the history of polygraphing that has not yet been generally recognized. It is one in which the courts foreseeably will (and assuredly should) experience a rapidly growing incidence of federal and state litigation by middle-class American workers against employers and their polygraphers for harm suffered as a consequence of polygraphing. Anglo-American common law has thus brought into effect its incremental social reforms without great fanfare, but inexorably. Several harbinger cases will serve our purposes here.

The legal armoury

The legal problems that radiate from the nature and practices of polygraphing are the result of the coincidence of several factors: (1) the uncontested incapacity of the machine to produce objective judgements about deception; (2) the consequent technological necessity to rely upon subjective human intelligence to make those judgements; (3) the designation by an employer or a law enforcement official of a polygrapher to make that judgement; (4) the propensity of polygraphers, entrapped in a simplistic technology, to make a significant proportion of assertively accurate but factually erroneous accusations of deception; and (5) the widening concern for the plight of innocent people who nonetheless continue in criminal and civil proceedings to be induced or compelled to choose between submitting to polygraphing or endangering their liberty or livelihood.

The wide range of concepts of liability ('causes of action') that are responsive to those circumstances do not pose theoretical difficulties in their application to polygraphing. One might infer that the curious dearth of cases in the past is due in part to the skimpy economics of blue-collar litigation that has discouraged contingent-fee lawyers, and partly to a lack of recognition of the extensiveness of the legal armoury available in cases of the infliction of harm by polygraphing. If utilized, they would be amply protective of the civil liberties of persons who have been harmed as a result of polygraphing. For much of what polygraphers routinely do in their practice, these causes of action would impose liability on them and, since they act as agents in legal contemplation, on the persons or institutions that commission their tests – their principals – as well as, to a certain extent, on the manufacturers and distributors of the equipment utilized.

However conceptual or ambiguous they may appear in their formulation, it is essential to bear in mind that rationales of legal liability are situation-specific, responsive to the immediate circumstances in which harm has been experienced. The practices and technology of polygraphing suggest several lines of inquiry.

How have the legal rationales of liability been applied at the behest of plaintiffs who have been injured by having submitted to being polygraphed? Without attempting to engage in a complete survey of the causes of action consequent upon polygraphing, it will suffice to give some of the more crucial highlights as follows.

Battery

According to classic tort law, in order to be liable for battery the defendant must have done some intentional act which must cause, and be intended to cause, an unpermitted contact that has been harmful or offensive (Prosser, 1966: 39–42).

Polygraphing unavoidably involves physical contacts with the body of the person who is being tested. The process puts the polygrapher in direct manipulative contact with the body of the suspected person ('subject' is the euphemism used by polygraphers to refer to the suspect). A rubber tube is strapped across the chest, a pressure band is placed around an arm, and electrodes are attached to the hands. Without the consent of that person, this assuredly would constitute the tort of battery for which compensatory and punitive damages may be recoverable. If the suspect is involuntarily submitting to the test, the additional tort of false imprisonment is implicated because she is obviously restrained both by the apparatus and by her perception of the compulsion of the situation.

However congenial may have been the nature of the prior relational situation, the suggestion or requirement of polygraphing on suspicion of wrongdoing drastically alters its psychology. It becomes an adversarial relationship which, without doubt, would be highly offensive to any normal person who is innocent of wrongdoing, experiencing considerable embarrassment and humiliation at being enmeshed in this unpleasant situation. This perception may well be more acutely sensed by a woman than by a man since the process of strapping on the apparatus is typically done by a male polygrapher in the course of which the actuality of physical contact is clearly more fraught with the possibility of causing the apprehension or the reality of sexually motivated contact. That can be a legal hazard as much for a righteous as for a licentious polygrapher.

Thus in a recent New York case an employer was held liable in damages for sexual harassment due to the misconduct of a polygrapher who asked 'highly personal questions' and made 'considerable physical contact' with several women whom he was polygraphing for their employer under a contract to test job applicants and current employees. Imposing liability on the employer as well as the polygrapher, the court rejected the employer's defence that it was not responsible for what happened. The court held that the polygrapher was the employer's 'agent', not merely an 'independent contractor'. For the polygrapher's misconduct the employer was held liable under the doctrine of *respondeat superior*. In addition to monetary damages for the woman, the court ordered the employer not to conduct further tests of women unless a female observer was present throughout and would do the attaching of the apparatus to the woman being tested (*People v. Hamilton*, 1985). Interestingly, aside from the merits of that case, polygraphers apparently may direct sexually inquisitive questions at women to be used as control questions which would foreseeably elicit sharp emotional reactions that might then be recorded on the charts to be compared with the recorded reactions to the graphed 'did you do it' relevant questions.

If a suspected employee or a criminal suspect is coerced, or her consent is fraudulently induced to submit to being tested, then the contacts with that person's body are 'unpermitted' in legal contemplation. That is because of lack of actual or 'informed' consent. No physically measurable harm is required for that cause of action to lie against the polygrapher. The experience of personal indignity that is involved is sufficient. The criterion is whether this would be offensive to an ordinary person who is not unduly sensitive about personal dignity. The tortious intent required to be established on the part of the polygrapher is only the intent to bring about the physical contact. Liability will then depend upon whether the potential plaintiff has consented to the physical contact or there is some reason that should function as a legal privilege to excuse from liability the person who has made the unpermitted contact.

In these circumstances, the best defence available to the polygrapher who is acting according to routine practice is that the suspect had consented to submit to the test. In general, the consent of a person against whom an otherwise actionable invasion is inflicted must be 'effective' in order to avoid liability for battery. The polygrapher will normally be able to produce a signed release, ostensibly recording that person's consent, as well as the express waiving of any cause of action against himself and whomever has commissioned the polygraphing. Although consent ordinarily bars recovery for intentional interferences with person or property, there are several conditions which, if they exist, will render that apparent consent nugatory and no defence.

First, if the conduct to which consent is given is violative of some public policy of substantial import, the consent will be held to be void. One cannot be held to have lawfully consented to engage in an act that is unlawful or, even if not expressly so, contravenes some public policy of consequence. Such a void 'consent' is therefore no defence against an action by that person for having been injured by the defendant's having done what would otherwise have been deemed to have been authorized by that person. In some state jurisdictions (Pennsylvania, for example) polygraphing is held to be contrary to public policy. In such a jurisdiction the question would arise whether the consent to submit to the test would be held to be void and no bar to the recovery of consequential damages.

Second, the willingness to be polygraphed may exist only because the suspect realistically feels threatened with adverse consequences that might otherwise ensue. It has been convincingly argued that submission to polygraphing is not voluntary if the subject is motivated by the desire to avoid being harmed by those who administer it. Realistically,

> there are very few situations in which a person with nothing to hide is likely to volunteer freely for a lie-detector test known to carry a risk. A rational person will not place herself at risk unless she has reason to fear what others may do to her, or refuse to do for her, if she does not submit to it. What counts in determining whether an act is voluntary is a person's baseline situation, the courses of events that would be normal or expected if no such opportunity were presented. One who agrees to take the test only because she believes that she will be worse off if she declines is not a volunteer, whether or not there is truly a risk. (Simon, 1983: 10)

Third, the written consent by one who is uninformed of the specific risk to innocent persons that is involved will not shield the polygrapher from liability for battery in either of two situations. In the one, he will incur liability if he knew or should have known of her mistaken or ignorant confidence in the accuracy of the test process, yet failed to disclose to her the serious controversy in which scientists are challenging the validity of polygraphing because of the risk to innocent persons of being erroneously accused of wrongdoing. The validity controversy itself is a common topic of discussion among polygraphers, as is evident in any current issue of the American Polygraph Association's newsletter. Reinforcing the presumptive awareness of the seriousness of that controversy is the further fact of which all polygraphers are presumptively aware. That is the fact that practically all federal and state courts continue to refuse to admit in evidence the results of the tests because of the lack of scientific validation. If the polygrapher's jurisdiction happens to be one of them, should he not be obligated to disclose that negative aspect of public policy to her as part of his duty to outline, to inform her, of the risk to which she will expose herself should she decide to agree to take the test?

In the second situation of his exposure to liability for failing to inform the prospective subject of the risk of being tested, he will incur liability in battery if he has induced her mistaken confidence in the accuracy of the process by representations which he knew, or should have known, were false. What could be more common among polygraphers than the practice in pretest interviews of asserting, in one form of words or another, the substantial infallibility of the test? It is well known among polygraphers that persons will frequently volunteer to be polygraphed 'to clear myself', only thereafter to learn from sad and costly experience of the problem of accuracy (Jones, 1981).

Misrepresentation

The torts of misrepresentation may result from conduct that is intentional or unintentional. In its intentional mode it is often referred to as the action of deceit; when it is unintentional it is called negligent misrepresentation. There are two principal factual predicates in polygraph situations, both of which are comparable to those that are involved in the causes of action in battery. One is the failure to disclose relevant and material information to someone whose consent is thereby improperly secured to submit to the procedure and who thereafter experiences consequential harm. The other situation involves false inducements. They arise when a polygrapher has made representations that are false in fact in order to induce someone to submit to being tested, or to disclose actions or thoughts which are of an intimately private nature. One example: 'You can't beat it if you're guilty, but if you're innocent, it's your best friend.'

Dean William Prosser has described intentional and negligent misrepresentations thus:

> The intent involved is intent to mislead, to deceive; and it requires something in the way of knowledge or belief that what is misrepresented is in fact false . . . The negligence involved is a failure to exercise reasonable care to make sure that the representation is true, even where the defendant honestly believes it to be true. (Prosser, 1966: 233)

Of the action of deceit, all American 'courts have extended it to include representations made by one who is conscious that he has no sufficient basis of information to justify them' (Keeton et al., 1984: 742). In the light of the extensively reported controversy about the validity of polygraphing, with repeated references to the plight of innocent suspects, it might be somewhat difficult for a polygrapher on cross-examination to sustain the appearance of ignorance.

> A defendant who asserts a fact as of his own knowledge or so positively as to imply that he has knowledge, under circumstances where he is aware that he will be so understood, when he knows that he does not know whether what he says is true, is found to have the intent to deceive, not so much as to the fact itself, but rather as the extent of his information. (Prosser, 1966)

That last is essentially a factual description of the typical polygrapher talking to the typical suspect about the infallibility of the machine. A federal court described a similar scene in the course of granting a writ of habeas corpus to a 30-year-old 'relator' who had confessed to murder at the age of fifteen after eight days of isolated interrogation, including several hours and several sessions of polygraphing by a well-known polygrapher, Richard Arthur. Wrote the court:

> Arthur admonished relator that the lie detector was capable of catching him in a lie ... Polygraph examiner Arthur was as much a part of the interrogation process as were the detectives ... The effect of the lie detector as an instrument of coercion was enhanced by Arthur's warning to relator that it would uncover a falsehood. Since the unreliability of lie detectors as a means of discovering the truth is a matter of wide judicial recognition, the examiner's warning amounted to a misrepresentation of scientific fact. Though not tantamount to trickery, the misrepresentation under the circumstances was improper and a factor to be considered in connection with Due Process standards. (*United States ex rel. Monks v. Warden*, 1972: 32, 34)

As one polygraph textbook advises, to the statement: 'I hear these "machines" can be beat,' the answer is 'There is no way you can "beat" the polygraph instrument unless you take a hammer to it.' If a suspect says, 'Suppose I tell the truth and the machine says I'm lying?', the answer is, 'It will never happen. Contrary to popular belief, the polygraph instrument does not say lie, does not say truth ... Neither can it put out lie recordings to truthful answers. Anyone who tries to convince you otherwise can be little more than a plain kook ... Misinterpretation by the examiner is rare because of the numerous counter-measure techniques at his disposal. When it does occur in preemployment, it is usually calling a deceptive person truthful' (Ferguson and Gugas, 24–6). In turn, Reid and Inbau counsel their readers to tell the suspect during the pretest interview 'something like the following: "You know, of course, that we're checking on (this thing). If you did this thing, I'm going to know about it as soon as this examination is over"' (Reid and Inbau, 1977: 17).

How could these authors or their readers possibly know if those assertions of infallibility are true or false? Yet they unhesitatingly state it as fact. To the contrary, the scientific evidence drawn from field studies is steadily confirming quite the opposite as it graphically discloses the serious record of false accusations of innocent suspects. What the polygrapher in the field realizes very well is that the suspect to whom he is spinning that yarn will normally believe him without question when he tells her that his 'machine is infallible and knows the truth just like God and you' (*People v. Leonard*, 1977: 15).

Polygraphers are well aware of that gullibility. Cynically or naively, as the case may be, polygraphers use lies to try to catch liars. They do so at the risk, indeed, of the cost of falsely accusing innocent suspects. As Sisela Bok observed in her study of moral choice in public and private life, 'If the choice is one of importance for others, or if, even though it seems trivial in itself, it forms part of a practice of deceit, then greater accountability should be required' (Bok, 1978: 105).

An actionable misrepresentation need not be intentional. It 'may be an entirely honest one, but may be negligently made, because of lack of reasonable care in ascertaining the truth, or carelessness in the manner of expression, or want of the skill and competence required by a particular business or profession' (Prosser, 1966: 234). That encompasses the situation of the polygrapher who may be truly ignorant of the state of the art and wholly unaware of the hazard to innocent persons or of the significance of the fact that the courts of his jurisdiction will not admit polygraph evidence because it is viewed to be scientifically unreliable.

In the nature of the polygraphing situation, there is a special relationship of dependency and dominance created by the very circumstances. The suspect, anxious or not, must be attentive to the will of the polygrapher; her clearance is wholly dependent upon him. The employer or some law enforcement official has committed her to his power and dominance, itself an impressive ratification of the process. In addition to all that, it is routine practice for the polygrapher to encourage, even induce, the suspect's trust in the power of the process.

In these circumstances it would be reasonable to expect the usual suspect to rely on what is being said by the polygrapher about the validity of the process. The courts do not hesitate to impose a duty to exercise reasonable care to avoid harming that reliant person. That duty will be breached should there be a failure to exercise reasonable care to avoid misrepresenting the state of the art. At the least, that requires exerting reasonable efforts to keep informed of the facts – for example, the risk to innocent suspects of false accusations – or in disclosing known facts (Keeton et al., 1984: 745).

'Wrongful' or regulatory discharge

In the United States thousands of unpublished decisions are made annually – as many as 30,000 – by labour arbitrators interpreting the negotiated 'just cause' collective-bargaining agreement standard for employer discipline. A decision by an arbitrator, jointly selected by the employer and the union representing the employees, may result in reinstatement with or without retroactive pay if the decision is that the employee was not discharged for just cause. But unlike the courts, no further damages are normally recoverable in arbitration. (On the other hand, unlike arbitration, courts rarely order an employee reinstated who is found to have been wrongfully dismissed, damages being the judicial remedy.) Most arbitrators who have encountered the polygraph issue have reinstated employees with back pay who have been discharged either for refusing to be polygraphed or on the basis of adverse findings by polygraphers (Jones, 1978). About 15 percent of American workers are covered by collective bargaining agreements, the rest being legally regardable as 'at will' employees who for decades have had no recourse at common law when they have been discharged for any reason or no reason at all.

In recent years, however, American courts have been developing a hybrid cause of action that has directly affected polygraphing (*Tameny v. Atlantic Richfield Co.*, 1980). It melds tort and contract principles to impose liability on employers for the 'wrongful' or 'retaliatory' discharge of 'at will' employees in violation of some public policy protective of the employee. In states where the legislatures have declared that public policy restricts or prohibits polygraphing, actions may be expected to succeed. In Pennsylvania, for example, a state statute made it a misdemeanour to require 'as a condition for employment or continuation of employment that an employee or other individual shall take a polygraph test or any form of a mechanical or electrical lie detector test'. The federal court of appeals, reversing the lower court, declared that 'the discharge of an employee at will because of a refusal to submit to a polygraph examination required by an employer gives rise to a cause of action for tortious discharge under Pennsylvania law'. The plaintiff Perks had been terminated when he refused to undergo a polygraph test after coming under suspicion of wrongdoing because of a supplier's accusation of having accepted his gift of a prostitute's services. The court relied upon the New Jersey Supreme Court's analysis of a like statute. That court had stated:

> There is no judicial control when an employer subjects his employee to a lie detector test and there is no licensing or other objective method of assuring expertise and safeguard in the administration of the test and the interpretation of its results. Nor is there any assurance of true voluntariness for the economic compulsions are generally such that the employee has no realistic choice. Organized labour groups have often expressed intense hostility to employer requirements that employees submit to polygraph tests which they view as improper invasions of their deeply felt rights to personal privacy and to remain free from involuntary self-incrimination. (*State v. Community Distributors Inc.*, 1974: 699)

The court of appeals accordingly concluded that there was a valid cause of action and sent the case back to be tried on its merits (*Perks v. Firestone Tire & Rubber Co.*, 1979).

Firestone Tire was involved in another polygraphing matter which seems to typify how these cases occur and the pressures that are created. An audit turned up a shortage of seventy tyres at a retail outlet in 1977. The store manager decided to polygraph all seven employees. On the way to the motel room where it was to be done, the manager told the seven, 'Don't worry about the chicken shit stuff. All we're worried about is the tyre thief.' He knew and had condoned the taking of occasional cans of wax or oil for the immediate personal use of the employees. At the outset of the session the polygrapher handed out the routine consent forms which each employee signed. During the session, however, in addition to the tyre-specific relevant questions, each was asked if he or she had taken anything, and if so was it oil, or wax, or whatever. The test did not determine anyone to be deceptive; the tyre thief was not disclosed. But during each post-test interview, the polygrapher asked, 'If you inherited a million dollars, how much would you give back to the store to cover the wax and oil and stuff that you've taken?' Each employee answered the question, the answers ranging from $1.00 to $100.00. All seven were dismissed for admitted thefts.

Complaints to their union resulted in offers of $350 for a release of liability and no reinstatement. Six signed, took the $350 and left. The seventh was angry and got a young lawyer. He filed a lawsuit in which he had counts for tort for wrongful discharge, defamation, intentional infliction of mental distress, and asked for punitive as well as compensatory damages. He arranged for David Lykken to come to Pittsburgh to testify as an expert witness about the polygraph. Very shortly before the trial date in 1979, the employer settled, paying $80,000.

Finally, in this little trilogy of Pennsylvania cases is Bonnie Polsky's. It illustrates how the typical encounter goes with a nervous employee and her polygrapher; but also what the litigational realities often turn out to be.

After Bonnie Polsky had worked for just over a year at Radio Shack, a multi-state marketer of electronic equipment, she was promoted to be manager of a Philadelphia area store staffed by herself and two other employees. One morning she opened the store and discovered that about $1,500 worth of merchandise had been stolen. Because there was no evidence of forced entry, her employer surmised that the theft had been an 'inside job'. So her boss, the district manager, decided that all three employees would be polygraphed.

Bonnie's account of what happened was that, when he informed her of the decision, she said, 'I don't want to take the polygraph, but if I have to do it to keep my job, I will take the polygraph.' He said, 'You have to take the polygraph.' She said, 'If I have to, I have to.' He said, 'You have to.' She did.

The polygrapher's conclusion that she had been deceptive was reported to her employer and she was terminated. She brought an action against Radio Shack on the claim that her discharge was unlawful because it was based on the results of a polygraph test obtained in violation of Pennsylvania's statute prohibiting an employer requiring an employee to submit to polygraphing 'as a condition for employment or continuation of employment'.

On Radio Shack's motion for summary judgment, the district court dismissed the action. The court held that '[w]here, as here, the release signed by plaintiff advised her of her rights under [the polygraph statute], and she was not compelled physically to sign, she may not later renounce the statement contained in the release and contend she was compelled to sign it in order to preserve her job'. The appellate court reversed, concluding that her evidence demonstrated a genuine issue as to whether she had been required to sign the release as a condition of continued employment (*Polsky v. Radio Shack*, 1981: 825).

On a motion for summary judgment, her pre-trial description of what had occurred is assumed to be true in determining if such facts would support a cause of action for damages. As she described it, her encounter with the polygrapher was perfunctory.

> He sat me down and said, 'We can get underway as soon as you put your name there, and you put your name there,' where he had already checked ... He made it perfectly clear to sign and let's get underway, because he said, 'You are here on a very serious charge.' He made me quite nervous.

She did not respond, nor did she ask for an opportunity to read the long (thirty-eight printed lines) release form that he put before her to sign. That was because

> I felt extremely threatened and harassed and I wanted to get it over with as quickly as possible ... If I didn't sign it, they wouldn't give me my polygraph, which I had to take in order to keep my job ... What I thought it might have was that, you know, he's Mark Hoffman and I am Bonnie Polsky, he is giving me a polygraph test on this date. I thought it was just a formalization of what was happening. I didn't read it, nor did he give me the time to. After signing my name, he went into ten or eleven questions. (*Polsky v. Radio Shack*, 1981: 826–7)

The release recited that under the cited state statute

I may not be required to take a Polygraph (Lie Detector) examination as a condition of my employment or continued employment. With full know-ledge of these rights, and without duress, coercion, force or promise of immunity or reward, I do hereby request a Polygraph examination to be given to me by [the polygraph firm] for the mutual benefit of myself and Radio Shack [handwritten] . . . Intending to be legally bound, I remise, release, waive and forever discharge all and each of the above corpora-tions, firms and individuals from any and all actions or cause of action, claim or demand, liability or legal actions which I have now or may ever have resulting directly or indirectly or remotely both from my taking said examination and the oral and written opinions rendered because of said examination.

The polygrapher directed her to sign at two places on the release before he would proceed, first at the end of the above text, and then below some further text on the same page that read:

Having submitted myself freely to this examination, I hereby re-affirm my agreement as expressed above. I swear that during said examination, I was well treated and remained of my own free will, knowing I could leave at any time I so desired. I also swear and certify that there were no threats or harm done to me or any promises made to me during the entire time I have been here, either in connection with the examination or the signing of this form.

When she signed the release form did she thereby evidence her consent to be tested? Or was her signing the result of being involun-tarily placed in a situation so imbued with compulsion that it could not truly be said that she had registered her voluntary consent? The evidence of her lack of consent was sufficient in the federal court's view to reverse the lower court's dismissal and send her case to trial to let her claims be assessed on their merits.

Polsky v. Radio Shack (1981) is a good harbinger case because it focuses attention on the critical question of whether it is realistic to assume that an employee's willingness to sign such a release should be credited as evidencing voluntary consent to submit to polygraphing. The appellate court was realistic in accepting the legislature's 'recog-nition of the uniquely vulnerable position in which such an employee is placed. As the New Jersey Supreme Court recognized, "there (is no) assurance of true voluntariness for the economic compulsions are generally such that the employee has no realistic choice" (*State v. Community Distributors Inc.*, 1974: 699).'

The US Supreme Court has identified a protected 'zone of privacy'. In *Whalen v. Roe* (1977: 598), Justice Stevens wrote that

The cases sometimes characterized as protecting 'privacy' have in fact involved at least two different kinds of interests. One is the individual interest in avoiding disclosure of personal matters, and another is the interest in independence in making certain kinds of important decisions.

Anyone familiar with polygraphing will recognize that both of those privacy interests are implicated in polygraphing situations. As to the first, the polygrapher, going by the book, routinely undertakes to probe personal matters, often of the most intimate sort, including sexually explicit sensitive questions. That is done in the effort to frame 'control' questions that will provoke measurably significant symptoms of arousal and thereby enable evaluative comparisons to be made with those reactions registered during the subject's answers to the presumably more arousal-producing guilt-pointing 'relevant' questions. The interest in avoiding disclosure of personal matters is put in direct jeopardy when a job-insecure or jail-fearful subject feels involuntarily compelled to submit to the test in order to avoid either a looming discharge or criminal prosecution, or possibly both.

The second privacy interest identified by Justice Stevens – independence in making 'certain kinds of important decisions' – is also directly implicated in the usual polygraph pretest interview. To the extent that the person either is coerced ('You take this test or you lose your job!') or is duped ('The machine will clear you if you're innocent or it'll nail you if you aren't!'), being polygraphed under either set of circumstances is invasive of the privacy of the person.

Justice Stevens's analysis for the Court in *Whalen v. Roe* (1977) of the dual nature of the constitutional right of privacy should be supportive of an effort by federal employees to enjoin the federal government from implementing a plan to subject them to polygraphing, whether of a 'We're just checking on your honesty' sort, or in some situation-specific investigation. But *Whalen v. Roe* also demonstrates that a given invasion of privacy may still survive challenge if it constitutes a reasonable exercise of the sovereign's police powers. Determining what may be reasonable uses of polygraphing in that context leads inevitably to an inquiry into the technology and practices of polygraphing. Based on an evidentiary demonstration of the flawed technology and the invasive practices of polygraphing, a federal district court will be asked to determine if resort to that process as an exercise of police power is to be deemed 'reasonable' when it demonstrably puts innocent persons disproportionately at risk of their liberty or livelihood. If the court concludes that it is an unreasonable exercise of police power, an injunction barring it would issue.

The Supreme Court of West Virginia had before it in 1984 the discharge of two cleaning maids by a Holiday Inn. They had been required as applicants for employment to sign an agreement that 'unless prohibited under local laws, I will take a polygraph examination prior to, during, or at the termination of my employment'. There was no state polygraph statute. In 1982 the employer notified its employees that it was instituting a tri-monthly polygraph programme with names of those to be tested being drawn 'lottery style'. When their turn came, the plaintiffs refused to be tested and they were dismissed as at-will employees.

The court reviewed the *Perks* and *Community Distributors* decisions 'relating to the protection of areas of an employee's life in which an employer has no legitimate interest', together with its own cases which had emphasized that 'certain areas of an individual's life are entitled to protection from unwarranted intrusion'. So it decided to 'hold that it is contrary to the public policy of West Virginia for an employer to require or request that an employee submit to a polygraph test or similar test as a condition of employment and ... the public policy against such testing is grounded upon the recognition in this State of an individual's interest in privacy' (*Cordle et al. v. General Hugh Mercer Corp.*, 1984: 117).

Intentional infliction of mental distress

Moniodis v. Cook (1985) is an example of the extremity of mental distress required by the courts to be shown by successful plaintiffs in polygraph cases. But the case also graphically demonstrates the severity of the remedial response once a sceptical court becomes convinced of the egregiousness of the employer's conduct and the pathetic results that ensued.

A Maryland appellate court described the plight of Marguerite Cook, a 'middle-aged lady' who was employed by Rite-Aid Stores, a retail chain. Concerned about inventory shortages, it announced that it would require the polygraphing of several employees whose work locale brought them under suspicion, including Mrs Cook, even though she was one who 'took her duties quite seriously', and was known to have 'dedication to her work'. By telling her that it wanted her to be polygraphed, the court concluded, her employer had 'challenged the trustworthiness of Mrs Cook and her value as an employee'.

Along with several others of her fellow employees, she evidently refused to take the test. The employer then had to consider a state statute that provided as follows: 'An employer may not demand or require any applicant for employment or prospective employment or any employee to submit to or take a polygraph, lie detector, or similar test or examination as a condition of employment or continued employment.' An employer who violated that statute would be guilty of a misdemeanour and subject to a fine 'not to exceed $100'. In addition, the state attorney general was authorized to 'prosecute all civil cases arising hereunder' that might be referred by the state Commissioner of Labor. In fact, the attorney general did file a civil action on behalf of Mrs Cook and twenty-one other terminated employees which, we may infer, was settled in due course for some nominal sum; but the court noted that Mrs Cook and three other employees had 'elected not to join in the settlement reached in that case but to continue with this action'. As it turned out, she was well advised, and the employer less so.

Rite-Aid implemented what someone misguidedly must have thought to be a truly Machiavellian plan to cope with such unco-operative employees as Mrs Cook and her peers. Its essence was described by a former manager who testified that he had been 'told, with regard to an employee other than the appellees, "Well, we can't fire her outright but what I want to do is cut her hours back until there is no longer any value for her to work here. She will become frustrated."' It put that plan to work in the case of Mrs Cook by transferring her, reducing her hours of work, taking away her store keys, finally thereby succeeding, as anticipated, in getting her to quit in frustration.

The testimony credited by the jury showed that she became deeply disturbed. Her husband found her at home weeping and wringing her hands. She had had a prior 'nervous condition' which had not interfered with her work; but now her emotional state deteriorated significantly. She took greater amounts of medication, began to sleep most of the time, became a recluse. Her relatives had to come to the house to tend to the household chores. She took pains to avoid contact with her neighbours who might ask her why she no longer worked for Rite-Aid Stores. This went on for at least a year.

The appellate court held that she had been 'constructively discharged' because her employer purposefully created conditions of employment that, as it had inferably calculated, became so intolerable that she, as would a reasonable person in her circumstances, felt compelled to resign. It concluded that the 'jury could properly conclude from this evidence that the appellant's conduct went far beyond the realm of "petty oppressions", and amounted to a complete denial of Mrs Cook's dignity as a person'. The court construed the statutory prohibition of required polygraphing to be a 'a clear mandate of public policy' which, when violated, would support a cause of action for the wrongful discharge of an employee otherwise readily dischargeable as an 'at will' employee. The cost for Rite-Aid: damages for 'intentional infliction of emotional distress' and for 'wrongful discharge' awarded by the jury and affirmed by the appellate court in the sums of $300,000 as compensatory and $1,000,000 as punitive damages.

Moniodis v. Cook (1985) is a good harbinger case because it so effectively dramatizes two less than obvious complementary aspects about the relationship between a run-of-the-shop employee and a much more economically secure employer bent on having his way regardless of the cost to the employee. First, there is the obvious plight of some innocuous person who undoubtedly appears to be among the weakest, most vulnerable and least resistent or threatening to the overreaching will of that employer. But, second, there is the latent strength of reprisal for the infliction of harm that is vested in that employee by those tort concepts which threaten such great cost to the employer who does not give some prudent cost-benefit thought to heeding their teaching. Tort law strikes once again in its quiet and effective manner, performing its historic function of incremental social reform.

Defamation
The kind of exposure to liability for defamation to which employers (and polygraphers in proper circumstances) may be vulnerable in polygraph cases is suggested by a Texas railroad drug case. Involved was an erroneous report of the presence of drugs in a switchman's urine. Wherry, the employee, had fainted while working, cutting his face. He was sent to a physician who ran diabetes and drug screening tests to learn why he had fainted. The lab report indicated a trace of methadone, a synthetic drug used to treat heroin addiction. The doctor informed the company's safety superintendent of the lab results. He stated that he could not say the employee was a user but further investigation might be indicated. None was undertaken. But the superintendent wrote an internal accident report in which he stated that Wherry's urine specimen was positive for methadone. He consulted another physician who performed a test which disclosed that his urine contained a compound similar to but not the same as methadone.

Nonetheless, the company dismissed Wherry and he sought assistance from the Veterans Administration. In due course the company labour relations director responded to a government inquiry with a letter stating that after his fainting his system was found to contain traces of methadone. Under the Railway Labor Act he appealed his discharge. But a Public Law Board (comparable to arbitration) upheld his discharge as for just cause. Wherry then filed suit for defamation against the company, the superintendent and the labour relations director based on the accident report and the letter, both of which were found by a jury to defame Wherry. It awarded him $150,000 in compensatory and $50,000 in punitive damages. On appeal, the verdict was affirmed against the company but reversed as to the individual officials (*Houston Belt & Terminal Railway Co. v. Wherry*, 1977). The outcome suggests that where the report of a polygrapher of 'deception' by an employee leads to a dismissal, and the former employee is later determined by a trier of fact to have been innocent, that employee may therefore be deemed to have been defamed.

That is what happened in *O'Brien v. Papa Gino's of America Inc.*, a 1986 case. By September 1982 John O'Brien had worked over nine years for Papa Gino's, a 'fast food' restaurant chain. He was earning a salary of $37,000 as an area supervisor responsible for twenty-eight stores and 450–550 employees. After a dispute with higher management over his refusal to promote the godson of the company president, he was confronted with allegations of rumours that he had been seen using drugs outside of work. When he denied it, he was told that he would lose his job unless he consented to take a polygraph test to demonstrate his innocence. Fearful of losing his job, he submitted to being tested. During it, he answered questions relating to his alleged drug use. After the test the polygrapher reported to the employer that O'Brien was lying when he denied using drugs. He was discharged on 7 September 1982.

O'Brien filed a lawsuit against his employer (but did not name the polygrapher as a defendant) charging that his was a 'wrongful discharge' in violation of public policy, that being compelled to be polygraphed had invaded his privacy, and that the polygrapher's report that he had lied about drug use, and the employer's discharge of him based on it, had defamed him. The jury in special verdicts concluded that no specific New Hampshire public policy barred O'Brien's discharge based on being compelled to submit to polygraphing; nevertheless the defendant employer's 'actions ... with reference to allegations of drug abuse by plaintiff O'Brien and the methods adopted by the defendant in its investigation of such allegations would be highly offensive to a reasonable person and were invasive of the plaintiff's privacy'. The jury awarded and the appellate court sustained $398,200 as damages for the invasion of privacy and $50,000 on the defamation claim. The jury did so, according to counsel, even though O'Brien admitted on the witness stand both that he had lied during the polygraph examination and he had used drugs.

O'Brien v. Papa Gino's (1986) is a good harbinger case because it exposes the vulnerability of employers and polygraphers (even though the latter was not named in the suit) to liability when an employee, for fear of the loss of his job, will feel compelled to submit to participating with the polygrapher in a discussion of his possible wrongdoing, a blunt and insensitive probing of his conscience – surely the most private of domains – while feeling unhappily constrained to answer invasive questions posited on, at the least, the suspicion if not the expectation of his wrongdoing.

Products liability

The courts for a couple of decades have been evolving rationales of 'products liability' which, regardless of good or bad efforts or intentions, impose liability on those who put products into the marketplace that are functionally injurious to persons. In particular, a manufacturer or other seller is subject to liability for failing to warn about a risk inherent in the way a product is designed and related to the intended and reasonably foreseeable uses that may be made of the product. The two social interests served by the requirements of warnings are risk reduction and protection of individual autonomy in decision-making (Keeton et al., 1984: 685).

In the case of the polygraph, the manufacturers and distributors of these machines that are sold for the 'detection of deception' will find themselves exposed to liability to the extent that someone is injured because of their failure to give adequate warnings about the risk of false accusations against persons innocent of any wrongdoing whose consent to being polygraphed will foreseeably be sought. At the least, manufacturers of polygraph equipment should affix prominently to the equipment – plainly visible to persons about to be polygraphed – and incorporate in their sales and product literature information phrased something like the following: 'This machine cannot detect deception. When properly operated, it will measure and record physiological data. Whether those data may warrant a finding that the person being examined is or is not being deceptive requires a judgement that can only be made by someone who examines the data generated by the proper operation of this machine.'

Civil Rights Act Section 1983

One of the post-Civil War congressional statutes, Section 1983 of the Civil Rights Act of 1871, has in the past decade become an important resource in protecting people against the conduct of state officials and private persons – such as polygraphers – acting in conjunction with them 'under color' of state law that subjects anyone 'to the deprivation of any rights, privileges, or immunities secured by the Constitution and laws'. Section 1988 of the Act provides for attorney's fees for the prevailing party in a Section 1983 suit.

In *Thorne v. City of El Segundo et al.* (1983) Ms Thorne applied for a police officer's position after having worked in the police department as a clerk-typist for several years. In addition to written and oral examinations (she scored second highest), a physical agility test (she passed) and psychological screen testing (she passed), she was required to submit to a polygraph examination as a necessary condition of her employment as a police officer.

Before commencing the examination, the polygrapher gave her forms explaining the procedure and a questionnaire to be filled out before proceeding. One form informed her that she could refuse to answer questions; but another warned that any reluctance to answer personal questions would be interpreted by the examiner as an indication of serious emotional or sexual problems. She reported on the questionnaire that she had been pregnant and had suffered a miscarriage.

During the polygraphing, the court found, the polygrapher had asked for details about this event, including whether she had had an abortion, and who was the father. Although she expressed reluctance to reveal the information, he persisted in questioning her. So she told him that it had been a former officer of the department with whom she had had an affair. When he continued to press her on the subject, however, evidently because the lines on the chart continued to indicate arousal, she finally disclosed that it had been a married officer who was still with the department. She asked him to keep that fact confidential. He also asked a number of other questions about her sexual activities, including when she had first had sex, and with whom, and whether she had had relationships with other members of the department.

Upon completion of the examination, he told her that she might not be able to complete the rigorous programme at the police academy and that she should think carefully before quitting her present job to enter the programme. The polygrapher then gave the police chief a 'confidential report' in which he discussed her affair with the officer and the resultant pregnancy and miscarriage. He also reported his conclusion that she lacked sufficient 'aggressiveness, self-assuredness, or probable physical ability'.

In due course she was notified that her name had been removed from the eligibility list. In addition to a Title VII sex discrimination claim against the city, she filed a Section 1983 action against the polygrapher and two others (the police chief and an investigator) in which she charged that the administration and handling of the polygraph examination and its results had, 'under color' of state law, invaded her constitutionally protected rights of privacy and free association.

Reversing the trial court's dismissal of her Section 1983 claim, the federal court of appeals rejected the polygrapher's argument that he could not be held liable because he was an independent contractor rather than a state employee. Instead, the court concluded that he had been acting under color of state law within the intent of Section 1983 when he administered the examination; he had done so on behalf of the city and was paid by it.

The court found that 'it is impossible to conclude that Thorne's participation in the polygraph examination was anything other than a necessary condition of her employment as a police officer', and that included answering highly invasive questions regarding her sexual association (p. 469). It held that the city had no legal right to require her thus to surrender her privacy in order to be eligible to get the job. 'A potential employee of the state may not be required to forego his or her constitutionally protected rights simply to gain the benefits of state employment.' Her ostensible consent, first to submit to the polygraphing, and then to answer the polygrapher's unduly intrusive questions, was no consent legally because it was improperly obtained. That reasoning led to the question whether what the polygrapher did constituted an unlawful invasion of her privacy violative of Section 1983.

The court held that it did.

> The constitution protects two kinds of privacy interests. 'One is the individual interest in avoiding disclosure of personal matters, and another is the interest in independence in making certain kinds of important decisions.' Both are implicated in this case. Thorne presented evidence that defendants invaded her right to privacy by forcing her to disclose information regarding personal sexual matters. She also showed that they refused to hire her as a police officer based in part on her prior sexual activities, thus interfering with her privacy interest and her freedom of association. (p. 468)

The court sent the case back to the district court to determine the amount of damages recoverable by her in both the Title VII and Section 1983 actions. But it added the cautionary note that

> The court's finding that Thorne had presented no credible evidence of damages is clearly erroneous. At a minimum, she has lost the wages she would have received as a police officer. Thorne also testified that she suffered emotional distress, humiliation, and loss of sleep due to defendants' actions, damages which defendants concede are available under Section 1983. (p. 472)

While *Thorne v. City of El Segundo et al.* (1983), as a Section 1983 case, is applicable only to state governmental officials or persons like polygraphers who act in conjunction with them, it is a harbinger of legal developments in the private sector because it underscores the basic public policy.

Bivens actions
Complementing Section 1983's restraint on wrongdoing by state officials, the Supreme Court has developed similar protections against overreaching federal officials for the violation of constitution-

al rights emanating from the ten amendments of the Bill of Rights. In 1971 the Supreme Court held in *Bivens v. Six Unknown Named Agents* (1971) that an action for damages was impliable as a private remedy for injuries due to a violation of the Fourth Amendment's command against unreasonable searches and seizures. The court has since held that damages could be recovered due to the violation of the Fifth Amendment guarantee of equal protection (*Davis v. Passman*, 1979) and that of the Eighth Amendment against cruel and unusual punishment (*Carlson v. Green*, 1980).

In the Carlson case, beyond just compensating victims, the court emphasized two factors to be particularly supportive of 'the Bivens remedy'. First, 'it is almost axiomatic that the threat of damages has a deterrent effect, surely particularly so when the individual official faces personal financial liability'. Second, it held punitive damages to be available, stating that they 'are especially appropriate to redress the violation by a Government official of a citizen's constitutional rights'. Finally, the court in *Carlson*, noting that a 'state official contemplating illegal activity must always be prepared to face the prospect of a Section 1983 action being filed against him', declared that 'A federal official contemplating unconstitutional conduct similarly must be prepared to face the prospect of a Bivens action.'

Bivens actions have yet to be applied to polygraphing conducted in violation of the Fourth Amendment (unreasonable search and seizure), the Fifth Amendment (self-incrimination; and due process of law) or the Sixth Amendment (displacing the jury's or the court's responsibility for the subjective determination of credibility with that of the polygrapher). But there is no reason to expect that they will not be available in a suitable case. Bivens remedies are expanding rapidly, as one federal court of appeals observed in applying the case to conduct by a federal prosecutor which allegedly had violated the plaintiff's Sixth Amendment right to the effective assistance of counsel (*Briggs v. Goodwin*, 1983).

When it becomes generally recognized how thoroughly and irremediably polygraphing is permeated by the subjective opinions of polygraphers, a Bivens polygrapher case will be just over the horizon of that recognition. Another court of appeals has applied Bivens to sustain a cause of action arising from the First Amendment when a public university professor was allegedly dismissed due to protected expressions of political import (*Peacock v. Duval*, 1983).

Fourth Amendment
The Fourth Amendment protects persons against 'unreasonable

searches and seizures', and directs that 'no Warrants shall issue, but upon probable cause'. Its strictures, applicable to the states through the Fourteenth Amendment, have been applied to the conduct of federal and state governmental officials in various civil activities. It protects our 'interests in human dignity and privacy' from bodily intrusive searches for evidence (*Schmerber v. California*, 1966). The court recently stated that 'Our cases establish that ... Fourth Amendment rights are implicated only if the conduct of ... officials at issue ... infringed "an expectation of privacy that society is prepared to consider reasonable"' (*O'Connor v. Ortega*, 1987). But the court has held that an expectation of privacy is not reasonable where the evidence obtained without a warrant has been open to constant public view (*Cupp v. Murphy*, 1973). Thus the required disclosure of a voice sample was held not violative of the Fourth Amendment (*United States v. Dionisio*, 1973); nor was a handwriting exemplar (*United States v. Mara*, 1973); nor is fingerprinting because it 'involves none of the probing into an individual's private life and thoughts that marks a search' (*Davis v. Mississippi*, 1969). Blood tests, X-rays, hair samples and the like are deemed to constitute searches requiring warrants (Craig, 1984: 906–8).

Would the court be apt to hold that, without a warrant, it constitutes a Fourth Amendment unreasonable search and seizure for there to be – during guilt – significant 'relevant' and 'control' questioning – an involuntary strapping on of the polygraph apparatus to a suspect's body for the taking and recording of changes in the calibrations of breathing, blood pressure, perspiration, heart beat, and whatever additional physically manifested symptoms of anxiety that may yet become technologically extractable and recordable? Suppose, for example, it became economically feasible tomorrow (it being technically possible today) to make concurrent video recordings of a suspect's conduct during the strapped-on questionings, including a close-up filming of the eyes to display changes in pupillary dilations and retinal shiftings about as questions are asked and answered, the whole being subjected to simultaneous computer correlation, enhancement and analysis, complete with an instantaneous screened terminal display for each question and answer of 'DECEPTION!' or 'TRUTHFUL!' In the context of whether a plaintiff so treated by governmental officials (and their agent, the polygrapher) should have a *Bivens* cause of action against them as individuals, in formulating a Fourth Amendment answer to those questions, what should be the decisional significance of the fact that proof of the results of those polygraphings is inadmissible as evidence for the prosecution or the defence in a court of that jurisdiction?

Fifth Amendment

Self-incrimination. Michael Simon has succinctly expressed the essence of why polygraphing violates the Fifth Amendment privilege against self-incrimination:

> Lie-detector tests exist to serve the interests of those who do not have to take them. Like other investigatory procedures, they are applied only to those in the position of having to demonstrate that they do not deserve to be denied something that others have the power to control. They differ from other methods in that they diminish human capacities. The success of the lie-detector technique, like that of coercive measures, depends on causing subjects to lose the ability to control their communication. It is a way of overriding and defeating the will. (Simon, 1983: 10)

Justice Potter Stewart wrote for the court that 'the basic purpose of a trial is the determination of the truth but, by contrast, the Fifth Amendment's privilege against self-incrimination is not an adjunct to the ascertainment of truth. That privilege, like the guarantees of the Fourth Amendment, stands as a protection of quite different constitutional values – values reflecting the concern of our society for the right of each individual to be let alone' (*Tehan v. United States*, 1966: 416).

In *Schmerber v. California* (1966) the court was concerned with the Fifth Amendment significance of the extraction of a blood sample by a physician at the direction of a police officer acting without a warrant and despite the defendant's refusal, on advice of counsel, to consent to the blood withdrawal and testing. The reasoning of the court so directly implicates the uses of polygraphing that it warrants quoting the opinion of Justice Brennan at some length. He wrote 'that the privilege [against self-incrimination] protects an accused only from being compelled to testify against himself, or otherwise provide the State with evidence of a testimonial or communicative nature'. The court accepted the officer's actions as constituting compulsion.

> The critical question, then, is whether petitioner was thus compelled 'to be a witness against himself' . . . In sum, the privilege is fulfilled only when the person is guaranteed the right 'to remain silent unless he chooses to speak in the unfettered exercise of his own will'. The privilege reaches an accused's communications, whatever form they might take . . . [but] it offers no protection against compulsion to submit to fingerprinting, photographing, or measurements, to write or speak, to stand, to assume a stance, to walk or to make a particular gesture. The distinction which has emerged . . . is that the privilege is a bar against compelling 'communications' or 'testimony', but that compulsion which makes a suspect or accused the source of 'real or physical evidence' does not violate it.

The court observed in a significant passage that

> There will be many cases in which such a distinction is not readily drawn. Some tests seemingly directed to obtain 'physical evidence', for example, lie detector tests measuring changes in bodily function during interrogation, may actually be directed to eliciting responses which are essentially testimonial. To compel a person to submit to testing in which an effort will be made to determine his guilt or innocence on the basis of physiological responses, whether willed or not, is to evoke the spirit and history of the Fifth Amendment. Such situations call to mind the principle that the protection of the privilege 'is as broad as the mischief against which it seeks to guard'.

Because the involuntary blood donor's 'testimonial capacities were in no way implicated', the court concluded that he was not entitled to claim the privilege (*Schmerber v. California*, 1966: 761–5).

The crux of polygraphing is that the physiological symptoms of the suspect are irrelevant and of no interest whatsoever unless they may be correlated with questions being asked. Indeed, one technique of polygraphing is to instruct the person not to speak out but only think 'yes' or 'no' in silence as the questions are asked. The physiology is inextricably enmeshed with the testimonial responses of the suspect as recorded on the machine.

Interestingly, the *Schmerber* court emphasized its concern for the manner in which the blood withdrawal was accomplished. It foresaw 'serious questions' if 'a search involving use of medical technique, even of the most rudimentary sort, were made by other than medical personnel or in other than a medical environment'. Of course, one immediately thinks of the affinity for the quasi-medical 'diagnosis of deception' terminology that polygraphers manifest. They are uncomfortably close to the truth in that respect, however, in the sense that the substantive determinations that they make are the sort of complex issues about mental function that are of continuing concern and research for psychologists and psychiatrists in laboratories and hospitals. But the skills and education of the prototypical polygrapher are those of a lab technician, not of the scientist conducting the studies.

Due process. It appears that the drug cases are going to make significant constitutional law before polygraph cases do. *National Treasury Employees Union v. Von Raab* (1986) is illustrative. The US Customs Service commissioner promulgated a drug screening programme in 1986, the basic premise of which was that 'Drug screening through urinalysis is a condition of employment for placement into positions covered by the program.' Customs employees who tested positive 'are subject to loss of consideration for the position applied for ... [and] ... are subject to removal from the service'. If a tentative selectee refused to undergo drug screening, he or she 'will lose consideration for that position'. A 'collector' is physically present in the lavatory during urination albeit 'close but not direct'. Subjects are required to fill out a pretest form stating any medications taken within the last thirty days and any circumstances in which he or she may have been in contact with illegal substances during that time.

The National Treasury Employees Union sued to enjoin any further implementation of the plan. The court concluded that the plan was an unconstitutional programme of warrantless searches violative of the Fourth Amendment, and even more intrusive of privacy than a search of a home. It rejected the argument that Customs employees had voluntarily waived their constitutional right to refuse to consent, holding it to be 'unconstitutional for the government to condition public employment on "consent" to an unreasonable search where the price of not consenting is loss of government employment or some other government benefit'.

Further, the court found the plan in violation of the Fifth Amendment privilege against self-incrimination, dubiously reasoning that it met the *Schmerber* test of 'evidence of a testimonial or communicative nature'. However dubious that conclusion may be, the court spoke emphatically and rightly when it declared that: 'This gross invasion of privacy constitutes a degrading procedure that so detracts from human dignity and self respect that it "shocks the conscience" and offends this Court's sense of justice'. That led the court to conclude that the plan 'unconstitutionally interferes with the penumbral rights of privacy held by Customs workers', as set forth by the Supreme Court in its decision in *Griswold v. Connecticut* (1965), reasoning. Finally, the court found the plan to be 'far from an infallible system' and

> so fraught with dangers of false positive readings as to deny the Customs workers due process of law when they apply for promotion into superior positions. Furthermore, in balancing the legitimate law enforcement, societal and governmental interests of the defendant against the severity of the intrusiveness, the unreliability of the testing further convinces the Court that the drug testing plan is unreasonable and not rationally related to achievement of the governmental interests. (*National Treasury Employees Union v. Von Raab*, 1987)

On appeal, the fifth circuit court of appeals vacated the injunction (*National Treasury Employees Union v. Von Raab*, 1987). But its reasoning does not bode well for the users of polygraphing. First, it concluded that the test programme was a 'search' under the Fourth Amendment. But it was not a constitutionally 'unreasonable' one for reasons that underscore the vulnerability of polygraph usage to constitutional challenge. Only Customs employees seeking transfer to sensitive positions are tested. The test results are either positive or negative for the presence of drugs, 'leaving no room for discretion in interpreting the tests'; the GC/MS test 'is almost always accurate' and the Service has put a quality-assurance feature in place to monitor accuracy. The court also observed that the test was 'to some extent, consensual', in the sense that an employee need not apply and could withdraw his application without prejudice prior to being tested. It cautioned, however, that the government cannot undertake searches of its employees 'simply by making consent a condition of employment'. In addition, to be 'reasonable' a Fourth Amendment search must 'be a "sufficiently productive mechanism" for achieving its purposes, for no privacy invasions should be permitted unless some good end is served'.

In contrast, polygraph conclusions are consistently based on variable subjective interpretations; are incapable of consistently yielding clearcut positives or negatives; and have an unacceptably high number of false positives erroneously accusing innocent persons of wrongdoing. They are also most frequently used on a 'sweep' basis unrelated to individualized suspicions. Quality assurance, in the sense of rectification of error within a reasonable time period, is impossible to achieve.

Turning to the Fifth Amendment, the appellate court first found no violation of the privilege against self-incrimination because a urine sample is not 'testimonial' evidence that would disclose 'any knowledge [the person tested] might have'. In contrast, of course, polygraphing is resorted to in order to cause thoughts to be disclosed which the suspect wishes to retain undisclosed in privacy. The polygrapher seeks to transform the verbal utterance of the suspect's denial of wrongdoing into an involuntary physiological exposure of an unvoiced thought.

Secondly, the court concluded that 'the drug-testing program is not so unreliable as to violate due process of Law'. It thereby acknowledged that the requirement of reliability (the judicial synonym for validity) must be met, or constitutional due process will not be satisfied. Indeed, the dissenting judge on this three-judge panel based his disagreement with his brethren on his conclusion that the testing programme was an 'ineffective method' of achieving the employer's goal and therefore was an unreasonable invasion of the employees' Fourth Amendment rights.

The implications for polygraph analysis are clear: the inherent fallibility of polygraphing, with its unacceptably high level of false positives, flunks the Fifth Amendment tests of due process and self-incrimination as well as the reasonableness requirement of the Fourth Amendment.

Conclusion

In the evolution of the torts of polygraphing, we are in that early phase of an emerging area of legal accountability in which harbinger cases brought by successful plaintiffs begin to appear and proliferate, foreshadowing the depth and directions in which litigation is likely to develop. Isolated instances as they appear, harbinger cases enable the identification of workable rationales of liability that are responsive to patterns of conduct and harm that are attributable to the newly recognized tortfeasors. Reports of success in pursuing those causes of action spread and, as more persons become aware of their rights in the resultant publicity, the volume of cases begins to grow, as the evolution of product liability doctrines well documents, and as the 'retaliatory discharge' cases are currently exemplifying. Over decades and centuries Anglo-American common law has thus effectuated its incremental social reforms without great fanfare, but inexorably.

It would be polyannish, however, to assume that the recognition of the applicability of those causes of action to polygraphing situations can alone achieve the needed reforms to any significant extent. Success in that regard will depend upon how the economic realities of blue-collar civil litigation evolve as hard-nosed contingent-fee lawyers, aware of those legal theories, may assess the prospects for converting them into recoveries for their clients of sufficient damages to make their own investment of time and effort worthwhile.

With all these actions in the armoury one must still realize that sound legal theories, indispensable to be sure, mean only that the plaintiff's case, if taken into court by a lawyer, will not be summarily dismissed as legally groundless. There remains the necessity to try the case. For that our would-be plaintiff needs an attorney. In these polygraph situations, the blue-collar economic realities being what they are, the lawyer who takes his case will almost always be doing so on a contingent-fee basis whereby she gets nothing for spending her time and effort before and during the trial unless he wins his case. That prompts her to assess his chances as realistically as she can. Once in the courtroom, she well realizes, her client will have to be believed by the trier of fact as he tries during direct and cross-examination to describe what occurred during the polygraph session and, depending on the trial circumstances, perhaps whatever he may have done or not done to arouse suspicions in the first place. The point of this closing foray into the practicalities of blue-collar litigation, of course, is to underscore the reality that even when legal theory is wholly on the side of the person harmed by polygraphing, justice may still remain unattainable.

So it may well be that federal legislation prohibiting employment polygraphing, pre-emptive of the various state policies, will turn out to be the only effective solution to the increasingly evident need for reform.

14

A British trade union view

Ken Jones

In 1984 the British Trades Union Congress carried a composite resolution on civil liberties which referred, inter alia, to the use of the polygraph. The relevant part of the resolution stated that:

> Congress . . . expresses its total opposition to the use of polygraph (or 'lie detector') machines as a violation of human rights and privacy, calls for an immediate end to the use of polygraph machines at GCHQ and calls for a law banning the use of these machines in both the public and private sectors.

I should like to explain why trade unions in Britain are opposed to the use of polygraph machines. In doing so I shall draw heavily on three union documents in particular. These are: firstly, written evidence submitted in 1983 by the Council of Civil Service Unions to the House of Commons Select Committee on Defence (Council of Civil Service Unions, 1983); secondly, a booklet entitled *The Case against the Polygraph* published in 1983 by the Society of Civil and Public Servants (1983); and thirdly, written evidence submitted in 1984 by the Council of Civil Service Unions to the House of Commons Select Committee on Employment (Council of Civil Service Unions, 1984).

In Britain the Civil Service unions have been in the forefront of opposition to the polygraph. This is because the first significant step towards the introduction of polygraph testing came in the Civil Service, at the Government Communications Headquarters (GCHQ). As well as looking at the nature of the arguments which the unions have deployed against the polygraph I shall briefly discuss the possible connection between polygraph trials and the ban on trade unions at GCHQ announced in January 1984. Although nothing in the nature of proof may become publicly available for decades, the evidence regarding such a connection is already very strong, and adds further weight to the argument that polygraph testing is not only an attack on individual liberty in its own right, but is also a threat to democratic procedures wherever it is introduced.

The Geoffrey Prime affair

If one man may be held responsible for the introduction of polygraph testing in Britain, it is Geoffrey Prime. His conviction on spying charges in 1982 set in train a sequence of developments which led directly to the first polygraph trials.

Prime was no ordinary spy. He was employed at GCHQ, one of the most sensitive security establishments in Britain. In the words of the Security Commission report on his case: 'the damage inflicted by Prime was of a very high order', and 'United States secrets [were] no less gravely compromised than our own'. But the Prime affair also represented a disastrous failure of the 'positive vetting' procedures used in the Civil Service to identify possible security risks. Prime was actually undergoing training in spy techniques in East Berlin for a week during the time that he was being investigated by a positive vetting team. He made a number of other visits to East Berlin and Vienna to make contact with Soviet intelligence. He expressed pro-Communist sympathies to colleagues at work. He was also a social and sexual 'misfit' who, in addition to his sentence for spying, received three years in gaol for sexual offences against children. Yet at no time did his behaviour arouse the suspicions of those responsible for security in his department. Indeed he was only arrested after his wife approached the police in 1981, four years after Prime had resigned from GCHQ (Security Commission, 1983).

As is customary in serious spy cases, the Prime affair was referred to the Security Commission. A large number of witnesses were examined, including some working in the United States Defense and State Departments and in its intelligence and security agencies. From the start it was clear that the Commission would be looking, to quote one of the chapter headings in the final report, for 'possible major innovations in personnel security procedures in the intelligence and security agencies'. It must be remembered that the Prime affair had exacerbated the already tense relationship between the British and United States Governments at that time: there had been disagreements over the Falklands War, and popular feeling in Britain against the deployment of cruise missiles was running high. GCHQ is essentially a joint US–British operation: it acts as a clearing house for intelligence information, much of which is simply passed on to the United States. The United States pays for a large part of the GCHQ operation, on which thousands of jobs depend. The Prime affair, adding to other doubts about Britain's political and security 'reliability', would have strengthened the hand of those in the United States who wanted a big shake-up at GCHQ. Well before the Security Commission report was published, press articles began to appear suggesting that the introduction of the polygraph machine – an essentially American device – was being considered.

Evidence to the Defence Select Committee

The Council of Civil Service Unions (CCSU) is the umbrella body bringing together trade unions in the non-industrial Civil Service. The constituent unions of the CCSU represents about 500,000 people in total, including those working in the Ministry of Defence, GCHQ, Foreign and Commonwealth Office, Diplomatic Service and other security-sensitive areas in the Civil Service. The CCSU was invited in late 1982 to give evidence on security vetting procedures to the House of Commons Select Committee on Defence, which had decided to conduct its own examination in the wake of the Prime Affair.

The CCSU took the opportunity provided by the Committee, and by the press leaks, to express its total opposition to the use of polygraph testing in the Civil Service. The principal grounds of opposition were summarized as follows:

> Lie detectors (or polygraphs)
>   have little or no scientific or theoretical base;
>   are inaccurate;
>   display a disturbing propensity to find innocent people guilty;
>   are ineffective at catching the determined spy;
>   threaten an unwarranted invasion of an individual's right to privacy;
>   could be used by unscrupulous governments to test the 'loyalty' of civil servants.

The unions went on to substantiate each of these claims in greater detail. On the question of the scientific basis of lie detection, the CCSU quoted from Lykken (1981), Skolnick (1961), and a research study by Irving and Hilgendorf for the Royal Commission on Criminal Procedure (1980). All these sources question whether there is any scientific reason for thinking that the polygraphs may be reliable. The CCSU pointed to the fact that polygraphs were developed not by scientists, but by policemen and lawyers.

On the question of accuracy, the CCSU quoted first the 12 percent error rate discovered by Irving and Hilgendorf in the laboratory tests. It then referred to the work done by Lykken related to real-life situations, in which the error rate was found to be between 28 and 37 percent.

Worse still, the CCSU pointed out, there was evidence that polygraph tests were biased *against* the truthful subject. References were made to work done by Pyle (1982) and Barland. In one test, half of the suspects who were independently known to be telling the truth were 'accused' of lying by the polygraph. The CCSU also drew on the

Tilson case to support its argument. In 1982 the Pentagon had fired manpower executive John Tilson after polygraphers alleged that he had 'failed' three lie-detector tests; Tilson had denied leaking an embarrassing budget estimate. Tilson was later reinstated when the journalist involved submitted a sworn statement declaring that he was not the source. The CCSU asked: 'If lie detectors are introduced as an aid to positive vetting, how many innocent civil servants will be refused PV (positive vetting) clearance? If lie detectors are introduced into the British Civil Service for security purposes, how long will it be before lie detectors will be used by governments to track down the sources of purely embarrassing "leaks"?'

The CCSU also argued that polygraph tests were ineffective at catching spies – which, after all, is their main ostensible purpose. Lykken (1981) and Venables (1982) were quoted in evidence for the view that a trained liar or a psychopath could fool the polygraph machine. Relatively simple techniques such as clenching one's toes, tensing the abdominal muscles, biting one's tongue or hiding a tack in one's sock and pressing on it at the appropriate time could make it possible to produce 'polygraphic perturbations'. Drugs were another possibility mentioned – a research team at the Institute of Pennsylvania Hospital had enabled subjects to deceive their polygraphers by taking the drug Meprobamate (Waid, Orne, Cook and Orne, 1981; see also Chapter 10 above, by Gudjonsson).

Finally the CCSU raised the issue of civil liberty, and in particular the implications of polygraph testing for the right to privacy:

> It is inherent in the design of the polygraph examination that the subject of the test is faced with searching and potentially embarrassing (control) questions ... Thus a civil servant in the Ministry of Defence could be faced with taking a lie detector test without knowing which were control questions and substantive questions. Nor would the civil servant know which questions and answers might be noted (or perhaps recorded), and included at some stage in a report to his or her superiors. Questions may cover a wide range of areas including those bearing on the civil servant's attitudes and loyalty to the government of the day. It would be all too easy therefore for lie detectors to become an instrument of intimidation, and a test of the civil servant's loyalty to a particular set of policies.

SCPS campaign

The Security Commission Report, published in May 1983, made eight recommendations for improving the security procedures at GCHQ. One of these was that a pilot scheme should be undertaken to test the feasibility of polygraph screening; the scheme should, the Security Commission said, 'embrace at least those probationers and existing staff of the Security Service itself and GCHQ who have or will have access to information of the highest classification'. The Prime Minister announced that the Government accepted this and all the other recommendations.

The Society of Civil and Public Servants (SCPS) is the second largest constituent union of the CCSU, representing around 85,000 members in middle-ranking executive grades. The SCPS annual conference, held shortly after the publication of the Security Commission Report, passed an emergency motion condemning the Government's decision to proceed with the pilot scheme, and pledging full support to any member who did not wish to co-operate with polygraph screening. The conference also decided to push for a wider campaign, involving the TUC and other bodies, to highlight the social issues raised.

The SCPS proceeded in the following months to generate publicity unfavourable to the polygraph and, in particular, its bias against truthful subjects. These and other arguments were brought together in a pamphlet in October 1983 entitled *The Case against the Polygraph*; the pamphlet was distributed to all SCPS members at GCHQ, as well as other trade unions and Members of Parliament. In his introduction to the pamphlet the SCPS General Secretary, Gerry Gillman, said:

> We believe that the overwhelming weight of scientific evidence shows polygraph screening to be unreliable and heavily biased against completely innocent subjects. Moreover, its introduction into the British Civil Service will do little or nothing to assist in the detection of trained spies, as there exist many techniques that can be employed to beat the polygraph. Worse still, there will be a risk that a trained spy, once having taken and passed a polygraph test, will face much less rigorous investigation through security methods that might otherwise have revealed doubts about security clearance. Although at this stage it is proposed to confine the introduction of the polygraph to GCHQ and the Security Service, experience in the United States of America must arouse fears that once introduced, on however a limited scale, the use of the polygraph will spread throughout the Civil Service and into commerce and industry. Our hope is that this pamphlet, by careful analysis of the techniques and problems associated with polygraph security screening, will assist in persuading the Government not to go ahead with the use of the polygraph in security vetting.

The pamphlet made an important distinction between the guilty knowledge test and the control question test:

> Whilst the Guilty Knowledge Test appears from the research to have general scientific credibility, considerable controversy surrounds the validity of the Control Question Test. This is important as the polygraph screening proposed for GCHQ and the Security Service will almost certainly be based on the Control Question Test.

Attacking the reliability of the control question test (CQT), the SCPS again quoted from the findings of Lykken and of Irving and Hilgendorf. It also referred to work done by Waid and Orne of the University of Pennsylvania, who quote a field study in which the CQT correctly identified 98 percent of deceptive subjects, but *at the expense* of erroneously identifying 55 percent of innocent subjects as deceptive (Barland and Raskin, 1976). Discounting the Security Commission recommendation that an adverse polygraph reading should not, on its own, be treated as a disqualification for security clearance, the SCPS went on to argue:

> There can be no doubting that an adverse polygraph reading will remain as a damaging question mark on a civil servant's security record. It is not difficult to imagine the pressures on promotion boards being such that many better qualified candidates will be passed over in favour of those less well qualified because of a single unsubstantiated doubt raised by a polygraph screening test.

In further sections of the booklet the SCPS discussed a number of personal and social factors known to affect the accuracy of polygraph testing. These included emotional and psychiatric disturbance (with reference to research done by Gudjonsson) and electrodermal lability (that is, variations between individuals' tendency to sweat). The booklet described some of the main mental, physical and chemical/pharmaceutical techniques open to guilty subjects for deliberately providing false readings during a polygraph test, and concluded by saying:

> Whilst it can be argued that any form of security vetting is by its nature bound to be intrusive, and that this is the price that civil servants know they have to pay when working in security areas, it cannot be denied that the polygraph is unjust, unreliable and counter-productive . . . Faced with having their security worthiness assessed by reference to an unreliable test, the morale and commitment of many key civil servants will suffer.

In December 1983 the SCPS took its campaign a stage further and organized a public conference in London on 'The Polygraph, Security Procedures, and Civil Liberties'. Guest speaker was Professor Lykken. The conference was attended by 125 delegates drawn from Civil Service unions, academic specialists (in psychology, physiology and the law), the National Council for Civil Liberties, journalists, Members of Parliament, and two representatives from the polygraph industry. Addressing the conference, SCPS Deputy General Secretary Campbell Christie warned that many loyal and valuable civil servants would have their careers blighted by a test of trustworthiness that was 'little better than tossing a coin'. Commenting on the wider implications of the introduction of polygraph screening in Britain, he said:

> Whatever assurances the Government may give now, if they get away with trying out the polygraph on staff at GCHQ, it will only be a matter of time before civil servants in every government department may be forced to answer questions on all aspects of their personal lives and their political views as part of a polygraph screening. Such developments are already happening in America. Beyond the Civil Service we will see a flood of American agencies seeking to export their various brands of polygraph tests for use in the private sector. As already happens in America unemployed workers may be forced to submit to humiliating polygraph interrogation on their union sympathies and sexual preferences, just to get a job. In the 1950s this country avoided the worst excesses of the McCarthy era. We pride ourselves on our freedoms and our avoidance of Big Brother methods of intimidation and investigation. Polygraph screening has the nasty smell of both McCarthyism and Big Brother. We urge the government to cancel the introduction of the polygraph in the British Civil Service.

Evidence to the Employment Select Committee

In April 1984 the House of Commons Select Committee on Employment decided to undertake an inquiry into the implications for industrial relations and employment of the introduction of the polygraph. This afforded the CCSU an opportunity to restate its opposition to the polygraph and (since by then the GCHQ trade union ban had been announced) to comment on the relationship between the decision to conduct a pilot test of the polygraph at GCHQ and the decision to ban national Civil Service trade unions from GCHQ.

The CCSU submitted a written memorandum, in which it was made clear that the union opposition was based primarily on the *unreliability* of the polygraph machine, and the consequent risk of unfair treatment for those subjected to it. The CCSU also went on to express its fear that, in using the polygraph for security screening, there would be a general reduction in the effectiveness of screening, in that more traditional measures would either be dropped or given less credence. The CCSU suggested that there should be an independent evaluation of the pilot test at GCHQ and in the security services, in view of 'widespread uncertainty about the reliability and accuracy of the polygraph'.

The CCSU expressed its deep concern about the possible spread of polygraph testing to other parts of the Civil Service. There are over 60,000 posts in the Civil Service which are the subject of the positive vetting procedure – the technique of enquiry into an individual's personal background and history, consisting of establishing *positive* evidence of their reliability on securing grounds. The CCSU said:

Either a future spy scandal or, more likely, the general attrition usually involved in the development of security screening, will probably ensure the extension of polygraph testing to all positively vetted posts in the Civil Service. With the current schedule of quinquennial reviews of positively vetted posts, plus the usual testing of new entrants to positively vetted posts, it is possible that up to 20,000 polygraph tests a year would be necessary if the polygraph were to become a regular feature of the positive vetting procedure.

The CCSU then commented on the possible extension of polygraph testing beyond existing positively vetted posts:

> Recent [official secrets] cases have shown the depth of ministerial concern at unauthorized disclosure of confidential material, and also the lengths employed (e.g. the use of senior police detectives, normally engaged on the investigation of serious crimes) in tracking down those responsible. The use of polygraph testing could appear as a short-cut method in trying to identify culprits, particularly if any alleged saving of police and other investigative resources could be demonstrated. Polygraph testing could, therefore, be used in routine enquiries of this kind, or, more likely, be introduced before any civil servant is given a post involving access to classified material, but not normally subject to the positive vetting procedure. Potentially, this would cover all civil servants in headquarter offices, together with a high proportion of those in operational outstations. Thereafter, it would be but a short step to the use of the polygraph on the wide scale which is currently envisaged in the United States Federal Civil Service.

The CCSU concluded its general comments by broadening the argument to cover the question of Government–Civil Service relations:

> There is a further and more general consideration that lies behind our opposition to the polygraph. This is the overriding ethos that guides and motivates civil servants in carrying out public business. The crucial relationship between civil servants and the government of the day is based upon trust: a feeling that should be mutual, but which, in the view of many civil servants, is significantly absent at present. The use of the polygraph anywhere in the Civil Service, even on a highly limited basis, is seen by all civil servants as an indication of lack of trust in them by the government of the day.

The point was also stressed that, in the more general employment field outside the Civil Service, the development of the use of the polygraph was bound to affect industrial relations adversely. The CCSU felt that no employer with pretensions to be a good employer would use a method such as polygraph testing even in the most extreme circumstances. Accordingly the CCSU recommended to the Employment Committee that a total ban should be introduced on the use of polygraph testing in any form of employment in the United Kingdom.

The report of the Employment Committee was published in February 1985 (House of Commons Employment Committee, 1985a). It concluded by saying:

42. We consider that the use of the polygraph in employment situations is undesirable and of insufficient reliability. We *recommend* that the Government keeps the position under review and introduces, either immediately, or, if the use of the polygraph were to increase, a strict licensing system for polygraphers supported by a code of practice approved by Parliament. We are in no doubt that the use of the polygraph has unwelcome implications for employment practice and for the rights of individuals.

43. The field of national security presents special problems. Following the report of the Security Commission on the Prime case the Government have set in train a pilot scheme at GCHQ to test the feasibility of polygraph security screening in the intelligence and security agencies. We *recommend* that at the end of the pilot scheme at GCHQ it should be evaluated by appropriate independent persons who have had experience of national security matters.

The polygraph and the GCHQ trade union ban

What were the attitudes towards the polygraph of trade union members at GCHQ itself? We can build up a picture by looking at the experiences of the three SCPS branches at GCHQ. The SCPS had around 800 members at GCHQ, including cypher staff, linguists and general administrative grades; a very high proportion would have been subject to positive vetting and many were in line for inclusion in the polygraph trial.

When the report of the Security Commission was published in May 1983, the SCPS Co-ordinating Committee at GCHQ (representing the three branches) held a meeting of all members at GCHQ to obtain their views on the possible use of the polygraph in the positive vetting procedures. A letter was sent to GCHQ management requesting any information that was available to support the validity of the polygraph testing. Management replied saying it was unable to provide documentation on reliability, but did give the following assurance: 'I [Mr Screaton] am happy to confirm E3's verbal assurance that the Department has no intention of dismissing any member of staff who refuses to cooperate [*sic*] in the polygraph pilot scheme.'

A consultative meeting of SCPS members was held on 16 June 1983. Around 230 attended, of whom 170 voted against the use of the polygraph and 39 in favour, with 21 abstentions. This was a clear endorsement of the SCPS national policy of no co-operation with the pilot scheme.

In January 1984 a questionnaire was sent to SCPS members in

order to get an updated picture. The questionnaire forms were sent out on 23 and 24 January but most were never delivered. On 25 January the Foreign Secretary announced in the House of Commons that all civil servants working at GCHQ were to be deprived of their trade union rights. Union leaders were given ten minutes' notice of the announcement. With immediate effect, GCHQ staff lost all their rights under employment protection legislation, including the right to appeal to an industrial tribunal against unfair dismissal. Staff were also told that the right of trade union membership at GCHQ would be withdrawn with effect from 1 March. Those who agreed to sign an official form surrendering their rights were to be paid £1,000. Those who refused to sign were threatened with dismissal.

A broad spectrum of opinion reacted by condemning the Government in the strongest possible terms for an act which was a clear violation of freedom of association, and which flew in the face of international labour and human rights conventions. Condemnation came from all the opposition parties in Parliament, virtually all the national press, senior civil servants, a recent former head of the Civil Service, the trade union movement, and (according to opinion polls) a large majority of public opinion.

Obviously it is not possible, given the current state of public knowledge, to be sure about the precise role played by the polygraph issue in the decision to ban unions at GCHQ. This is a game played according to the Government's own rules: the official justification for the ban is that the activities of trade unions at GCHQ threatened national security, and the rules on official secrecy about matters connected with national security deny us access to the information which would allow us to say definitely whether or not the Government is telling the truth. The best we can do is look at the circumstantial evidence.

Following the Prime Affair, the Government and the security establishment were desperate to placate the United States over the situation at GCHQ. It was decided to embark on a pilot test using the polygraph machine – a device in widespread use in the United States, particularly in the security and intelligence services, but almost unknown and without credibility in Britain. The pilot test was due to begin in the security service in January 1984, and in GCHQ in the spring. The trade unions involved made known their opposition to polygraph testing and their policy of no co-operation with the pilot test. The ban on trade unions was announced on 25 January 1984, along with the withdrawal of the GCHQ employees' right of access to industrial tribunals in cases of unfair dismissal. The notice to staff said that 'GCHQ staff will continue to be subject to the security regulations and procedures prescribed by the Government and by

Director GCHQ from time to time. These will include any recommendations of the Security Commission accepted by the Government.'

One of the Security Commission recommendations accepted by the Government was, of course, that polygraph testing be introduced at GCHQ. The Government's action cleared the way for anyone at GCHQ who refused a polygraph test to be sacked, and made it impossible for the dismissal to be challenged – and therefore the reliability of the polygraph to be exposed to scrutiny – before either an industrial tribunal or a court of law.

Any reasonable observer would, I believe, be driven to conclude that the unions' opposition to polygraph testing was in fact the major reason for the ban. The alternative version offered by the Government is that the unions were banned because of sporadic industrial action between 1979 and 1981 involving some GCHQ staff – mostly over pay and conditions. But this is scarcely credible. The union ban came two and a half years after the last instance of industrial action referred to – but only weeks before the start of polygraph testing. Even if we accept and endorse the Government's stated reasons, a trade union ban would have been a more than sufficient remedy; the removal of employment protection rights was overkill – but extremely convenient in suppressing public and legal scrutiny of the polygraph.

Conclusions

Trade union opposition to the polygraph has focused largely on the question of its unreliability. This is surely the correct strategy. If the polygraph is unreliable, it poses a tangible threat to all trade union members concerned. Trade unions must base their policies on protecting the legitimate interests of their members.

It is also important for trade unions to be able to show that they take a responsible position on questions affecting national security. As anyone with any knowledge of history will be aware, British trade unions have always played a highly patriotic role, but in recent times the Thatcher governments have not scrupled to portray the labour and trade union movements as containing sinister forces prepared to undermine the nation's defences. This has produced electoral dividends. It has also diverted attention from the fact that traitors almost invariably emerge from within the ranks of the 'establishment' itself. Finally, it provides a useful scapegoat when the security services are guilty of one of their recurrent lapses, as in the Prime affair. The unions have therefore been tactically right not to overdo the arguments against polygraph testing based more generally on the need to protect civil liberties. And they have been right to emphasize the ways in which the polygraph will actually be *counterproductive* in terms of protecting national security.

I have included a short discussion of the GCHQ trade union ban because the wider civil liberties question is nonetheless an extremely important one. This goes beyond the issues of individual privacy. We have to ask ourselves whether the role played by the polygraph at GCHQ was not corrosive of natural justice, democratic rights, and – ironically enough – the truth.

References

Abrams, S. and Ogard, E. (1986) 'Polygraph Surveillance of Probationers', *Polygraph*, 15: 174–82.

American Psychological Association (1987) 'Polygraphs Unsuitable for Employment Screening, APA tells Congress', APA Press Release, 5 March, Washington DC.

Anastasi, A. (1976) *Psychological Testing* (4th Edition). New York: Macmillan.

Ansley, N. (1984) 'Statement Presented at Hearings on Polygraphs for Counterintelligence Purposes in the Department of Defense', Committee on Armed Services, United States Senate, 7 March.

Arena, J.G., Blanchard, E.B., Andrasik, F., Cotch, P.A. and Myers, P.E. (1983) 'Reliability of Psychophysiological Assessment', *Behaviour Research and Therapy*, 21: 447–69.

Balloun, K.S. and Holmes, D.S. (1979) 'Effects of Repeated Examinations on the Ability to Detect Guilt with a Polygraphic Examination: A Laboratory Experiment with a Real Crime', *Journal of Applied Psychology*, 64: 316–22.

Barland, G.H. (1981) *A Validity and Reliability Study of Counter-Intelligence Screening Test*. Security Support Battalion, 902d Military Intelligence Group, Fort George G. Meade, Maryland.

Barland, G.H. (1984) 'Statement Presented at Hearings on Polygraphs for Counterintelligence Purposes in the Department of Defense', Committee on Armed Services, United States Senate, 7 March.

Barland, G.H. and Raskin, D.C. (1975) 'An Evaluation of Field Techniques in Detection and Deception', *Psychophysiology*, 12: 321–30.

Barland, G.H. and Raskin, D.C. (1976) *Validity and Reliability of Polygraph Examinations of Criminal Suspects*. US Department of Justice Report No. 76–1, Contract 75–NI–99–0001. Salt Lake City, UT: Department of Psychology, University of Utah.

Beary, J.F. (1984) Statement, the President's National Security Decision Directive 84 and Department of Defense Directive on the Use of Polygraphs, 1983: Hearings Before the Legislation and National Security Sub-Committee of the House Committee on Government Operations, 98th Congress, First Session 5.

Bem, D.J. and Allen, A. (1974) 'On Predicting Some of the People Some of the Time: The Search for Cross-situational Consistencies in Behavior', *Psychological Review*, 81: 506–20.

Benussi, V. (1914) 'Die Atmungssymptome der Lüge', *Archiv für die Gesamte Psychologie*, 31: 244–73. English translation published 1975, 'Respiratory Symptoms of Lying', *Polygraph*, 4: 52–76.

Bersh, P.J. (1969) 'A Validation Study of Polygraph Examiner Judgments', *Journal of Applied Psychology*, 53: 399–403.

Bivens v. Six Unknown Named Agents of the Federal Bureau of Narcotics (1971) 403 US 388.

Block, J. (1971) *Lives Through Time*. Berkeley, CA: Bancroft.

Block, E.B. (1977) *Lie Detectors: Their History and Use*. New York: David McKay.

Bok, S. (1978) *Lying: Moral Choice in Public and Private Life*. New York: Pantheon.

Bradley, M.T. and Ainsworth, D. (1984) 'Alcohol and the Psychophysiological Detection of Deception', *Psychophysiology*, 21: 63–71.

Bradley, M.T. and Warfield, J.F. (1984) 'Innocence, Information, and the Guilty Knowledge Test in the Detection of Deception', *Psychophysiology*, 21: 683–9.

Brandeis, J. (1928) In *Olmstead v. United States*, 277 US 438, 478.

Brett, A.S., Phillips, M. and Beary, J.F. (1986) 'Predictive Power of the Polygraph: Can the "Lie Detector" Really Detect Liars?' *The Lancet*, 8 March, 544–7.

Briggs v. Goodwin (1983) 698 F.2d 486 (D.C. Cir.).

British Psychological Society (1985) 'A Code of Conduct for Psychologists', *Bulletin of The British Psychological Society*, 38: 41–3.

British Psychological Society (1986) 'Report of the Working Group on the Use of the Polygraph in Criminal Investigation and Personnel Screening', *Bulletin of The British Psychological Society*, 39: 81–94.

Bull, R. (1983) 'The Truth about Lie-detection', *Police Review*, June, 1190–1 and 1246–8.

Carlson v. Green (1980) 446 US 14.

Chaplin, W.F. and Goldberg, L.R. (1984) 'A Failure to Replicate the Bem and Allen Study of Individual Differences in Cross-situational Consistency', *Journal of Personality and Social Psychology*, 47: 1074–90.

Copeland, M. (1978) *The Real Spy World*. London: Sphere.

Cordle et al. v. General Hugh Mercer Corporation (1984) 325 S.E.2d 111 (W. Va. S. Ct.).

Cornwell, R. and Staunton, M. (1985) *Data Protection: Putting the Record Straight*. London: National Council for Civil Liberties.

Correa, E.J. and Adams, H.E. (1981) 'The Validity of the Pre-employment Polygraph Examination and the Effects of Motivation', *Polygraph*, 10: 143–55.

Council of Civil Service Unions (1983) *Memorandum to House of Commons Defence Committee*. London: Council of Civil Service Unions.

Council of Civil Service Unions (1984) *Evidence to House of Commons Employment Committee*. London: Council of Civil Service Unions.

Craig, J.K. (1984) 'Note, The Presidential Polygraph Order and the Fourth Amendment: Subjecting Federal Employees to Warrantless Searches', *Cornell Law Review*, 69: 896.

Cronbach, L.J. (1981) *Essentials of Psychological Testing* (4th Edition). New York: Harper & Row.

Cunningham, C. (1972a) 'International Interrogation Techniques', *Royal United Services Institute of Defence Studies Journal*, September.

Cunningham, C. (1972b) 'Interrogation', *Medico-Legal Society Journal*, 41: 49–62.

Cupp v. Murphy (1973) 412 US 291.

Davidson, P.O. (1968) 'Validity of the Guilty-Knowledge Techniques: The Effects of Motivation', *Journal of Applied Psychology*, 52: 62–5.

Davidson, W.A. (1979) 'Validity and Reliability of the Cardio Activity Monitor', *Polygraph*, 8: 104–11.

Davis v. Mississippi (1969) 394 US 721.

Davis v. Passman (1979) 442 US 228.

Dawson, M.E. (1980) 'Physiological Detection of Deception: Measurement of Responses to Questions and Answers During Countermeasure Manoeuvres', *Psychophysiology*, 17: 8–17.

Department of Defense (1984) *The Accuracy and Utility of Polygraph Testing*. Washington, DC: Department of Defense.

Department of Defense (1986) *Department of Defense Polygraph Program: Report to Congress for Fiscal Year 1986*. Washington, DC: Department of Defense.

De Paulo, B. and Pfeifer, R. (1986) 'On-the-job Experience and Skill at Detecting Deception', *Journal of Applied Social Psychology*, 16: 249–67.

De Paulo, B.M., Stone, J.I. and Lassiter, G.D. (1985) 'Deceiving and Detecting Deceit', in B.R. Schlenker (ed.), *The Self and Social Life*. New York: McGraw-Hill.

Dorsen, N. (1984) 'A Transatlantic View of Civil Liberties in the United Kingdom', in P. Wallington (ed.), *Civil Liberties 1984*. Oxford: Martin Robertson.

Dudycha, G.J. (1936) 'An Objective Study of Punctuality in Relation to Personality and Achievement', *Archives of Psychology*, 29: 1–53.

Dulewicz, V. (1984) 'The Use of the Polygraph for Personnel Screening: A Statement by the Society Issued by the Scientific Affairs Board'. Leicester: British Psychological Society.

Ekman, P. (1985) *Telling Lies: Clues to Deceit in the Marketplace, Politics and Marriage*. New York: W.W. Norton.

Ekman, P. and Friesen, W. (1969) 'Nonverbal Leakage and Clues to Deception', *Psychiatry*, 32: 88–106.

Ekman, P. and Friesen, W. (1974) 'Detecting Deception from the Body or Face', *Journal of Personality and Social Psychology*, 29: 288–98.

Ekman, P., Levenson, R.W. and Friesen, W.V. (1983) 'Autonomic Nervous System Activity Distinguishes Among Emotions', *Science*, 221: 1208–10.

Elliott, D.W. (1982) 'Lie Detector Evidence: Lessons from the American Experience', in E. Campbell and L. Waller (eds), *Well and Truly Tried: Essays in Honour of Sir Richard Eggleston*. Melbourne: Law Book Company.

Epstein, S. (1979) 'The Stability of Behaviour: 1. On Predicting Most of the People Much of the Time', *Journal of Personality and Social Psychology*, 37: 1097–126.

Farwell, L.A. and Donchin, E. (1986) 'Can the P300 be Used in the Detection of Deception?', paper presented at the annual meeting of the Society for Psychophysiological Research, October, Montreal, Canada.

Ferguson, R.J. and Gugas, C. (1984) *Preemployment Polygraphy*. Springfield, IL: Charles C. Thomas.

Foot, P. (1986) *Murder at the Farm: Who Killed Carl Bridgewater?* London: Sidgwick & Jackson.

Forman, R. and McCauley, C. (1986) 'Validity of the Positive Control Polygraph Test Using the Field Practice Model', *Journal of Applied Psychology*, 71: 691–8.

Frye v. United States (1923) 293 F. 1013 (DC Cir. 1923).

Fukumoto, J. (1982) 'Psychophysiological Detection of Deception in Japan: The Past and the Present', *Polygraph*, 11: 234–8.

Gallup Organization (1982) *Survey of Members of the American Society for Psychophysiological Research Concerning their Opinion of Polygraph Test Interpretation*. Princeton, NJ: Gallup Organization.

Garwood, M. (1985) 'Two Issues on the Validity of Personnel Screening Polygraph Examinations', *Polygraph*, 14: 209–16.

Giesen, M. and Rollison, M.A. (1980) 'Guilty Knowledge Versus Innocent Associations: Effects of Trait Anxiety and Stimulus Content on Skin Conductance', *Journal of Research in Personality*, 14: 1–11.

Ginton, A., Daie, N., Elaad, E. and Ben-Shakhar, G. (1982) 'A Method for Evaluating the Use of the Polygraph in a Real-life Situation', *Journal of Applied Psychology*, 67: 131–7.

Green, B.F. (1978) 'In Defense of Measurement', *American Psychologist*, 33: 664–70.

Griswold v. Connecticut (1965) 381 US 479.

Gudjonsson, G.H. (1983) 'Lie Detection: Techniques and Countermeasures', in S.M.A. Lloyd-Bostock and B.R. Clifford (eds), *Evaluating Witness Evidence*. Chichester: John Wiley.

Gudjonsson, G.H. and Sartory, G. (1983) 'Blood–injury Phobia: A "Reasonable Excuse" for Failing to Give a Specimen in a Case of Suspected Drunken Driving', *Journal of the Forensic Science Society*, 23: 197–201.

Gugas, C. (1979) *The Silent Witness: A Polygraphist's Casebook*. Englewood Cliffs, NJ: Prentice-Hall.

Hammond, D.L. (1980) 'The Responding of Normals, Alcoholics, and Psychopaths in a Laboratory Lie-detection Experiment', unpublished Doctoral Dissertation, California School of Professional Psychology.

Hampson, S.E. (1982) *The Construction of Personality: An Introduction*. London: Routledge & Kegan Paul.

Hampson, S.E., John, O.P. and Goldberg, L.R. (1986) 'Category Breadth and Hierarchical Structure in Personality: Studies of Asymmetries in Judgments of Trait Implications', *Journal of Personality and Social Psychology*, 51: 37–54.

Hartshorne, H. and May, M.A. (1928) *Studies in Deceit*. New York: Macmillan.

Her Majesty's Stationery Office (HMSO) (1981) *Report of the Royal Commission on Criminal Procedure* (Cmnd 8092). London: Her Majesty's Stationery Office.

Her Majesty's Stationery Office (HMSO) (1983) *Report of the Security Commission* (Cmnd 8876). London: Her Majesty's Stationery Office.

Herbold-Wootten, H. (1982) 'The German Tatbestandsdiagnostik; A Historical Review of the Beginnings of Scientific Lie Detection in Germany', *Polygraph*, 11: 246–57.

Herriot, P. (1984) *Down from the Ivory Tower*. Chichester: John Wiley.

Herriot, P. and Wingrove, J. (1984) 'Decision Processes in Graduate Pre-selection', *Journal of Occupational Psychology*, 57: 269–75.

Hewitt, P. (1977) *Privacy: The Information Gatherers*. London: National Council for Civil Liberties.

Hewitt, P. (1982) *The Abuse of Power*. Oxford: Martin Robertson.

Hodgson, R. and Rachman, S. (1974) 'II. Desynchrony in Measures of Fear', *Behaviour Research and Therapy*, 12: 319–26.

Honts, C.R. (1982) 'The Effects of Simple Physical Countermeasures on the Physiological Detection of Deception', unpublished Masters Thesis, Virginia Polytechnic Institute and State University.

Honts, C.R. and Hodes, R.L. (1982a) 'The Effect of Simple Physical Countermeasures on the Detection of Deception', *Psychophysiology*, 19: 564 (SPR Abstract).

Honts, C.R. and Hodes, R.L. (1982b) 'The Effects of Multiple Physical Countermeasures on the Detection of Deception', *Psychophysiology*, 19: 564 (SPR Abstract).

Honts, C.R., Hodes, R.L. and Raskin, D.C. (1985) 'Effects of Physical Countermeasures on the Physiological Detection of Deception', *Journal of Applied Psychology*, 70: 177–87.

Honts, C.R., Raskin, D.C. and Kircher, J.C. (1983) 'Detection of Deception: Effectiveness of Physical Countermeasures Under High Motivation Conditions', *Psychophysiology*, 20: 446 (SPR Abstract).

Honts, C.R., Raskin, D.C. and Kircher, J.C. (1984) 'Effects of Spontaneous Countermeasures on the Detection of Deception', *Psychophysiology*, 21: 585 (SPR Abstract).

Honts, C.R., Raskin, D.C. and Kircher, J.C. (1986) 'Countermeasures and the Detection of Deception', paper presented at the meeting of the American Psychological Association, Washington, DC, August.

Horvath, F.S. (1977) 'The Effect of Selected Variables on Interpretation of Polygraph Records', *Journal of Applied Psychology*, 62: 127–36.

Horvath, F.S. and Reid, J.E. (1971) 'The Reliability of Polygraph Examiner Diagnosis of Truth and Deception', *The Journal of Criminal Law, Criminology and Police Science*, 62: 276–81.

House of Commons Employment Committee (1984) *The Implications for Industrial Relations and Employment of the Introduction of the Polygraph* (Minutes of Evidence: Dr D. Carroll and others). London: Her Majesty's Stationery Office.

House of Commons Employment Committee (1985a) *The Implications for Industrial Relations and Employment of the Introduction of the Polygraph* (Third Report from the Committee Session 1984–85. Together with the Proceedings of the Committee). London: Her Majesty's Stationery Office.

House of Commons Employment Committee (1985b) *The Implications for Industrial Relations and Employment of the Introduction of the Polygraph* (Second Special Report from the Committee. Observations by the Government on the Third Report of the Committee in Session 1984–85). London: Her Majesty's Stationery Office.

Houston Belt & Terminal Railway Company v. Wherry (1977) 548 S.W.2d 743 (Ct. Civ. App. Texas).

Hunter, F.L. and Ash, P. (1973) 'The Accuracy and Consistency of Polygraph Examiners' Diagnosis', *Journal of Police Science and Administration*, 1: 370–5.

Iacono, W.G., Boisvenu, G.A. and Fleming, J.A. (1984) 'Effects of Diazepam and Methylphenidate on the Electrodermal Detection of Guilty Knowledge', *Journal of Applied Psychology*, 69: 289–99.

Iacono, W.G. and Patrick, C.J. (1987) 'What Psychologists should Know about Lie Detection', to appear in A.K. Hess and I.B. Weiner (eds), *Handbook of Forensic Psychology*. New York: John Wiley.

Inbau, F. (1965) 'The Case against the Polygraph', *American Bar Association Journal*, 51: 857–9.

Irving, B. and Hilgendorf, L. (1981) *Police Interrogation: The Psychological Approach* (Royal Commission on Criminal Procedure, Research Study No. 1). London: Her Majesty's Stationery Office.

Jones, E.A. Jr (1978) ' "Truth" When the Polygraph Operator Sits as Arbitrator (or Judge): The Deception of "Detection" in the "Diagnosis of Truth and Deception" ', in J.L. Stern and B.D. Dennis (eds), *Truth, Lie Detectors, and Other Problems in Labor Arbitration*, Proceedings of the 31st Annual Meeting, National Academy of Arbitrators.

Jones, E.A. Jr (1981) 'Clark County, Nevada, v. International Association of Firefighters', Commerce Clearing House, 82–1 ARB par. 8097.

Judge, A. (1984) 'No, you don't Have to Take the Truth Test, but What have you got to Hide?' *Police*, January: 18–20.

Kaganiec, H.J. (1956) 'Lie Detector Tests and the Freedom of the Will in Germany', *Northwestern University Law Review*, 51: 446–60. Condensed version published (1957) in *Journal of Criminal Law, Criminology, and Police Science*, 47: 570–84.

Karst, K.L. (1986) 'Right of Privacy', in L.W. Levy, K.L. Karst and D.J. Mahoney (eds), *Encyclopedia of the American Constitution*. New York: Macmillan.

Keeler, E. (1984) *Lie Detector Man*. Boston, MA: Telshare Publishing.

Keeler, L. (1931) 'Lie Detector Applications', in *Proceedings of the International Association of Chiefs of Police*, p. 184. Reprinted in D.C. Dilworth (ed.), *Silent Witness: the Emergence of Scientific Criminal Investigations*. Gaithersburg, MD: International Association of Chiefs of Police.

Keeton, P.W., Dobbs, D.B., Keeton, R.E. and Owen D.G. (eds) (1984) *Prosser and Keeton on Torts*. New York: West Publishing.

Kircher, J.C. and Raskin, D.C. (1982) 'Cross-Validation of a Computerized Diagnostic Procedure for Detection of Deception', *Psychophysiology*, 19: 568–9.

Kleinmuntz, B. and Szucko, J. (1984a) 'A Field Study of the Fallibility of Polygraphic Lie Detection', *Nature*, 308: 449–50.

Kleinmuntz, B. and Szucko, J. (1984b) 'Lie Detection in Ancient and Modern Times: A Call for Contemporary Scientific Study', *American Psychologist*, 39: 766–76.

Kohnken, G. (1987) 'Training Police Officers to Detect Deceptive Eyewitness Statements: Does it Work?', *Social Behaviour*, 2: 1–17.

Kramer v. Drinkhall (1982) Civil Action No. 80–3324 (DC District, US Federal Court).

Kubis, J.F. (1962) *Studies in Lie Detection: Computer Feasibility Considerations* (Technical Report 62–205, prepared for Air Force Systems Command, Contract No. AF 30, Project No. 5534). New York: Fordham University.

Larson, J.A. (1932) *Lying and its Detection*. Chicago, IL: University of Chicago Press. Reprinted (1969) Montclaire, NJ: Patterson Smith.

Law Commission (1974) *Breach of Confidence* (Working Paper No. 58). London: Her Majesty's Stationery Office.

Lazarus, R.S., Coyne, J.C. and Folkman, S. (1984) 'Cognition, Emotion and Motivation: The Doctoring of Humpty-Dumpty', in K.R. Scherer and P. Ekman (eds), *Approaches to Emotion*. Hillsdale, NJ: Lawrence Erlbaum.

Lombroso, C. (1881) 'Describing Experiments on Criminals with the Sphygmograph, to Test Sensibility to Pleasure and Pain and to Suggest Medico-legal Possibilities', *Arch. di psichiat.*, 23: 539. Cited at p. 434 in J.A. Larson (1932), *Lying and its Detection*. Chicago, IL: University of Chicago Press.

Lombroso, C. (1895) *L'Homme Criminel* (2nd Edition). Paris: Felix Alcan.

Lykken, D.T. (1959) 'The GSR in the Detection of Guilt', *Journal of Applied Psychology*, 43: 385–8.

Lykken, D.T. (1974) 'Psychology and the Lie Detection Industry', *American Psychologist*, 29: 725–39.

Lykken, D.T. (1981) *A Tremor in the Blood: Uses and Abuses of the Lie Detector*. New York and London: McGraw-Hill.

Lykken, D.T. (1983) 'Polygraphic Interrogation: the Applied Psychophysiologist', in A. Gale and J.A. Edwards (eds), *Physiological Correlates of Human Behaviour Vol. 1: Basic Issues*. London: Academic Press. pp. 243–56.

Lykken, D.T. (1984a) 'Dear Abby', *Los Angeles Times*, 22 February.

Lykken, D.T. (1984b) 'Polygraphic Interrogation', *Nature*, 307: 23.

Lykken, D.T. (1985) 'The Probity of the Polygraph', in S. Kassin and L. Wrightsman (eds), *The Psychology of Evidence and Trial Procedure*, Beverly Hills, CA: Sage.

Lykken, D.T. (1987) 'The Validity of Tests: Caveat Emptor', *Jurimetrics* 27: 263–70.

Marston, W.M. (1938) *The Lie Detector Test*. New York: Richard R. Smith.

Masterman, Sir John (1972) *The Double Cross System*. New Haven, CT: Yale University Press.

Mervis, J. (1986) 'Council Takes Stand on AIDS, Polygraph; Creates Science Post', *American Psychological Association Monitor*, March, 11.

Mischel, W. (1968) *Personality and Assessment*. New York: John Wiley.

Moniodis v. Cook (1985) 64 Md. App. 1, 494 A.2d 212.

More, H.W. (1966) 'Polygraph Research and the University', *Law and Order*, 14: 73–8.

Mosso, A. (1878) 'Über die gegenseitige Beziehung der Bauch- und Brustatmung', *Archiv für die gesamte Physiologie*, 18: 441.

Münsterberg, H. (1908) *On the Witness Stand*. New York: McClure.

National Treasury Employees Union v. Von Raab (1986) 649 F. Supp. 380 (E.D.La.)

National Treasury Employees Union v. Von Raab (1987) 816 F.2d 170 (5th Cir.) vacating 649 F. Supp. 380 (E.D.La.).

Newcomb, T.M. (1929) *Consistency of Certain Extravert–Introvert Behavior Patterns in 51 Problem Boys*. New York: Columbia University, Teachers College, Bureau of Publications.

Ney, T. and Gale, A. (1987) 'A Critique of Laboratory Studies of Emotion with Particular Reference to Psychophysiology', to appear in H. Wagner (ed.), *Social Psychophysiology: Theory and Clinical Applications*. Chichester and New York: John Wiley.

Nikolaichik, V.M. (1964) 'Truth Serum and the Lie Detector, a Return to the Inquisitions' (in Russian), *Soviet State and Law*, 12: 120–6.

O'Brien v. Papa Gino's of America Inc. (1986) 780 F.2d 1067 (1st Cir.).

O'Connor v. Ortega (1987) *US Law Week*, 55: 4405, 31 March.

Office of Technology Assessment (1983) *Scientific Validity of Polygraph Testing: A Research Review and Evaluation*. Washington, DC: Congress of the United States.

Olmstead v. United States (1928) 277 US 438.

Orne, M.T. (1983) Transcript of Evidentiary Hearing, *US v. DeLorean*, CR 82–910(B)–RMT (C.D. Cal.), 17 November.

Peacock v. Duval (1983) 694 F.2d 644 (9th Cir.).

People v. Hamilton (1985) H–49547, RIA Employment Coordinator par. EP–21, 726 (N.T. Sup. Ct.).

People v. Leonard (1977) 59 A.D.2d. 1 (N.Y. App. Div.).

Perks v. Firestone Tire & Rubber Company (1979) 611 F.2d 1363 (3rd Cir.).

Peters, R.B. (1982) 'A Survey of Polygraph Evidence in Criminal Trials', *American Bar Association Journal*, 68: 162–5.

Peterson, J.L., Fabricant, E.L. and Field, K.S. (1978) *Laboratory Proficiency Testing Research Program*. Washington, DC: National Institute of Law Enforcement and Criminal Justice.

Podlesny, J.A. and Raskin, D.C. (1978) 'Effectiveness of Techniques and Physiological Measures in the Detection of Deception', *Psychophysiology*, 15: 344–59.

Polsky v. Radio Shack (1981) 666 F.2d 824 (3rd Cir.).

Ponting, C. (1985) *The Right to Know: The Inside Story of the Belgrano Affair*. London: Sphere.

Prosser, W.L. (1966) 'Misrepresentation and Third Parties', *Vanderbilt Law Review*, 19: 231.

Pyle, C.J. (1982) 'Statement before the Committee on the Judiciary, US House of Representatives', 9 December 1982.

Radio Moscow (1980) 'Interview with Dr Igor Karpets, head of a research institute of the Soviet Ministry of the Interior' (20 April), *Summary of World Broadcasts*, Monitoring Service of the British Broadcasting Corporation, SU/6402/B/1, 23 April 1980.

Raskin, D.C. (1976) *Reliability of Chart Interpretation and Sources of Error in Polygraph Examinations* (US Department of Justice Report No. 76–3, Contract 75–NI–99–0001) Salt Lake City, UT: University of Utah.

Raskin, D.C. (1979) 'Orienting and Defensive Reflexes in the Detection of Deception', in H.D. Kimmel, E.H. Van Olst and J.F. Orlebeke (eds), *The Orienting Reflexes in Humans*. Hillsdale, NJ: Lawrence Erlbaum.

Raskin, D.C. (1982) 'The Scientific Basis of Polygraph Techniques and Their Uses in the Judicial Process', in A. Trankell (ed.), *Reconstructing the Past: The Role of Psychologists in Criminal Trials.* Stockholm: Norstedt & Soners. pp. 319–71.

Raskin, D.C. (1984a) Testimony in *TSEU et al. v. Texas Department of Mental Health Mental Retardation et al.,* Austin, TX, April.

Raskin, D.C. (1984b) 'Statement Submitted to Committee on Armed Services', United States Senate, 7 March.

Raskin, D.C. (1986a) 'The Polygraph in 1986: Scientific, Professional and Legal Issues Surrounding Application and Acceptance of Polygraph Evidence', *Utah Law Review,* 1: 29–74.

Raskin, D.C. (1986b) 'Testimony before the Committee on Labor and Human Resources', 23 April 1986, United States Senate (Hearing on S. 1815, Polygraph Protection Act of 1985). Washington, DC: Government Printing Office.

Raskin, D.C., Barland, G.H. and Podlesny, J.A. (1977) 'Validity and Reliability of Detection of Deception', *Polygraph,* 6: 1–39.

Raskin, D.C. and Hare, R.D. (1978) 'Psychopathy and Detection of Deception in a Prison Population', *Psychophysiology,* 15: 126–36.

Raskin, D. and Kircher, J. (1987) 'The Validity of Lykken's Criticisms: Fact or Fancy?', *Jurimetrics,* 27: 271–7.

Reid, J.E. (1945) 'Simulated Blood Pressure Responses in Lie Detection Tests and a Method for their Detection', *Journal of Criminal Law, Criminology and Police Science,* 36: 201–4.

Reid, J.E. and Inbau, F.E. (1977) *Truth and Deception* (2nd Edition). Baltimore, MD: Williams & Wilkins.

Rovner, L.I., Raskin, D.C. and Kircher, J.C. (1979) 'Effects of Information and Practice on Detection of Deception', *Psychophysiology,* 16: 197–8.

Sackett, P.R. and Decker, P.J. (1979) 'Detection of Deception in the Employment Context: A Review and Critical Analysis', *Personnel Psychology,* 32: 487–506.

Saxe, L., Dougherty, D. and Cross, T. (1985) 'The Validity of Polygraph Testing', *American Psychologist,* 40: 355–66.

Schmerber v. California (1966) 384 US 757.

Security Commission (1983) *Report of the Security Commission, May 1983* (Cmnd 8876). London: Her Majesty's Stationery Office.

Simon, M.A. (1983) 'Shall We Ask the Lie Detector?', *Science, Technology and Human Values,* 8 (Summer): 1–13.

Skolnick, J.H. (1961) 'Scientific Theory and Scientific Evidence: An Analysis of Lie Detection', *Yale Law Journal,* 70: 694–728.

Slowik, S.M. and Buckley, J.P. (1975) 'Relative Accuracy of Polygraph Examiner Diagnosis of Respiration, Blood Pressure, and GSR Recordings', *Journal of Police Science and Administration,* 3: 305–9.

Society of Civil and Public Servants (1983) *The Case Against the Polygraph.* London: Society of Civil and Public Servants.

State v. Community Distributors Inc. (1974) 64 N.J. 479, 317 A.2d 697 (N.J. Sup. Ct.).

Stern, R.M., Breen, J.P., Watanable, T. and Perry, B.S. (1981) 'Effect of Feedback of Physiological Information on Responses to Innocent Associations and Guilty Knowledge', *Journal of Applied Psychology,* 66: 677–81.

Symonds, P. (1931) *Diagnosing Personality and Conduct.* New York: Century.

Tameny v. Atlantic Richfield Company (1980) 164 Cal. Reptr. 839 (Sup. Ct.).

Tehan v. United States, ex rel. Shott (1966) 382 US 406.

Tent, L. (1967) 'Psychologische Tatbestandsdiagnostik (Spurensymptomatologie, Lügendetektion)', in U. Undeutsch (ed.), *Forensische Psychologie,* Vol. 11. Göttingen: Verlag für Psychologie. pp. 185–259.

Thorne v. City of El Segundo et al. (1983) 726 F.2d 459 (9th Cir.).

Thornton, P. (1984) 'Hypnosis – Which Way should the Pendulum Swing?' *Rights*, 7: 5.

Thornton, P. (1985) *We Protest – the Public Order Debate*. London: National Council for Civil Liberties.

Thornton, P. (1987) *Public Order Law*. London: Financial Training Publications.

Undeutsch, U. (1975) 'Die Verwertbarkeit unwillkürlicher Ausdruckserscheinungen bei der Aussagenwürdigung', *Zeitschrift für die gesamte Strafrechtswissenschaft*, 87: 650–62.

Undeutsch, U. (1979) 'Die Leistungsfähigkeit der heutigen Methoden der psychophysiologischen Täterschaftsermittlung', *Monatsschrift für Kriminologie und Strafrechtsreform*, 62: 228–41.

United States v. Dionisio (1973) 410 US 1.

United States v. Mara (1973) 410 US 19.

United States ex rel. Monks v. Warden (1972) 339 F. Supp. 30 (D.N.J.)

United States Code, 42 USC (1871) Sections 1981 et seq.; (1964) Title VII, Sections 2000e et seq.

Venables, P.H. (1982) Quoted in 'Lie Detectors Can Tell Lies' by Brian Silcock, *Sunday Times*, 5 December 1982.

Waid, W.M., Orne, E.C., Cook, M.R. and Orne, M.T. (1981) 'Meprobamate Reduces Accuracy of Physiological Detection of Deception', *Science*, 212: 71–3.

Waid, W.M., Orne, E.C. and Orne, M.T. (1981) 'Selective Memory for Social Information, Alertness, and Physiological Arousal in the Detection of Deception', *Journal of Applied Psychology*, 66: 224–32.

Wertheimer, M. and Klein, J. (1904) 'Psychologische Tatbestandsdiagnostik', *Archiv für Kriminal-Anthropologie und Kriminalistik*, 15: 72–113.

West, N. (1981) *MI5*. Oxford: Bodley Head.

Whalen v. Roe (1977) 429 US 589.

White, L.T., Lopez, M. and Haney, C. (1982) 'To Polygraph or Not: The Effects of Preemployment Polygraphing on Work-related Attitudes', *Polygraph*, 11: 185–99.

Wicklander, D.E. and Hunter, F.L. (1975) 'The Influence of Auxiliary Sources of Information in Polygraph Diagnosis', *Journal of Police Science and Administration*, 3: 405–9.

Widacki, J. and Horvath, F.S. (1978) 'An Experimental Investigation of the Relative Validity of the Polygraph Technique and Three Other Common Methods of Criminal Identification', *Journal of Forensic Sciences*, 23: 596–601.

Zuckerman, M., De Paulo, B. and Rosenthal, R. (1981) 'Verbal and Non-verbal Communication of Deception', in L. Berkowitz (ed.), *Advances in Experimental Social Psychology*, Vol. 14. New York: Academic Press.

Annotated bibliography

Many of the key papers in the field of polygraph assessment and related issues are cited in the References. The following limited selection is designed to help the reader who wishes to follow up the themes addressed in the book in more detail.

Anastasi, A. (1976) *Psychological Testing* (4th Edition). New York: Macmillan.
A standard textbook taking a straightforward conventional line on various technical issues. The early chapters are particularly relevant to the question of standardization, rapport, reliability and validity.

Ansley, N. (1984) *Quick Reference Guide to Polygraph Admissibility, Licensing Laws, and Limiting Laws*. Linthicum Heights, MD: American Polygraph Association.
Ansley, N., Horvath, F. and Barland, G. (1983) *Truth and Science: A Comprehensive Index to International Literature of the Detection of Deception and the Polygraph (Lie Detector) Technique* (2nd Edition). Linthicum Heights, MD: American Polygraph Association.
As the titles indicate, these are comprehensive accounts and bibliographies of the legal standing of polygraph testing within the USA, and the extensive literature on research into the polygraph test.

Arena, J.G., Blanchard, E.B., Andrasik, F., Cotch, P.A. and Myers, P.E. (1983) 'Reliability of Psychophysiological Assessment', *Behaviour Research and Therapy*, 21: 447–69.
A study of the reliability and interrelationships between physiological measures of psychological state, revealing the general lack of relationship among measures and the variations in reliability within measures over similar and different testing conditions.

British Psychological Society (1986) 'Report of the Working Group on the Use of the Polygraph in Criminal Investigation and Personnel Screening', *Bulletin of The British Psychological Society*, 39: 81–94.
A report of a special working party established by the Scientific Affairs Board, this is the official statement of The British Psychological Society in relation to the use of the polygraph. It covers, in brief, most of the issues addressed in this book. Obtainable as a separate from the Society's offices at Leicester.

Copeland, M. (1978) *The Real Spy World*. London: Sphere.
American espionage operations, but with many references to MI5, its organization, successes and failures.

Cronbach, L.J. (1981) *Essentials of Psychological Testing* (4th edition). New York: Harper & Row.
A textbook by one of the leading contributors to the theory of psychological measurement. Cronbach's account of technical issues is sophisticated but accessible.

Cunningham, C. (1972a) 'International Interrogation Techniques', *Royal United Services Institute of Defence Studies Journal*, September.

Cunningham, C. (1972b) 'Interrogation', *Medico-Legal Society Journal*, 41: 49–62.
A clear description of interrogation techniques by one of the authors of the present volume. Defuses a number of myths about interrogation techniques and 'brainwashing'.

Ekman, P. (1985) *Telling Lies: Clues to Deceit in the Marketplace, Politics and Marriage*. New York: W.W. Norton.
Claimed by its author as the very first book to explore the many dimensions of lying – the markings of a successful liar, why so many of us become willing victims – and to offer straightforward and cautious methods for uncovering deception. Attractively written, with particularly good discussion of Ekman's own work on the microstructure of facial expression.

Ekman, P., Levenson, R.W. and Friesen, W.V. (1983) 'Autonomic Nervous System Activity Distinguishes among Emotions', *Science*, 221: 1208–10.
This should prove to be a landmark study since it has rekindled the possibility of physiological differentiation of emotions.

Elliott, D.W. (1982) 'Lie Detector Evidence: Lessons from the American Experience', in E. Campbell and L. Waller (eds), *Well and Truly Tried: Essays in Honour of Sir Richard Eggleston*. Melbourne: Law Book Company.
A thorough critical survey, by a distinguished British lawyer, of the United States experience of the forensic use of lie detectors, including a historical account, and an analysis in depth of the technicalities and use of the polygraph. The first published detailed evaluation of the polygraph test by a British lawyer.

Green, B.F. (1978) 'In Defense of Measurement', *American Psychologist*, 33: 664–70.
A summary of the status of personality testing in the aftermath of the behavioural consistency debate.

Hampson, S.E. (1982) *The Construction of Personality: An Introduction*. London: Routledge & Kegan Paul.
An introduction, by one of the authors of the present volume, to personality psychology emphasizing the social construction approach.

Harnon, E. (1982) 'Evidence Obtained by Polygraph: An Israeli Perspective', *Criminal Law Review*, 340–8.
A discussion of the report in Israel of a special advisory committee in 1981. The advisory committee recommended limited admission of polygraph evidence.

Hodgson, R. and Rachman, S. (1974) 'II. Desynchrony in Measures of Fear', *Behaviour Research and Therapy*, 12: 319–26.
One of the first studies to address itself to the notion of desynchrony between different measures of emotion.

House of Commons Employment Committee (1985a) *The Implications for Industrial Relations and Employment of the Introduction of the Polygraph* (Third Report from the Committee Sessions 1984–85. Together with the Proceedings of the Committee). London: Her Majesty's Stationery Office.
This is the key report of the Select Committee on Employment, which briefly reviews the evidence taken orally and in writing. Together with several other reports, including details of the evidence presented and examination of witnesses, it represents the most comprehensive British account of the scientific evidence and industrial relations aspects of polygraph use.

Iacono, W.G. and Patrick, C.J. (1987) 'What Psychologists should Know about Lie Detection', to appear in A.K. Hess and I.B. Weiner (eds), *Handbook of Forensic Psychology*. New York: John Wiley.
   An excellent survey that also provides a first report of important new research by the authors. Gives a first-rate critique of the research on the validity of the polygraph. The authors call for a higher level of rigour in lie-detection research.

Kleinmuntz, B. and Szucko, J. (1984b) 'Lie Detection in Ancient and Modern Times: A Call for Contemporary Scientific Study', *American Psychologist*, 39: 766–76.
   They argue that until recently psychologists have neglected the scientific investigation of polygraphic lie detection. They claim that across the centuries a number of simplistic assumptions have been made about lie detection and that although these may have widespread public acceptance, they do not stand up to informed psychological opinion based on sound scientific research.

Lazarus, R.S., Coyne, J.C. and Folkman, S. (1984) 'Cognition, Emotion and Motivation: The Doctoring of Humpty-Dumpty', in K.R. Scherer and P. Ekman (eds), *Approaches to Emotion*. Hillsdale, NJ: Lawrence Erlbaum.
   As well as providing an updated account of the cognitive appraisal theory, this recent article contains references of several earlier articles by Lazarus. Included in the references are articles which are in opposition to a cognitive interpretation of emotion.

Lykken, D.T. (1981a) *A Tremor in the Blood: Uses and Abuses of the Lie Detector*. New York and London: McGraw-Hill.
   The first critical appraisal of the history, theory and practices of polygraphic interrogation. Accessible to the general reader and still relevant. An entertaining and easily read book.

Lykken, D.T. (1981b) Review of 'The Science and Art of the Polygraph Technique' by A. Matte, *Contemporary Psychology*, 26: 479–81.
Lykken, D.T. (1986) Review of 'Preemployment Polygraphy' by R. Ferguson and C. Gugas, *Contemporary Psychology*, 30: 880–1.
   The two book reviews attempt to convey the viewpoint and quality of thinking of two leaders of the polygraph industry in the United States.

Masterman, Sir John (1972) *The Double Cross System*. New Haven, CT: Yale University Press.
   How the British secret services took control of German espionage operations in Britain and neutral countries during the Second World War by 'turning' agents or controlling the information they were passing back to Germany.

Maxwell, A.E. (1970) *Basic Statistics in Behavioural Research*. Harmondsworth: Penguin.
   Lives up to its title, and gives a good brief account of reliability and validity. The chapter on 'Types of Investigation' has some good material relevant to the evaluation of the polygraph.

Office of Technology Assessment (1983) *Scientific Validity of Polygraph Testing: A Research Review and Evaluation*. Washington, DC: Congress of the United States.
   This publication gives one of the best authoritative and objective evaluations of the polygraph evidence. It covers the use of the polygraph in different settings and suggests directions for future research.

Raskin, D.C. (1979) 'Orienting and Defensive Reflexes in the Detection of Decep-

tion', in H.D. Kimmel, E.H. Van Olst and J.F. Orlebeke (eds), *The Orienting Reflexes in Humans*. Hillsdale, NJ: Lawrence Erlbaum.
This paper provides the reader with the application of the concepts of orienting and defensive reflexes in understanding the processes that underlie the effectiveness of the control and guilty knowledge techniques.

Raskin, D.C. (1982) 'The Scientific Basis of Polygraph Techniques and Their Uses in the Judicial Process', in A. Trankell (ed.), *Reconstructing the Past: The Role of Psychologists in Criminal Trials*. Stockholm: Norstedt & Soners. pp. 319–71.
A detailed description of various polygraph techniques, the scientific evidence concerning their reliability and accuracy, and issues concerning their uses in judicial proceedings.

Raskin, D.C. (1986a) 'The Polygraph in 1986: Scientific, Professional and Legal Issues Surrounding Application and Acceptance of Polygraph Evidence', *Utah Law Review*, 1: 29–74.
This paper gives up-to-date information about the wider issues (scientific, legal and practical) surrounding the polygraph test's effectiveness and application. It provides a useful account of recent counter-measure research. Many case illustrations are described, including abuses by examiners and scientific experts.

Raskin, D. and Kircher, J. (1987) 'The Validity of Lykken's Criticisms: Fact or Fancy?' *Jurimetrics*, 27: 271–7.
Read together with the article criticized and Lykken's reply, this article provides a good example of the current controversy surrounding the issue of polygraph testing.

Sackett, P.R. and Decker, P.J. (1979) 'Detection of Deception in the Employment Context: A Review and Critical Analysis', *Personnel Psychology*, 32: 487–506.
An assessment of the validity of different methods of detecting deception, including the polygraph.

Shelley, D. and Cohen, D. (1986) *Testing Psychological Tests*. London: Croom Helm.
A light, entertaining but informative account which takes a tilt at a wide range of psychological tests, unpacking a whole range of important issues.

Tapper, C. (1985) *Cross on Evidence* (6th Edition). London: Butterworth.
The leading UK text on the law of evidence. It contains a short passage on 'Statements Validated by Scientific Means', concerned with polygraphs, truth drugs and hypnosis, which concludes: 'The unproven reliability of these techniques, together with the danger of the jury's attributing more weight to such unfamiliar scientific evidence than it deserves, would justify the English courts in following the examples of their counterparts in the rest of the common law world in excluding such statements' (p. 269).

United States Department of Defense (1984) *The Accuracy and Utility of Polygraph Testing*. Washington, DC: Department of Defense.
This presents the Defense Department's views on the accuracy and utility of federal polygraph examinations. It contains a review of the research literature as well as examples of the effectiveness of the polygraph. (Available from the Research Division, Defense Polygraph Institute, Fort McClellan, Alabama 36205, USA.)

United States Department of Defense (1986) *Department of Defense Polygraph Program: Report to Congress for Fiscal Year 1986*. Washington, DC: Department of Defense.

A 33-page report with the results of the test programme on polygraph security screening, with case histories. (Available from same address as previous item.)

West, N. (1981) *MI5*. Oxford: Bodley Head.
A historical account of the organization and operations of MI5 up to 1945.

West, N. (1986) *MI5 1945–72. A Matter of Trust*. London: Coronet.
A description of some operations and defections within MI5 following the Second World War. Some speculation, with emphasis on high-level cases and well-known defectors, but includes information about the organization and weaknessess of the British system of vetting.

Guide for students

The following questions are designed to guide the reading of psychology students who wish to get to grips with the range of problems surrounding the use of the polygraph for the detection of deception. They may also be of value to other readers. There is no clear answer to many of the questions; however, all have been asked at one time or another, in alternative forms, within the debate over the alleged benefits or accuracy of the polygraph lie-detection test.

- What are the key interrogation methods used by polygraphic examiners?
- Do the different methods have an equivalent rationale?
- What are the key contexts and circumstances in which the polygraph test is employed?
- Are all interrogation methods equally appropriate and/or successful in all such contexts?
- How are subjects prepared for the polygraph test procedure?
- How are the questions to be posed to the subject prepared?
- Are certain sorts of questions considered to be unacceptable as part of the interrogation procedure?
- Why is it sometimes necessary for the test procedure to be repeated?
- What precautions are taken to ensure that participation in the procedure is voluntary?
- Why is it claimed that the success of lie detection procedures depends upon the skill of the examiner?
- What elements of lie detection assessment procedures are objective and what elements are subjective?
- How do we know, in everyday circumstances, when someone is lying to us?
- How long is the typical training of polygraphic examiners?
- What is the content of training courses?
- Who becomes a polygraph examiner?
- What precautions could be taken by a registration body in setting guidelines for polygraph lie-detection practice?
- What are the different types of reliability measure taken by psychometricians, and to what extent do they apply to reliability studies of the polygraph test?
- What types of measurement error have been identified by psychometricians and which of these are salient in the context of polygraphic lie-detection procedures?
- What problems are there in establishing external criteria of accuracy in field studies?
- In what sense are laboratory studies poor simulations of real-life investigations?

- Which component of the polygraph testing procedure might account most for its alleged successes?
- Can studies be designed which enable partitioning of the effects of different components?
- Why are most authorities dissatisfied with the majority of research conducted on the polygraph test procedure?
- Why is there a controversy over estimates of accuracy?
- How are base rate data computed and what bearing do they have on estimates of accuracy of detection?
- What factors might account for the high rate of commission errors in several studies (i.e. false accusation of the innocent)?
- What factors might support the claims of advocates of polygraphic interrogation procedures that they are particularly successful in securing confessions?
- Can a polygraph test, at a pre-selection interview, assist in determining whether the candidate has general qualities of honesty and truthfulness?
- Are concepts of truth and honesty in some sense absolute or are they affected by social context and cultural norms?
- Are there consistent relationships between pre-transgression anxiety, anxiety during commission of prohibited acts, and/or post-transgression remorse?
- What is the relevance to chart interpretation, of psychophysiological data on the reliability of and interrelationships between the peripheral physiological measures employed in polygraph testing?
- What bearing do contemporary theories of emotional experience and emotional expression have upon the theoretical interpretation of polygraphic data?
- What factors need to be borne in mind in estimating the potential costs and benefits of polygraphic lie detection?
- Can subjects deceive the examiner?
- What methods can be used as counter-measures?
- Are different counter-measures appropriate for different test procedures (i.e. CQT versus CIT)?
- Why are there problems in designing a convincing laboratory study of counter-measure strategies and their degree of success in deceiving the examiner?
- In the context of state security, periodic screening of staff in sensitive posts, and security vetting generally, is the use of polygraphic testing likely to be cost-effective?
- What is the standing of polygraphic lie detection evidence in the British courts?
- Where polygraph test evidence is allowed in different legal systems, what constraints are imposed?
- Is the polygraph examiner regarded as an expert witness?
- Is it self-serving to obtain polygraph test evidence as to one's innocence?
- In what senses might the report of the polygraph examiner be considered hearsay?

Glossary

Base rate In order to assess accuracy of lie detection, one needs a measure of the true level of deception or lying within the sample or parent population. Base rates are likely to be different for different populations and contexts (for example, crimes *versus* job applications). There is controversy over the calculation of base rate and its implications for assessing the accuracy of different lie detection techniques.

Bias A source of systematic error in measurement which partially determines the direction of outcome. Bias may be a factor in examiner expectations, or an inadvertent characteristic of the testing procedure, or a characteristic of the population tested (for example, different ethnic groups have been shown to give more vigorous skin conductance responses). In formal experimental design and psychometric procedures, special precautions can be taken to reduce bias.

Biofeedback A group of methods designed to give the person information about the state of their bodily responses. For example, a subject may receive auditory information about their heart rate and be taught to increase or decrease heart rate at will. Particularly successful in the treatment of muscle tension disorders (for example, headache). Biofeedback methods could be part of counter-measure training to assist individuals in defeating the lie-detection test.

Cognitive processes Higher order processes such as thinking and self-reflection which structure our knowledge of the world. There is controversy over the relationship between cognition and emotion and the degree to which emotion may or may not be controlled by cognitive processes.

Concealed Information Test or CIT A class of lie-detection tests which focuses on the fact that only the respondent or those with special knowledge (for example, a police investigation team) could be party to the particular information concerned. The Guilty Knowledge Test (GKT) is a concealed information test.

Control Question Technique or CQT The principal technique of lie detection used in criminal investigation and for which polygraph examiners are trained. Comparisons are made between responses to questions which are: (1) relevant to the crime, (2) of concern to the respondent but not directly relevant to the crime, and (3) neutral questions. Skill is needed in constructing the schedule of questions and the examiner's judgements are based on comparing responses to the different type of questions.

Correlation coefficient A statistical measure of the degree of association between two variables or measures, varying from no association (correlation of 0.0) to complete association (+1.0 or −1.0). Variables may be positively or inversely related. Roughly speaking the square of the correlation indicates the amount of variation which is accounted for by the measures; thus a correlation of 0.9 although it appears high, means that some 20% of the variation (or one case in five) is not accounted for.

Counter-measures A variety of techniques which it is believed can be used successfully in defeating the polygraph test. These can include physical techniques (to amplify responses to all questions), self-administered drugs (to reduce responsiveness), and mental techniques such as imagination and dissociation (which either enable the person to give vigorous responses to all questions or which cut off the person's attention to them).

Discharge theory of emotion A theory of emotion which sees emotion as a sort of energy which must be released by the individual through some channel of expression and which 'leaks out' in spite of voluntary effort to prevent it. Thus emotion could be expressed physiologically, verbally, subjectively or in our tone of voice, and so on, in spite of attempts to conceal our feelings. The notion that emotion can be discharged through different channels means that individuals will vary in emotional expression. It also means that different channels may not correlate in their level of expression.

Electrodermal activity Activity of the sweat glands of the skin, consisting of inherent tonic fluctuations and phasic or responsive reactions to particular stimuli. Skin resistance or skin conductance responses are measures of electrodermal activity.

Event related potentials or ERPs A specific electrical response in the brain as a reaction to a stimulus. Early components of the response reflect physical characteristics of the stimulus (such as intensity), later components reflect psychological significance.

Facial feedback hypothesis A theory of emotion which suggests that the facial muscles have been 'wired in', during the course of evolution, to the emotional parts of the brain and that emotional experience necessarily involves facial expression. The hypothesis also suggests a positive correlation between different channels of emotional expression and can therefore contradict the discharge theory of emotion.

False negative Commission of a Type II error or the failure to detect an event which is truly present. In the case of lie detection it consists of identifying a guilty person as innocent.

False positive Commission of a Type I error or the detection of an event which is not truly present. In the case of lie detection it consists of falsely accusing an innocent person of guilt.

Guilty Knowledge Test or GKT A multiple choice procedure ('Was the victim wearing a dress which was green, red, black, white . . . ?') incorporating information which only the guilty person could know. A concealed information test which some authorities believe could be the basis of theoretically sound methods of physiological lie detection.

Heart rate The rate at which the heart beats, normally expressed in terms of beats per minute. Variations in heart rate may indicate the processing of information including emotional information. The polygraph examiner will interpret variations in rate which occur during the course of the examination, and in particular, compare heart rate responses to different questions.

Negative vetting A lower level of security vetting involving the checking of available information on record about an individual, including known associations with those who have already come to the attention of the security services.

Non-verbal behaviour Behaviours other than the content of speech yet which are said to convey meaning about the intentions or feelings of an individual. Facial expression, eye contact, inter-personal distance, posture, tone of voice and physiological responses such as blushing, are examples of non-verbal behaviour studied by psychologists. People may vary in the extent to which they *encode* information in this manner, or in their capacity to *decode* it.

Orienting reflex or response Called the 'What is it?' reaction by Ivan Pavlov, this is a complex of physiological, behavioural and subjective reactions to novel stimuli (a sudden sound) or a significant stimulus (hearing your name at a party). It is interpreted as a preparation of the body for the processing of further information.

Peak of Tension Test   A multiple choice test, similar to the Guilty Knowledge Test (GKT), in which the subject is presented with a crime-related item embedded in a series of crime-unrelated items. As the innocent suspect cannot recognize the critical item, the possibility of a false positive error is minimized. Unlike the GKT, the item is placed in the middle of the list (rather than at random), and the subject knows the item sequence. As the list presentation moves to the central item the subject experiences increased tension associated with a peak in physiological responses.

Personality coefficient   A derogatory description (coined by Walter Mischel) of findings in personality research which typically show a cross-situational consistency correlation of around 0.3, and which therefore accounts for less than 10 percent of the overall variance (see Correlation coefficient). Such findings are thought to undermine the claims of trait theorists.

Polygraph   A scientific instrument which provides several channels of information on a chart. It is used in psychophysiological research to study the relationships between psychological and bodily processes. In modern laboratories polygraphs are linked to powerful computers to assist in the quantification and analysis of physiological traces. Measures include the electrical activity of the brain (EEG or ERP), heart rate, blood pressure, electrodermal activity, and muscle activity (EMG).

Positive vetting   An active process of security vetting involving a thorough examination of the life of the subject and including interviews with both the subject and his/her associates and acquaintances. The subject is likely to be aware that such an investigation is underway.

Psychometrics   The theory and practice of mental testing as reflected in the development, administration and interpretation of tests such as personality, aptitude and intelligence tests and other performance measures. A specialist field involving training at a postgraduate level within psychology.

Psychopathic personality or sociopath   A deviant individual claimed by some authorities to be manipulative, persuasive and lacking in the tender emotions. Physiological explanations of psychopathy include the notion that psychopaths are slow to give physiological responses in certain situations, being individuals who are 'low-aroused' and unresponsive to methods of socialization which involve threats of punishment.

Psychophysics   A specialist branch of experimental psychology concerned with the relationships between sensory stimulation and physical and subjective responses.

Psychophysiology   The study of the relationships between psychological variables and bodily responses. Psychophysiologists are usually specialists in bodily processes such as the electrical activity of the brain or the cardiovascular system. The polygraph and the computer are essential tools of the trade.

Random error   Sources of error which might affect the outcome of experiments or psychological measurements in a random fashion. For example, a child taking an intelligence test may be suffering from a cold on that day. In experiments, the use of large samples can ensure that the impact of such errors may be negligible since they are assumed to cancel each other out. There are, of course, more systematic sources of error (*see*, for example, Bias).

Relevant control test   A procedure used in the screening of job applicants, which includes several questions, some of which are relevant ('Have you ever lied on a job application?'; 'Have you ever stolen from your employer?') and a few irrelevant questions such as 'Is it Monday today?' The answer should be 'No' to all questions and the rationale is that a more vigorous physiological response to relevant questions will indicate the subject has something to hide.

Relevant–irrelevant question procedure   Used by earlier polygraphers in criminal investigation and incorporating crime-related and crime-unrelated (neutral) questions. No longer used very much in this context since it is recognized that even an innocent person will respond more vigorously to questions relating to criminal activity as opposed to neutral questions. Displaced by the Control Question Technique.

Reliability   A technical term relating to the stability of measurement instruments. In psychometrics, reliability may refer to agreement between judges, agreement by a judge with his own earlier judgements, or more typically, the capacity of a test to give the same results on different occasions. Reliability is a *necessary* but not *sufficient* condition for validity.

Respiration   Measured on the polygraph using a device, fixed around the chest, which expands and contracts as the individual breathes. The pen record will show depth of inspiration and exhalation, as well as rate of breathing.

Right to silence   In some circumstances, a person is entitled to keep quiet, so that what he or she says may not be used as evidence which might count against them. Nor can the assertion of the right be used by others to infer guilt. In a criminal trial a person may not be required to speak against him- or herself. In the USA such rights are incorporated in the Fifth Amendment to the Constitution.

Skin conductance or skin resistance response (GSR)   A measure of sweat gland activity in response to psychological stimulation, as indicated by a change in a polygraph trace. A response takes the form of a decrease in skin resistance (or increase in its reciprocal, conductance) to a tiny imposed electrical current. Electrodes are usually placed on the fingers. A GSR is one of the responses which make up the orienting reflex.

Standardization   An important aspect of psychometric procedures ensuring that tests are administered in a constant fashion and that scoring methods are so objective that judgements will not vary as a function of who conducts the test. A key aspect of standardization is the provision of a test manual, containing information not only about procedures but about test score norms for appropriate populations of subjects.

Stimulation or stim test   A preparatory procedure recommended in some manuals of polygraph lie detection to 'soften up' the subject of the investigation with the aim of persuading them that it is pointless to lie. One simple technique is to show the subject that the polygraph can be used to identify a playing card they have chosen, when in actuality, the polygrapher has a fixed pack in which all the cards are the same.

Temporal and cross-situational consistency   Two important aspects of measurement and prediction. Temporal consistency means that under identical conditions, a subject will obtain a similar score or behave in a similar fashion. In cross-situational consistency the aim is to predict the individual's behaviour under a variety of conditions. Thus, in the case of employment selection procedures, the aim is not merely to predict how a person will react in a similar interview (temporal consistency) but how they will react in a variety of working situations. Critics of trait-based personality theories claim they show evidence of temporal but not cross-situational consistency (*see* Personality coefficient).

Tort   A civil wrong for which the law provides relief on behalf of the injured party. Designed to protect the person against personal harm or damage to property. Includes a variety of categories such as negligence, privacy, misrepresentation, interference with civil rights by a third person and slander.

Trait   A characteristic of the person, usually claimed to be genetic in origin, used to classify a set of typical behaviours. For example, the term *extraversion* refers to a set of dispositional attributes such as a desire for activity and social intercourse, as well as impulsivity and a need for change. Critics of such theories claim they have been unable to demonstrate cross-situational consistency of behaviour or to account for more than 10 percent of behaviour measured in particular contexts. A naive person might believe that a polygraph test, used as a pre-selection interview, might reveal traits such as 'honesty' or 'truthfulness' as a characteristic of the subject.

Validity   A technical term in psychometrics referring to the ability of a test to actually measure what it purports to measure. Stability or reliability of the test is an essential prerequisite for validity but does not guarantee it. Roughly speaking, reliability and validity, taken together, are equivalent to the lay notion of 'accuracy'. In polygraph lie detection, reliability (i.e. in the form of agreement between examiners as to a set of polygraph records) does not in itself guarantee validity (correct detection of guilty or innocent persons).

Index